Sex in Canada

Sex in Canada

The Who, Why, When, and How of Getting Down Up North

TINA FETNER

UBCPress · Vancouver

Printed in Canada on FSC-certified ancient-forest-free paper (100% post-consumer recycled) that is processed chlorine- and acid-free.

UBC Press is a Benetech Global Certified Accessible™ publisher. The epub version of this book meets stringent accessibility standards, ensuring it is available to people with diverse needs.

Library and Archives Canada Cataloguing in Publication

Title: Sex in Canada : the who, why, when, and how of getting down up north / Tina Fetner.
Names: Fetner, Tina, author.
Description: Includes bibliographical references and index.
Identifiers: Canadiana (print) 20230572448 | Canadiana (ebook) 20230572464 | ISBN 9780774869508 (hardcover) | ISBN 9780774869515 (softcover) | ISBN 9780774869522 (PDF) | ISBN 9780774869539 (EPUB)
Subjects: LCSH: Sex—Canada. | LCSH: Sex customs—Canada.
Classification: LCC HQ18.C2 F48 2024 | DDC 306.70971—dc23

Canada Council   Conseil des arts
for the Arts   du Canada

Canadä

BRITISH COLUMBIA ARTS COUNCIL

BRITISH COLUMBIA

UBC Press gratefully acknowledges the financial support for our publishing program of the Government of Canada, the Canada Council for the Arts, and the British Columbia Arts Council.

This book has been published with the help of a grant from the Canadian Federation for the Humanities and Social Sciences, through the Scholarly Book Awards, using funds provided by the Social Sciences and Humanities Research Council of Canada.

UBC Press is situated on the traditional, ancestral, and unceded territory of the xʷməθkʷəy̓əm (Musqueam) people. This land has always been a place of learning for the xʷməθkʷəy̓əm, who have passed on their culture, history, and traditions for millennia, from one generation to the next.

UBC Press
The University of British Columbia
www.ubcpress.ca

FOR LANE AND MAX

Contents

Figures

Acknowledgments

I am so grateful for all the support I received while doing this research and writing this book. The research was funded by the Canadian government through a grant from the Social Sciences and Humanities Research Council. It is part of a larger project we now call Sex in Canada (originally titled Social and Political Attitudes and Sexual Behaviours in Canada), which I developed in collaboration with my colleagues Michelle Dion, professor of political science at McMaster University, and Melanie Heath, professor of sociology at McMaster University. I am thankful for our collaboration on this project and for the support they have offered over the years. I am also very grateful to the participants who completed the survey, sharing the intimate details of their lives in anonymity. Thank you so much.

This project would not have been possible without the support of Debby Herbenick at Indiana University, whose research on sexual behaviour is an inspiration. Her generosity in sharing the questionnaire for the National Survey of Sexual Health and Behavior, which formed the basis of the Sex in Canada survey, is greatly appreciated. Her decision to do so was collegial and kind, and the survey instrument is the foundation for all the research this project will accomplish.

In addition, the larger Sex in Canada project was supported by a research team that included several graduate and undergraduate students at McMaster University, including Nicole Andrejek, Meghan Bird, Lexie Milmine, Sarah Newell, Mathieu Poirier, Max Stick, Megan Werger, and Thomas Wood. They brought energy, fresh ideas, and hard work to the project. Thanks much, also, to Tony Silva for his collaborations on the research. I thank the anonymous peer reviewers, as well as my editor at UBC Press, James MacNevin, for their kind and helpful feedback.

I owe a deep debt of gratitude to the very talented wordsmith and my good friend Letta Page. Her enthusiasm for this project was contagious, and I appreciate the energy that her upbeat attitude gave me when I needed it most. Letta refuses to let me calcify into a stodgy academic, even though that would be as comfortable as curling up with a good book. Instead, she lent her wit and humour to the project, as well as her substantial talent as an editor, helping me find my voice for this work. If you enjoy reading it as much as I hope you will, you can thank Letta. I certainly do.

I am especially grateful to my friend Miranda Hill. Miranda supported me in writing this book in many ways. She helped me figure out how to make time in my busy schedule, helped me think through the audience and the publication process. She let me use her home as a writing retreat when I needed a quiet space away from it all. I drank her tea, sat at her desk, and soaked up all the creative energies that she had written into that space. Thank you so much, Miranda.

I also want to thank my community of fellow academics whose own work, whether it is in my field or another, is an inspiration. Sometimes, their work is cited here, and I am grateful for the chance to engage with their scholarship. In other cases, though our work may not overlap, I have basked in the warmth and support of our friendship. When I got up early in the morning to write, I was bolstered by the thought that they were probably doing the same. Thank you to Karen Bird, Jessica Fields, Kieran Healy, Carrie James, Jennifer Lena, Tressie McMillan Cottom, C.J. Pascoe, Karen Robson, Stephanie Ross, Sarah Sobieraj, Marisa Young, and so many more. Thanks also to my sister, Tracy Robinson, who has been a steady presence throughout.

Finally, I must thank Lane Dunlop and Max Fetner Dunlop, who have been by my side (and indeed, stuck in the house with me) while I wrote this book. I feel all the love and support that you have always given me, and I am eternally grateful.

Sex in Canada

Introduction:
The Social Science of Sexuality

Who wouldn't like to learn more about sex? Sex and sexuality are central aspects of our lives. Discovering one's sexuality is an important part of the transition from childhood into adulthood. Sex is often the basis through which we make connections with others and learn more about ourselves. It is tangled up with falling in love, forming families, and having children. It can bring us pleasure and pain, and we can invest our sexual relationships with all our hopes and our fears. Despite being so important to our lives, sex was unmentionable not very long ago, something deeply personal to keep hidden and private. Music, film, and television were censored and rated to keep sexual content away from impressionable young listeners and viewers. The only appropriate space for talking about sex was with a trusted partner or friend in a quiet, intimate conversation. Parents understood that they were to break this taboo only once. They dreaded the arrival of "the talk" with their children, then suffered through it awkwardly.

Now, in this era of self-expression and social media, we have more opportunities to talk frankly and openly about our sexual identities, behaviours, desires, and fears. Indeed, sex seems to be everywhere in our culture.[1] Although we still have a rating system, movies and TV series routinely feature sex scenes, and sexually explicit material is all but unavoidable on the internet. Schools across the country offer sex education programs that teach children at various ages about the names of body parts, sexual and gender identities, birth control, and prevention of sexually transmitted infections. Recently, 2SLGBTQ+ people – a term for individuals with two-spirit, lesbian, gay, bisexual, transgender, queer, and other non-heterosexual identities – have come out of the closet to live their lives proudly and publicly. And sexual harassment and violence are being taken more seriously, with some public figures being held accountable for their actions. The era of sex taboos, it may seem, is behind us.[2]

Although much has changed in Canadians' willingness to talk about sex, the discomfort quickly returns when we scratch the surface. For example, chatting about the sexual relationships of elder populations, such as those in nursing homes, is still against the norm. Teen sex continues to worry adults. Unconventional sex practices, such as those involving costumes and role playing, may feel unfamiliar or unsettling. Experiences of low or absent sexual attraction, or asexuality, may be an uncomfortable subject for some. When we do discuss sex, we may avoid going into detail about behaviours or techniques, keeping to socially safer subjects such as romance and love. There are still norms against, for example, telling a friend what specifically turns us on or brings us to orgasm. All of this is to say that, although our culture has opened up significantly, silence remains the rule when it comes to some sexual topics.

Some of our ideas about sex have changed over time. For example, our thoughts on the morality of premarital sex experienced a sea change in the last century, as did our emphasis on the social relevance of women's virginity.[2] The taboos against masturbation have decreased dramatically as well.[3] Canadians' attitudes toward lesbian and gay people have become more positive over the decades, and same-sex marriage, which became legal in 2005, is widely approved.[4] At the time, it was quite controversial, but now it is not. All major federal political parties support it, and a large majority of Canadians do, too. The evidence from attitudes surveys suggests that Canadian morality around sex and sexuality emphasizes consent and honesty between partners, with a steady disavowal of extramarital sex, yet moral restrictions on sex before marriage or on remarrying after divorce have loosened considerably.[5]

Nonetheless, Canadians do not agree on every issue. For example, abortion is a thorny topic. Although a strong majority – about three out of four Canadians – supports legal abortion, a vocal minority thinks it should be made illegal or at least highly restricted.[6] Sex education is also controversial. Most parents want schools to teach their children about sex and sexuality, but some think it is harmful to expose children to certain subjects, such as same-sex sexuality and birth control.[7] These disagreements are perhaps not as divisive as in other countries, but it would be a mistake to assume that Canadians all think alike on matters of sexuality.

Anthropologist Gayle Rubin explains that, culturally, "sexual acts are burdened with an excess of significance."[8] That is to say, sexuality and sexual behaviour are more meaningful to us than other common human traits and behaviours. We think we know more about someone if we learn how many sexual partners they have had than if we learn how often they snack on potato chips, for example. We see having sex for the first time as a critical milestone, whereas the age at which someone begins wearing eyeglasses seems of little consequence. This difference is owing to the special place that sexuality occupies in our value systems – the ways we judge whether we (and others) are good or bad, healthy or unhealthy, moral or immoral. When someone we know breaks a sexual norm, we can see it as proof of something larger, a character flaw. Further, each individual dimension of our sexual lives is regarded as relevant to weighing whether sexual behaviours are appropriate: whether we are married or single, whether we use only our bodies or include objects, whether we are by ourselves, in pairs, or in a group. Rubin argues that our inclination to divide "good" sex from "bad" helps us determine whether we are, at our very core, good or bad people. As a result, even sexual behaviours that are consistent with our own morality – for example, that are consensual, feel good, and harm no one – may still feel risky because we worry that we may run afoul of others' moral judgments. We want others to think we're good people.

Sexual behaviour, of course, is much more private and less visible than many other types of social behaviour. Because it is both private and morally significant, it is subject to deep curiosity, even as social norms become more inclusive. In fact, as more sexual behaviours become accepted, we want to know even more about what others are getting up to. For example, Rubin wrote about sex in 1984, when the 2SLGBTQ+ movement was taking some early steps toward social acceptance. Today, though 2SLGBTQ+ Canadians have some distance to go before they achieve full equality, they have made many gains. So, I wonder, have Canadians made similar shifts toward accepting non-monogamous relationships? Do they have an open mind about self-pleasure and masturbation? How common is intercourse, oral sex, or the use of sex toys? It can seem that sexual norms are always changing, but there really aren't any rigorous studies that give the basic facts about who is doing what.[9] Fortunately, the Sex in Canada study asked many of the questions that are still considered off-limits.

Stubborn controversies and silences around sex and sexuality can sometimes leave us with unanswered questions. We may wonder what is "normal" behaviour and whether what we do is the same as what the average Canadian does. We rarely have a sense, for example, of how often couples have sex or whether most people masturbate on a regular basis. We may ask what proportion of sexual relationships are monogamous or open, or whether being married or unmarried determines what a couple does in bed. Is anal sex just for gay men, or do straight couples do it, too? Does having children diminish your sex life? This book attempts to fill in such silent spaces to paint an accurate picture of sex in Canada.

It's important to remember that sociologists make a distinction between what is normal and what is average. Normal is related to norms, or social rules, of what is right and wrong, so we would understand normal behaviour to be consistent with those rules. On the other hand, average behaviours are practices and lived experiences that we can measure, more or less. In this book, we want to think about both averages and norms, so we consider behaviours and values. This book reports many averages for various sexual behaviours, and we can reflect on how this information might also tell us something about our social norms. For example, if the sexual behaviours of older Canadians differ from those of younger adults, this may suggest that norms have changed over time. Older Canadians were socialized into one set of norms as they came into adulthood and sexual activity, and younger Canadians who reached adulthood decades later were socialized into a different set. The same can be said of differences in sexual behaviours among differing groups of people; they might give us a hint at social divisions in the norms. For example, if the behaviours of members of a religious group differ from those of Canadians in general, we might infer that a religious norm is influencing them.

As useful as it is to report the behaviour of the average Canadian, it is important not to stop there. By design, averages obscure variation. This book will also pay attention to how sexual practices diverge among Canadians. In particular, it focuses on how social differences, such as level of education, residence in a certain region, or gender, might influence various sexual behaviours. A sociological perspective considers how broader social patterns organize our lives, nudging us into shared habits and providing us with opportunities and challenges that differ from those in distinct social locations. A sociological perspective on sexuality, then, expects that the same social differences that affect our lives will also affect our sexual experiences, shaping both opportunities and challenges. Thus, this research attends to the ways that social categories and divisions are reflected in the sexual behaviours, identities, and partners of Canadians. In other words, this book asks, How does our social world shape our sexual lives?

WHAT IS UNIQUE ABOUT CANADA?

For decades, social scientists have had reliable information about sexual behaviour in the United States, the United Kingdom, France, and other countries. In Canada, they have begun to include more questions about sexual behaviour in their surveys in recent years, but we are still behind other countries in generating a broad, informed picture.[10] When I teach a Canadian university course on the sociology of sexualities, I'm often obliged to rely on statistics from the United States to give students accurate information on the social organization of sexuality, and I'm never surprised when they object that perhaps the statistics are different here.

There are several reasons to believe that Canada might be different from the United States, or from other countries, in terms of sexual behaviour.

First of all, Canada has several policies in place that distinguish it from the United States. Some of its criminal law governing sexual behaviour is different, as is the case with sex work. In the United States, tens of thousands of sex workers are convicted every year, most of them women.[11] In Canada, sex work per se is not illegal, though a number of crimes are related to it, and there are far fewer arrests surrounding the practice.[12]

Human rights law related to sexuality distinguishes Canada, too. The Canadian Charter of Rights and Freedoms has been consistently interpreted by the courts such that 2SLGBTQ+ individuals should have equal treatment under the law and should be free from discrimination.[13] In the United States, they come under a patchwork of legal rights, in which some states prohibit discrimination, but others do not. In some states, consensual sex between two adults of the same gender was a crime as recently as 2003, when the Supreme Court declared these laws unconstitutional. In Canada, similar laws were removed from the books back in 1969. In the United States, new laws banning trans and nonbinary youth from participating in sports teams that are consistent with their gender identity have been implemented in multiple states in recent years, and a new wave of laws prohibiting doctors from providing gender-affirming care to trans youth has been proposed (and in some cases, passed).[14] In contrast, Canada passed federal legislation in 2017 to secure human rights for trans and gender-diverse people.[15]

Reproductive rights are more secure in Canada than in the United States. Although access to abortion remains a challenge for some Canadians, abortions are publicly funded regardless of the reason for the procedure.[16] And though Canada was late in approving the drugs that induce medical abortions (as opposed to surgical ones), these are now widely available with a doctor's prescription. Navigating the Canadian health care system to obtain an abortion may be difficult, but the situation in the United States is even more challenging. In 2022, a Supreme Court decision overturned the right to abortion for all Americans, leaving the legal status of reproductive rights in a hodgepodge of policies across the various states. The rights that had been in place for fifty years were eliminated as a result of a decades-long fight by anti-abortion activists.[17] Despite these policy differences, Canada is estimated to have a somewhat lower rate of abortion than the United States.[18]

Canadian culture relating to sexuality also seems somewhat different from that of the United States. For example, Canadians are less enthusiastic about marriage, and many long-term partners choose not to marry.[19] These common-law partnerships are often considered equivalent to marital partnerships, whereas in the United States, living together is generally seen as a first step toward marriage. The province of Quebec, and francophone culture more broadly, is also worth special attention as we consider the cultural differences between Canada and the United States. Sociologists have noted that though the attitudes of English-speaking Canada are similar to those of the United States, the French-speaking parts of the country are more socially liberal than either of these.[20] It is worth asking whether that applies to sexual attitudes or even to patterns of sexual behaviour – and we will, later in this book.

WHY DO A SEX SURVEY?

For all these reasons and more, it is clear that to really understand sex in Canada, relying on surveys from the United States simply will not do. The varied ways that Canadians express their sexuality are worthy of our attention, so we are going to need Canadian data. Fortunately, our survey provides a snapshot that can give a sense of what goes on in Canadian bedrooms, with whom, and how often. Our idea was to provide a broad foundation of knowledge on a wide array of behaviours and to establish a baseline for future studies that might consider trends in sexual behaviour over time. The survey offers a sense of the current state of social norms surrounding sexuality in Canada. And it lets us compare Canada to other countries around the world.

This research also helps us understand the social organization of sexuality in Canada. Sociologists know that the social world is not the same in every location; rather, social forces shape our world and influence how people react to their circumstances. Certain divisions, such as living in the countryside or in the city, affect how easy it is to meet a partner. Gender is a key predictor for many aspects of life, including sexuality, and income, education, race, and age can form boundaries that push our behaviour in one direction or another. Taken together, these forces shape the landscape of sexuality in Canada, and this book will consider the variety of Canadian perspectives regarding sex and sexuality.

This book is meant to present these findings in a readable and engaging format, while touching on controversial and complex topics. Because it is based on solid scientific evidence, we can shed new light on controversies and break down complexities to examine the situation as it stands today. A core feature of this book is that it offers no opinions on how sex in Canada should be but rather stays squarely within the realm of how it is currently.

THE SEX IN CANADA SURVEY
The Sex in Canada survey was completed in 2018. That's right; all the data that I use for this book were gathered before the 2020 global pandemic. In the midst of the pandemic, we limited our contact with others, typically spent much more time at home, and in many cases worked remotely and helped our children do their schooling from home as well. All of this, combined with the stress and grief of a major health crisis, likely affected our sex lives in the short run and possibly even caused shifts in the long run. This book cannot offer any insights into Canadian sexuality during the pandemic. However, as a snapshot of our sexual behaviour in a pre-pandemic world, it is an important baseline of information. We know what Canadians think and what they do sexually without the extra burden of stress that COVID-19 brought to their lives. Perhaps in the future, another survey will offer comparative data so that we can see if behaviour changed in the post-pandemic world.

To conduct the survey, our team of sociologists and political scientists used a quota-based sampling protocol that was developed and administered by the research firm Environics Canada. We recruited a sample of participants who matched the proportion of Canadians in each of the following categories, according to the most recent census: gender, age, region of residence, and visible minority status. For example, 51 percent of Canadian adults are women, and so 51 percent of our survey respondents were women, too. Since 6.6 percent of Canadians live in the Atlantic provinces, we made sure that 6.6 percent of our participants lived in these provinces, and so on. We conducted the survey in the two official languages of Canada, English and French, and let people choose which one they wanted to use. We delivered the survey in proportion to the census figures for anglophone and francophone Canadians – that is, 76 percent of the surveys were taken in English, and 23 percent were taken in French. This strategy produced a generalizable sample of Canadian adults; that means the answers of our participants can be understood to be representative of all Canadians. In total, the Sex in Canada survey was completed by 2,303 Canadian adults aged eighteen to ninety. More details on our methods are available in the appendix.

The data collection strategy I describe here would be sure to turn up Canadians of all kinds, but we wanted to collect reliable data from lesbian, gay, and bisexual Canadians as well. So, we took some extra steps to survey a pool of LGB people that was a bit larger than what we might expect to find in the general population. We call this oversampling, and it allows us to understand the behaviours and attitudes of this group, especially if they differ from those of straight Canadians. In the end, our survey included 300 Canadians who identified as lesbian, gay, or bisexual and 2,003 who identified as straight or heterosexual.

This approach of understanding sexuality through the lens of survey data has limitations. First of all, we must rely on the self-reports of participants. Were they telling the truth? We could not guarantee that all responses would be accurate, but we took many steps to ensure participants' truthfulness. First, we never asked them for their names or any identifying information. We made a point of telling them that the survey would ask personal questions, so that they could make sure they had privacy. Participants filled in the survey online, so they never had to speak to anyone on the phone or in person, which could potentially be embarrassing for them. Of course, I can't promise that everyone answered every question truthfully. However, I do feel that we did our best to create the conditions where they would feel comfortable to do so.

Which questions we choose to ask can shape our perceptions of sexuality. Even in the United States, where survey data on sexuality are more plentiful than in Canada, research shows that surveys are much more likely to ask about heterosexual, married, monogamous, and procreative sexuality than about any other types of sexual identities and activities.[21]

As social scientists ask their questions in hopes of discovering what sexual norms are, they are also inadvertently shaping those norms, in the eyes of the survey participants and within the audience of their research reports. For example, sexualities surveys, like sex education in schools, have focused more on risk than on pleasure.[22] We have only recently begun asking about same-sex relationships or LGB identity, which has fortified 2SLGBTQ+-movement claims for equal treatment and full social inclusion.[23]

In the Sex in Canada survey, we tried to focus on both risks and pleasure, and we avoided using any judgmental language to sway responses. However, our study was subject to certain pitfalls, many of which exist in other studies. Because we wanted to describe the sexuality of Canadians in general, we concentrated on what was widely shared. Sexual activities in which smaller numbers of people engage cannot be accurately captured with survey data, so this book has little to say about sex clubs, role play, or fetishes. Similarly, relationship forms that are favoured by small numbers of Canadians, such as polyamorous relationships and other types of consensual non-monogamy, are not well captured by a survey instrument like ours. There is no intent to imply a value judgment, but as Laurel Westbrook, Jamie Budnick, and Aliya Saperstein argue, by shining a spotlight on more numerous identities, activities, and relationships, we are also casting a shadow upon the rest. Fortunately, there is a lot of great social scientific work on sexual communities and practices that are not covered in these pages. I strongly recommend that you keep reading.

A NOTE ABOUT GENDER IDENTITY

As our understandings of gender are changing over time, so should our approaches to categorizing people in social science. For example, trans men and women, as well as nonbinary people, are not adequately represented by the usual male/female options on a survey. Some may not want to use gender categories to describe themselves at all. Social scientists who design survey questions are grappling with the issue of how to include everyone in their surveys, regardless of gender, and how to represent them well when presenting data. Consensus is emerging around the use of a two-step question sequence to capture sex and gender.[24] This is what we employed. We first asked our respondents what sex they were assigned at birth, and then we asked what their gender identity was now, including nonbinary options. About 1 percent chose trans and nonbinary gender options. This was a bit greater than the proportion of trans and nonbinary people reported by the 2021 census, which found that 0.33 percent of Canadians identify as trans or nonbinary.[25]

When I report on gender breakdowns in this book, I am using the second of our two questions to capture the gender identity of participants. So, when I say "men," this includes cisgender and transgender men. When I say "women," this includes cisgender and transgender women. There were not enough respondents in the nonbinary category for me to report them separately; nor were there enough trans respondents to make any reliable claims about the sexual behaviour of trans men and women. We need more research on these specific populations to have a complete understanding of gender and sexuality.

THREE STRANDS OF SEXUALITY

How do you measure sexuality? This question is more difficult than it may seem at first. "Sexuality" is a very broad term that covers many aspects of each of us, some deeply internal and personal, others that are shared and communicated with intimate partners or with the world. When a woman gets married to a man, she is communicating to her family and her community not only her long-term personal commitment, but also, as we tend to expect, her sexual commitment. We commonly assume that she is expressing a heterosexual identity, that she will have sex only with the groom, and that these aspects of her sexuality will remain consistent throughout her life. However, researchers have found that the situation is much more complicated.

Research has identified at least three strands that we can measure, more or less, to gain a picture of an individual's sexuality at a given point in time: sexual identity, behaviour, and desire. Sexual identity refers to the way that we present ourselves to the world. At this moment in Canadian culture, we may use the terms heterosexual, lesbian, gay, asexual, bisexual, two-spirit, or queer to capture our sexual identities. Sexual behaviours are the sexual actions that we take, with a partner or by ourselves. And sexual desire tries to capture our inner feelings – what turns us on or brings us pleasure, our fantasies and dreams. These strands are interwoven, but they are conceptually distinct aspects of how we understand ourselves as sexual beings.

One thing that is very clear in sexuality research is that we cannot measure only one strand and assume we know everything about the other two. For example, early research by Alfred Kinsey produced the "Kinsey Scale," which suggested that many people who present a heterosexual identity harbour some same-sex sexual desires.[26] Similarly, survey research by sociologist Edward O. Laumann and colleagues shows very clearly that the number of people who report having had sex with someone of the same gender is much larger than the number of people who identify as gay, lesbian, or bisexual.[27] Thus, when we ask about sexual identity, we are not getting an accurate understanding of people's sexual behaviour. So, we learned that we cannot just ask people about their sexual identity and think we know everything about their sexual behaviour or desires.

This book is attuned to the three strands. Our survey used a spectrum of questions to learn about sexual identity, behaviour, and desire. To broaden our understanding of sexuality, we also asked about pleasure, feelings of intimacy with a partner, and discomfort and pain. We want to know more than just what Canadians do in bed. We want to know how they feel about it.

HOW IS THE BOOK ORGANIZED?
This survey offers a rich picture of sex in Canada, presented in a series of topics that lead us through several ways to understand our sexual selves. Chapter 1 examines the role that sexual identity plays in shaping the world around us. The most familiar sexual identities are not universal; nor have they always been around. Still, they are powerful forces that shape our understandings of sexuality, while they influence our families, communities, and the social order.

Chapter 2 asks, How much sex are we having? It considers a number of myths. For example, we may think that single people are having all the fun, enjoying sex on a regular basis and perhaps with several partners, whereas married people struggle to find the time and energy for sex. We take a look into the differences in sexual behaviour between young people and older people, whose libidos, the story goes, have surely diminished over time. And we gain some insight into how often Canadians pleasure themselves, whether or not they are with a partner.

Chapter 3 considers the commitment between partners that may or may not accompany a sexual relationship. How committed are Canadians to their partners, how much cheating do they do, and how often are their relationships open to sexual exploration with outsiders? Plus, we look at how many people are having sex outside of relationships altogether. Casual sex in the form of hookup culture is all the rage among young urban adults, but is this also the case among the middle-aged or among seniors?

Chapter 4 turns to sexual behaviour. What are we doing the most, and what do we avoid? How many of us are having oral or anal sex? How many use sex toys and vibrators? How common is sex without the kissing and cuddling that we associate with love and intimacy? Does the script of penile-vaginal intercourse as the dominant form of heterosex limit the possibilities for straight couples more than for LGB couples? This chapter gives us a look into the sex acts of Canadians and how they might vary by gender, age, or sexual identity.

Sex can be a site of both pleasure and pain, and Chapter 5 examines the good and bad feelings that accompany it. What behaviours are the most pleasurable, arousing, and stimulating? What brings us to orgasm, and why do men climax more often than women in hetcroscxual scx? Is emotional intimacy between partners linked to sexual pleasure? This chapter also examines the pain of sex, as in feeling pressured or coerced into having it, or having sex that is physically uncomfortable, as well as the risk of poor sexual health outcomes. Out of respect for our participants, the Sex in Canada survey stopped short of asking them to describe any non-consensual sexual activity, so though we know it is all too common, we don't dive deeply into it here.

Chapter 6 considers the social organization of sexuality. That is, how does social location affect sexual behaviours? This chapter looks at the small differences in sexuality that exist across the regions of Canada and the larger differences between anglophones and francophones. We think about how religion shapes sexual behaviour and how education influences the choices we make in our sexuality. This chapter also considers the politics of sexuality, examining whether those who lean to the left on the political spectrum might engage in activities that, on average, differ from those who lean to the right.

Taken together, the findings presented in this book offer a solid empirical foundation for our knowledge about sex in Canada. By its end, we will understand how much and what kind of sex Canadians have on average and how they feel about it. We will also have a sense of the wide variety in their sexual behaviours, identities, and desires. In some instances, the analysis will give the answers we expected, whereas in others, the data hold a few surprises. And we will know how these averages vary, if at all, by social locations such as age, racial identity, level of education, and language group. In the end, this book is an overview of the social organization of sexuality – the way that social forces nudge us into patterns of sexual behaviour.

1

Thinking about Sexual Identity

Sexual identity is one of the most important social divisions that organize our sexual lives. It says something essential, not only about our attractions and desires, but also about our families and communities. It is a way for us to make sense of who we are and to communicate this sense to others.[1] When I say I am "straight" or "heterosexual," I am telling you a little something, but not nearly everything, about my sexual desires. I may be communicating the gender of my partner, but perhaps the full truth about my sexuality is more complex, or maybe it has changed over time. Some people experience their sexuality as an unalterable truth about who they are, whereas others feel that it is more fluid.

The 2SLGBTQ+ acronym, which combines a set of sexual identities that distinguish themselves from the straight identity, is now widely known. Two-spirit, lesbian, gay, bisexual, transgender, and queer identities have been claimed by people who were once labelled as deviant by powerful social actors in legal, medical, and psychological communities. Giving a positive set of names to that which has been demeaned by others has been central to the struggle for rights and equality, as has forming an inclusive community that broadens coalitions rather than limits them. For this reason, the acronym can be expanded to include additional identities. For example, the 2S in 2SLGBTQQIA+ refers to two-spirit Indigenous understandings of gender and sexuality. The second "Q" in QQ represents people who are questioning their sexuality, a recognition that for some, identities change over their lifetime. The "I" stands for intersex people, those whose sex at birth falls somewhere between the binary categories of male and female, and who have been fighting for the right to self-determination of their gender and sex. The "A" is for asexual people, who experience low or absent levels of sexual desire, and the plus sign "+" symbolizes other possibilities.

In this book, I most often refer to lesbian, gay, bisexual, and straight identity categories. They are the most numerous among the groups mentioned above and are thus most easily captured with survey methods. I will use the acronym LGB in discussing survey data about participants who claimed lesbian, gay, and bisexual identities. However, when I refer to the communities, social movements, and subcultures that formed around these sexual identities, I use the 2SLGBTQ+ acronym that is most prominent today. These are not simple choices. The language we use to represent these communities and their diverse members has been contested and debated, changing over time. It will continue to change. Sociologists know that sexual identity is much more than a label we choose to describe ourselves. These categories form divisions that shape our social world. In this chapter, I give a historical sketch of how we came to adopt these particular identity categories and discuss how they have become forces that affect our lives.

HISTORY OF SEXUAL IDENTITY

Those who have studied sexuality throughout history have found same-sex sexual activity to be universally present to some degree and in some form in all cultures for which there are historic records.[2] However, cultures vary widely in how they understand and interpret it. The categories of sexual identities that we use in Canada today can be traced back to nineteenth-century Europe, with the exception of two-spirit identity, which was crafted to represent Indigenous traditions. It is surprising to some that we cannot trace these identities further back than the 1800s, as they can seem to be natural and obvious. However, the terms "heterosexuality," "homosexuality," and "bisexuality" did not exist before the nineteenth century. They were invented then.[3]

If men have been having sex with men, and women with women, throughout time and across all cultures, how can LGB (and straight) identity have been invented only in nineteenth-century Europe? The key to understanding this mystery is seeing the sexual behaviour (what we do) and the identity category (who we are) as two separate things. The behaviour was always around, but our way of understanding what it means about who we are took on a unique form in Europe over the nineteenth century. Prior to this shift in thought, religious institutions were dominant in defining what sexuality meant, and their approach was to see it as either sinful or morally good, rather than as something that categorized individuals as one type of person or another. For example, a person who did something "wrong" sexually committed a sin or crime like any other: it was an aberrant behaviour that deserved a consequence.[4]

However, over the nineteenth and twentieth centuries, as science and medicine sought to replace religion as the primary lenses through which we understand sexuality, sexologists and psychologists began to view it differently. They saw sexual behaviour as revealing something about the core nature of individuals, grouping them into various "types" of people. Sigmund Freud's theories of psychosexual development were one key influence in this way of thinking, but he was not the only intellectual of his day to reimagine sexuality as central to the self and identity.[5] Freud was joined by a host of doctors, psychiatrists, and sexologists who approached sexuality as an expression of "who we are" as opposed to simply "what we do."

In particular, several sexologists were concerned with distinguishing normal, healthy sexuality from what they saw as abnormal, unhealthy variations.[6] Among their extensive efforts to document variations of all types, the terms "heterosexuality" and "homosexuality" became new ways to describe distinct categories of people. Over time, heterosexuality was understood to denote normal sexuality, and homosexuality was seen as mentally unhealthy. Although some who used these terms were activists fighting against the criminal laws that banned same-sex sexuality, their efforts at reform largely failed, and severe treatment of those who were diagnosed as homosexuals became the norm. Over the course of the twentieth century, many psychologists attempted to "treat" what they considered to be the mental illness of homosexuality with a variety of harsh and punitive techniques, including institutionalization, castration, and aversion therapies.[7] In this context, same-sex desire was something to keep secret, as its discovery was likely to result in very negative reactions, including expulsion from one's family, being fired from work, or being involuntarily committed to an institution.

In the twenty-first century, lesbian and gay communities began to resist this diagnosis and its accompanying punishments. A few psychologists began to rethink the categorization of homosexuality as a mental illness. One in particular, Dr. Evelyn Hooker, conducted a study in which she found that a panel of experts could not accurately diagnose homosexuality, an important work that showed homosexuals to be psychologically well adjusted.[8] By 1973, the protests of lesbian and gay activists had convinced the American Psychiatric Association to remove homosexuality from its diagnostic manual.[9] A large body of evidence was amassed demonstrating clearly that homosexual people were as mentally healthy as heterosexuals. The idea that same-sex attraction is a sign of mental illness has since been abandoned by psychiatrists and psychologists.

This history of the shameful treatment of homosexual people pushed many to reject the labels homosexual and heterosexual. In addition, gender and sexuality scholars began to question the categories themselves. When Michel Foucault wrote that the scientific categorization of sexuality as healthy or unhealthy was a political project in the service of power, he hinted at a rich array of possibilities for sexuality beyond heterosexual and homosexual.[10] Gender theorist Judith Butler's suggestion that gender is performative and fluid, producing infinite possibilities beyond the binary categories of man and woman, was similarly highly influential.[11] As activists resisted the psychological diagnoses embedded in the heterosexual/homosexual schema, theorists argued for more fluid understandings of gender and sexuality.[12]

However, even after all these changes, we still retain the underlying idea that the preference for one gender or another forms the principal basis of our sexual identities. We may refer to "gay and lesbian" rather "homosexual," may opt for "straight" rather than "heterosexual," and may use the word "bisexual" for people who do not fall into either camp. Today, this schema remains the primary (but by no means the only) way that we make sense of our sexual selves: through the genders of ourselves and of our partners. If I am a woman and my partners are men, I am straight; if my partners are women, I am a lesbian. And if some of my partners are men and others are women, I am bisexual. Simple, right? As we will see, not necessarily. Although these categories do not always capture the wide variety of sexual and gender experiences that people embody, they are the ones that, for the most part, we use to describe ourselves.[13]

HOW MANY CANADIANS ARE LGB?

It turns out that, as a rule, we are terrible at guessing the proportion of the population that is lesbian, gay, or bisexual. If I asked you to guess, what would you say? If you are like most Canadians, you might opt for something like 10 or 15 percent, which would substantially overestimate the LGB population.[14] In fact, only about 4 percent of Canadians identify as lesbian, gay, or bisexual: about 1 million people.[15] If you didn't know that, it's really not your fault. Government agencies that are tasked with tracking population dynamics have only recently begun counting LGB, trans, and nonbinary people.

The Canadian census began counting cohabiting same-sex couples in 2006, after same-sex marriage was legalized. As of 2011, there were over sixty-four thousand households with such couples, about 0.8 percent of all cohabiting couples in Canada.[16] Of course, by counting only households, we miss all those who are single and who are in a relationship but not living together. The census, the only survey that attempts to include everyone rather than just a representative sample, would give the most accurate figure, but Statistics Canada has included sexual identity questions on some very large-scale surveys, which provide highly reliable estimates. Note that at this point, surveys ask only about lesbian, gay, and bisexual identities. No large-scale estimates are available for queer, two-spirit, pansexual, or asexual identities.

One such survey administered by Statistics Canada, the Canadian Community Health Survey, did include a question on sexual orientation.

Statistics Canada used its various surveys to release a report in 2021 that estimates 4 percent of Canadians over age fifteen has an LGB identity.[17] Among this group, about one-fourth identify as gay men and about 17 percent as lesbian women. Over half of those in the LGB group (about 2–3 percent of the population) identify as bisexual, with women twice as likely than men to describe themselves in this way. There is some evidence that the proportion of Canadians who identify as LGB will grow over time, as young people are more likely than older age cohorts to do so. This pattern has also been documented in the United States.[18] It suggests that the shift away from the exclusion and marginalization of LGB people in recent decades is making more space for people to claim LGB identities.

Even though the census doesn't yet ask about sexual identity, this important counting tool did recently change the way it asks about sex and gender in order to establish the size of the transgender and nonbinary population. Canada was the first country to take this step, which activists and scholars had been advocating for years.[19] The census revised its sex question to a two-part series that first asks for sex at birth and then asks for current gender. The gender question includes male, female, and a third option that allows people to input their gender identity in their own words. In this first census to capture the trans population, Canada counted just over 100,000 trans and nonbinary people, or about 0.33 percent of the population.

As many members of the 2SLGBTQ+ community will argue, sexuality doesn't fit neatly into a series of checkboxes. The need to chronicle, count, and measure the LGBTQ+ population through scientific tools such as surveys imposes more order onto sexual identities than is called for by the way in which people live their sexual lives.[20] This is just as true for people with straight identities as for those who are LGB. We often assume there are clear and permanent lines between straight and lesbian or gay. That is, straight people are always and exclusively attracted to members of the other gender, and as soon as someone has sex with a same-gender partner, that means they are gay or lesbian, and they will remain so for the rest of their lives. Anyone who falls between these two situations, we might imagine, is "really" a bisexual. However, sexual behaviour and identity in the real world just don't work this way.[21]

For example, people's sexual identities don't always match up with the gender of their sexual or romantic partner.[22] In other words, some people experience a discordance between their sexual behaviour and their sexual identity.[23] Although having a sexual experience that doesn't match your identity might prompt you to rethink it, some Canadians feel comfortable in an identity that doesn't precisely match their behaviour.[24] This might be due to social pressure to stay in the closet or an understanding of the self that is distinct from one's sexual activity.[25] One research study that examined rural men who identified as straight despite having sex with other men found that they valued the sense of masculinity that was tied to a straight identity.[26]

In our survey, most of the women who identified as straight and who were currently in a relationship had a male partner. A small fraction, 1.9 percent, reported that their partner was female. You might think that they simply made a mistake when they filled out this part of the survey. That's not impossible, as we all know how easy it is to check the wrong box on a form. However, among the straight-identified men who were currently in a relationship, 3.9 percent stated that their partner was male. Similarly, 3.7 percent of the women who identified as lesbian reported that their partner was a man, and 6.5 percent of gay men said they were currently dating women. Figure 1.1 shows that sexual identities are only rough approximations of people's sexual and romantic lives.

This same mismatch between sexual identity and gender of partner also popped up when participants answered our questions about sexual behaviour. If you think that gay men have sex only with men and lesbian women with women, the information in Figures 1.2 and 1.3 may surprise you. In fact, 10 percent of gay men stated that, during the last year, one or more of their sexual partners was a woman. About 8 percent of lesbian women reported that one or more of their partners was a man.

If we focus on straight-identified people, we see a similar pattern. For example, 3 percent of straight women reported that one or more of their partners in the past year was a woman. The figure was higher for straight men who had sex with men. About 6 percent of them reported having one or more men as a sexual partner during the last year. This pattern is consistent with other surveys on sexual identity and partner choice.[27]

What this tells us is that sexual identity can be flexible and expansive.

FIGURE 1.1   **Sexual identity and gender of relationship partner**

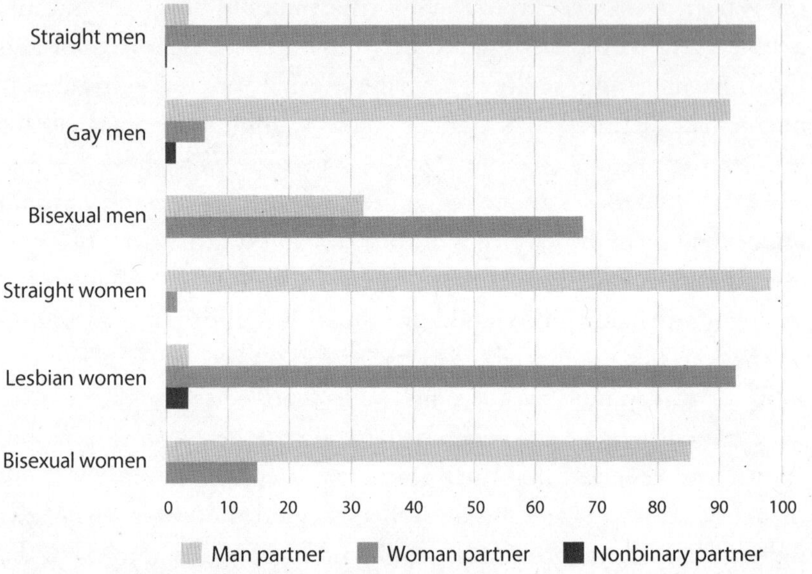

For a proportion of our participants, it did not map perfectly onto their partner's gender at the moment that they took our survey. We also know that many, but not all, people experience changes in their sexual desires over their life course. Some redefine their sexual identity, such as when lesbian or gay people come out of the closet, claiming a new identity to their friends and family. But identity changes can go in the other direction as well. For instance, women who have lived as lesbians for decades sometimes find a male partner later in life and take on a straight or bisexual identity.[28]

That sexual desire is fluid has been understood for some time. This idea has been advanced as an important corrective to Freudian approaches that situate sexuality as a deep truth about oneself, a uniquely core attribute of the self that determines many other aspects of personality and relationships. This very solid and unchanging concept of sexual identity works for some people, who feel that they have always known about the direction of their sexual desires, which express something important and real about who they are as individuals. However, the idea posited by Foucault, Butler, and other theorists – that gender and sexual-

FIGURE 1.2 **Gender of sexual partners of men**

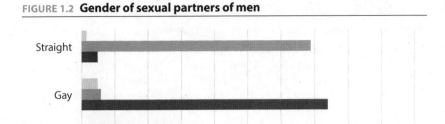

FIGURE 1.3 **Gender of sexual partners of women**

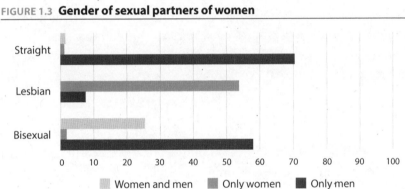

ity are always changing and emerging – feels right to others, whose desires do not necessarily fit well into the straight, lesbian, or gay check-boxes on a survey.[29] From this perspective, both sexuality and gender are, to some unknown degree, emergent and performative, unfolding through interactions in an ongoing way. Categories such as queer and pansexual, which avoid the constraints of traditional identity markers, emerged to make sense of sexuality in a new way, as I will discuss.

Although it may be tempting to pronounce on whether sexual identity is solid or fluid, the evidence shows that Canadians use both understandings. The Sex in Canada survey revealed that some people embraced a flexible understanding of their sexual identity. For others, having a solid understanding of their sexual identity is a useful tool to situate them in their social world. And this system of understanding does more than just describe the sexual orientations of individuals; it structures the social world.

SEXUALITY STRUCTURES OUR WORLD

Just like gender (and other social forces such as class, race, and ethnicity), sexuality orders and shapes the world around us.[30] It is social in that it groups people into "types," a process that can bring them together but that can also separate them. Sexual identities describe communities of people, gathering them together. They create neighbourhoods and community groups. They organize friendships and family ties. Assumptions about sexual identities are embedded in social policies and institutions.[31] In this section, we think about how most of the world is organized around heterosexuality. In response to this, communities, subcultures, and social movements have formed around sexual identities that do not conform to heterosexual expectations.

COMMUNITIES

It may be easiest to see how sexual identities shape the social world by thinking about 2SLGBTQ+ communities. For over a century, gay men, lesbian women, trans people, and those with queer sensibilities have formed neighbourhoods in cities, sometimes called "gaybourhoods."[32] Over time, 2SLGBTQ+ people move in. Businesses that cater to them, such as bookstores, bars, and clubs, cluster in these spaces.[33] Feminist bookstores have been important hubs for lesbian communities.[34] Health care clinics may post a rainbow flag in their windows. Annual pride parades both protest discrimination and celebrate 2SLGBTQ+ lives.[35] These neighbourhoods are visible because they are marked as 2SLGBTQ+: physically, culturally, socially. Sexual identity is central, not just to the individuals who live there, but also to the social institutions and to the larger community. Of course, 2SLGBTQ+ communities develop in other spaces as well, including small towns and rural areas.[36]

Just as these neighbourhoods are structured around sexuality, so are other neighbourhoods and communities. If you think about the visible markers that reveal how sexuality brings people together in a 2SLGBTQ+ neighbourhood, shapes their lives, influences how they connect, spend their leisure time, and so on, you can understand that the rest of the social world is similarly organized around sexuality, too. However, most of it revolves around heterosexuality. Just as gaybourhoods bring 2SLGBTQ+ people together, provide services for them, and create community, in most of the social world, heterosexuality is the somewhat invisible identity around which much of our life is organized. In fact, heterosexuality is so dominant that it may be a little difficult to detect. But if you look for it, you will see that it is everywhere all the time, a taken-for-granted part of life. The tacit assumption that everyone is heterosexual unless identified otherwise underlies much of the social world, from government agencies to mortgage applications to interactions at your local grocery store.

We call this heteronormativity to convey the idea that heterosexuality lies at the root of many norms.[37] Of course, heteronormativity is also intertwined with the way that gender organizes our lives.[38] Theorists refer to the sex/gender/sexuality system in highlighting that many gender expectations for men and women work in service of a world that is organized around heterosexuality.[39] The "normal" life that is set up for the nuclear family – a married heterosexual couple with children – is embedded in more of the social world than just neighbourhoods. It is baked into the way that businesses sell us products and services. Schools structure their curriculum and their extracurricular activities around heterosexuality.[40] Family events and neighbourhood gatherings often rely on differing expectations for mothers and fathers.

CULTURES AND SUBCULTURES
Sexuality can be understood in still more expansive terms, as an important force that organizes our culture. One way to think of culture is in concrete terms, as the films, books, and music that it produces. Heterosexuality is clearly a leading character in the media that we consume on a daily basis, although more room for 2SLGBTQ+-focused characters and plots has been created in recent decades. The imagined selves that are reflected back at us through creative media are now more

sexually diverse than they were fifty years ago, but they still primarily feature heterosexuality as the unremarkable expectation for families in particular and social lives in general.

Another way to think of culture is in its broadest sense, as the system of meanings that tell us who we are, what our shared beliefs and values are. These understandings are produced by interactions among individuals, as well as by institutions such as government, religion, and our health care system. This is how heterosexuality can be understood as culturally dominant. Everything from nursery rhymes through high school proms, from university dorms through retirement communities is grounded in an assumed heterosexuality that goes unmarked. LGB identity (or another sexual identity) must be claimed explicitly to overcome this presumption.

Many 2SLGBTQ+ subcultures have developed in response to the dominant position of heterosexuality. They have a rich history in the theatre, in campy drag shows, and in early film.[41] In art, music, film, and fashion, 2SLGBTQ+ subcultural styles can play with, mock, and criticize heteronormativity and gender norms. In the interplay between our dominant heterosexual culture and the 2SLGBTQ+ subculture, we have further evidence of the ways that sexuality shapes our shared experiences. Some aspects of gay men's subculture are distinct from that of lesbian women, but in many instances, shared subcultures create inclusive spaces for gay men, lesbian women, queer, trans, and gender-expansive people with systems of meaning that stand apart from the dominant culture.

BISEXUALITY

Do bisexual people also have subcultures? This remains an open question.[42] To this point in Canada's history, bisexuality has been more useful in reflecting the sexual preferences and expressing the personal identities of individuals than in forming social institutions, neighbourhoods, or community groups. Whereas bisexual people have been included in 2SLGBTQ+ community groups, organizations, and activism to varying degrees, they have also felt somewhat marginalized in these communities.[43] Many bisexuals claim that they do not feel fully embraced by either heterosexual cultural institutions or gay or lesbian subcultures. This lack of inclusion has a negative impact on their mental health.[44]

Over the decades, a number of cultural icons have been bisexual, but the development of bisexual community organizations and cultural institutions has been limited. However, bisexuality is on the rise. Recent population studies in the United States show that 5.5 percent of women and 2.0 percent of men identify as bisexual.[45] Younger generations are far more likely than previous ones to adopt a bisexual identity, along with other sexual identities such as queer and pansexual, all of which resist limiting attraction to either gender.[46] This may be a sign that, as social inclusion of lesbian and gay people increases, people are more willing to claim a sexual identity that is not restricted by gender preference.

INEQUALITY, ACTIVISM, AND CHANGE

To understand sexuality as a social force is also to see it as a mechanism of inequality. Our sexual identities place us in particular locations relative to other sexual identities, in either the dominant group or the marginalized group. The position of heterosexuality as self-evidently normal, good, and healthy is reflected not only in culture, but also in social structure. Inequality can be measured in various ways. For example, we might consider legal, political, and social exclusion and inclusion of heterosexual and LGB people as measures of inequality.

In the not very distant past, the inequalities between straight and 2SLGBTQ+ people were extreme. As recently as 1968, sex between two men was a criminal offence in Canada (indeed, arrests continued well after that date).[47] Homosexuality was formally defined as a mental illness, and both adults and minors could be institutionalized against their will for their sexuality. Gender presentation and identity have similarly been treated as both mental illnesses and crimes. Representations of 2SLGBTQ+ lives in popular culture were rare and often in the form of exaggerated negative stereotypes.[48]

Due to the decades-long struggle of 2SLGBTQ+ organizations and communities, the law, social institutions, and public opinion have significantly shifted toward inclusion and equality.[49] The coalition model of working together has been responsible for many of Canada's policy changes during the last several decades, such as the inclusion of sexual orientation and gender identity in non-discrimination law and the legal recognition of same-sex marriage. For example, although the Charter of Rights and Freedoms does not mention sexual identity directly, the courts have interpreted its provisions as standing for equal rights for lesbian, gay, and bisexual people. Canada legalized same-sex marriage in 2005, and Prime Minister Justin Trudeau officially apologized for Canada's mistreatment of 2SLGBTQ+ people in 2017. Anti-discrimination protections for transgender people were also passed in 2017. This distinguishes Canada from the United States, where some states and cities prohibit discrimination against 2SLGBTQ+ people, though others do not.

However, Canada's anti-discrimination laws have not solved the problem of sex-based inequalities, which become visible in social patterns across groups of people. For example, 2SLGBTQ+ people are underrepresented among our elected officials. Whereas some out lesbian and gay individuals have won elections, such as former Ontario premier Kathleen Wynne, this is still a relatively rare event. If sexual identity did not matter to elections, we would expect about 4 percent or so of elected officials to be LGB, to match the population. We may be moving in that direction, but we are not there yet.

Lesbian and gay people may make less money than their straight counterparts. In Canada, data on sexual identity are limited, so many questions about its link with wage inequality remain unanswered. However, we do have good data on the incomes of married and common-law couples. Analyses of these data reveal that gender and sexuality combine to affect income disparity among individuals. There is a sex/gender order to income inequality: straight men are better paid than gay men, who in turn make more than lesbian women, who make more than straight women.[50] In this analysis, there is a wage penalty for gay men relative to straight men. However, straight women are at the disadvantage relative to lesbian women. Sexuality seems to be an important part of the story of gender and wage inequality, but more research is needed.

Another way of thinking about inequality is in terms of risk of victimization. Members of the 2SLGBTQ+ community are at highest risk of harassment and targeted violence. In Canada, they are disproportionately victimized in violent crimes.[51] Lesbian women and gay men are 2.5 times more likely than heterosexuals to experience violence, and bisexuals are 4.0 times more likely. Trans people are also at heightened risk of violence. Although more data are needed, community surveys consistently report that they experience relatively high rates of violence. For example, the 2015 Trans PULSE report that surveyed trans Ontarians noted that 1 in 5 of them reported being assaulted, either physically or sexually.[52]

Nonetheless, social attitudes toward lesbian and gay people have substantially improved over time, a trend that has been particularly dramatic in Canada during the last forty years. Whereas Canadians once expressed strongly negative opinions of lesbian and gay people, Canada is now among a handful of countries with very positive attitudes.[53] This has come about because young people do not share the negative views of the older generation and because Canadians of all ages have revised their opinions.[54] However, such acceptance is not universal, and some young people are still harassed by their peers and rejected by their families.[55]

A sociological view of sexual identity sees these inequalities as part of our social structure, evidence that sexuality forms divisions and boundaries that order the world in much the same manner as gender, race, and class.[56] This perception means that sexual identity not only reflects the preferences or sexual desires of individuals, but also exists outside the individual, slotting us into neighbourhoods and community groups, setting expectations for how we conduct our lives, producing cultures and subcultures that give meaning to our lives, and causing inequalities along dimensions of sexual identity.[57]

KNOWLEDGE, POWER, AND SEXUALITY:
TWO-SPIRIT IDENTITY IN INDIGENOUS CULTURES

I note above that Canadian ideas about sexual identities came originally from Europe. It is important to understand that other cultures have their own understandings of sexual identity. In fact, many Asian, Latin American, and African cultures, as well as Indigenous cultures around the world, have developed ways of understanding gender and sexuality that differ from the heterosexual/homosexual model that is most familiar in Canada. Rather than engaging in cultural tourism by dropping a few examples of unfamiliar sexualities into a discussion that otherwise ignores them, exoticizing the people who don't conform to the Eurocentric model, I encourage you to read further on this topic.[58]

One alternative way of understanding sexuality, however, is worth mentioning because of its relevance in Canada: the two-spirit identity, which emerged as a form of resistance to colonization.[59] Indigenous peoples who live in Canada are not of a single culture; rather, they are many nations with many cultures. Before Europeans set foot on this continent, they had many different ways of understanding gender and sexuality. Colonizing forces attempted to eliminate these cultures as part of the larger project of occupying land and controlling the governance of the place we now know as Canada.

Surveillance and social control were central to that project. For example, colonization as a bureaucratic process included observing the sexual practices of Indigenous peoples and generating a historical record that marked them as unusual, deviant, and strange. The production of knowledge that mocks and dismisses Indigenous ways of being and knowing has been a core part of the colonial project of social and economic dominance, and gender and sexuality have featured heavily in it.[60] Portraying Indigenous peoples as sexually immoral, exotic, and strange served as one among several justifications for colonization.

In resisting colonization, which is still in place today, Indigenous people struggle to prevent the eradication of their cultures.[61] Individuals from many cultures form coalitions to resist the colonial practices that erase their ways of knowing and being. For example, some Indigenous peoples of North America use the term "two-spirit" to describe a particular Indigenous sexual and gender identity – one that colonizers had labelled with an offensive term.[62]

Producing a positive word to describe Indigenous sexuality and gender signals a refusal to be defined by colonialization. It demonstrates that Indigenous sexual and gender identities are best understood through a lens that respects Indigenous cultures and traditions. It acknowledges the European origins of the LGB categories that are common in Canada today and establishes a non-colonial possibility for Indigenous peoples to exist on their own terms. In other words, the framework for sexual identity that dominates Canadian culture – and the one that forms the basis of this book – cannot simply be imposed upon Indigenous traditions.[63] For this reason, I do not attempt to describe the sexual lives of two-spirit or other Indigenous people. Two-spirit communities should be allowed their own voice regarding their experiences of sexuality in Canada.

LGBTQQIA+ IDENTITIES
There have been many challenges, modifications, and additions to sexual and gender identity categories. For example, "queer" emerged in both intellectual and activist communities as a criticism of the LGB/straight identity system and the politics that such a system implies. The body of scholarly work known as queer theory has been highly influential in its claims. As it reminds us, the categories that provide us with sexual identities, but that also shape the social world, are just one possibility through which we might imagine ourselves.[64] Some queer theorists argue that identity categories imply a certain type of activist project that emphasizes equality and respectability rather than social transformation.[65] Then again, some individuals use "queer" to refer to a sexual identity. In certain cases, this denotes support for an expansive or radical political project; in other instances, it simply feels more comfortable than the words lesbian, bisexual, or gay.

TRANSGENDER AND NONBINARY GENDER IDENTITIES
"Transgender" refers to people whose gender differs from the sex they were assigned at birth. "Cisgender" is the opposite of transgender, describing people whose gender matches the sex they were assigned at birth. Although transgender people have existed throughout history, these particular terms are somewhat new, and they are being debated and changed over time. For example, some prefer "trans," arguing that it offers a broader umbrella for a community that understands gender and sex in a variety of ways.[66]

Some people adopt a nonbinary gender identity that is neither man nor woman. Imagining gender as a spectrum, rather than as two distinct categories of male and female, allows a range of possibilities for the presentation of self.[67] As gender is deeply embedded in both the English and French languages, new terms have been proposed to express non-binary pronouns for people who don't see themselves as fitting either "she" or "he." In English, the practice of using "they" as a singular, non-binary pronoun has gained ascendancy in recent years, becoming accepted by prominent style guides.[68]

Trans and nonbinary communities have been in, of, and around lesbian and gay communities for decades. Indeed, performing gender, playing with the multiple meanings of gender, and mocking traditional gender stereotypes have been important parts of gay and lesbian subcultures, art, and performance, and transgender people have been leaders in activism to produce social change. Today, the 2SLGBTQ+ acronym intends to capture the togetherness of communities who have been marginalized for their genders and sexualities but who have united in their struggle for change and inclusion.

INTERSEX IDENTITY

"Intersex" describes individuals who, due to a range of medical conditions, do not totally conform to male or female sex categories.[69] They have formed communities to resist the surgeries that alter genitalia to look more male or (more often) more female. These procedures are most likely to occur when intersex people are very young, often as infants. Intersex activists want intersex people to exercise consent over their own bodies, opposing medically unnecessary cosmetic surgeries on children.[70] They have succeeded in convincing some medical professionals that cosmetic genital surgeries are unnecessary, though the practice has not yet been banned by law. Intersex people have often found places in 2SLGBTQ+ communities and have worked with 2SLGBTQ+ activists to produce social change.

ASEXUAL IDENTITY

Of course, not all sexualities are covered by the LGB framework. Asexuality, for example, is a relatively emergent identity that describes low or no sexual desire.[71] Sometimes people combine an asexual or "Ace" identity with an LGB or straight identity to communicate that they have low sexual desire for a particular gender or genders. Others want to express a feeling of attraction accompanied by a lack of interest in sex.[72] Online communities have formed around Ace identities, enabling people to think through their sexuality in conversation with others who share a low or absent sex drive.[73] Asexuality should be distinguished from celibacy, which is best characterized as a choice to abstain from sex, rather than having little desire for it.

PANSEXUAL IDENTITY

"Pansexual" refers to an identity that is open to partners regardless of their gender identity or presentation. The word suggests a criticism of binary understandings of gender and of the rigidity of categories in the LGB system.[74] For this reason, pansexuality is slightly different from bisexuality, in that it acknowledges those with nonbinary gender. Those who feel that gender is not a central feature in what they find attractive in others may also choose to describe themselves as pansexual.[75]

Each of these sexual identities is both a personal and a political project that combines concerns over "who I am" with ideas about how the world is organized. The last several decades have seen profound change around sexual identity. Despite queer critiques and the rise of many new identities, most social and political change has occurred in the area of lesbian and gay rights. This is reflective of the social order described above, and the LGB framing of sexual identity has become increasingly institutionalized in laws and social practices. Transgender identity is also becoming institutionalized. Standards of care for gender transitions have been established in the medical system, and the law now recognizes the rights of transgender people. For example, federal passports allow people to change their gender when they transition. Canada also legally recognizes nonbinary gender in some institutional ways, such as providing for the option of a third gender, "X" in addition to "M" and "F," on legal documents.

This institutionalization of the 2SLGBTQ+ identity system does not necessarily mean that this way of knowing will forever organize our world. We have seen many changes over the last few decades, and the criticisms of these approaches, as well as the categories that have recently been produced, may become more prevalent in the future. For now, however, this way of knowing sexuality and gender forms the basis of our social life.

SEXUAL IDENTITY: BOTH PERSONAL AND SOCIAL

As sexual identity shapes the world in general, our own personal identity will influence how we engage with it, influencing where we live, what we do for fun, and who our friends are. Of course, we should also expect to see differences in sexual behaviour. For example, gay subcultures have sometimes embraced more expansive sexual norms than those of the heteronormative culture. They reject or modify expectations of monogamy in favour of sexual freedom.[76] Do gay men have more sex than straight men? And can we ask the same question for lesbian women, who are also part of the 2SLGBTQ+ subculture but who have formed distinctly women-centred subcultures of their own?

Sexual identity categories are not the perfect way to describe sexuality. They are the products of a particular time and place, like all social constructions. Embedded within them is an insistence that heterosexuality is central and that other orientations are marginal. They assume that sexual orientation is a core element of the self and is thus permanent and rooted in biology. However, human sexuality is complex. It is about more than just the gender of our partner, and sometimes sexual feelings change over time. The available identity categories are not always a perfect fit with the desires and feelings of every individual at every moment in their lives. Still, the system has important consequences for the social world. It has served as the basis for the formation of communities. It is an essential component of both the dominant culture and a set of vibrant subcultures. It is entrenched in the law and throughout our institutions. Although it may not fit each individual perfectly, it is a force that organizes the world.

It may seem too obvious to claim that sexual behaviour is also governed by sexual identity, but as the survey data show, sexual activity is influenced but not determined by sexual identity. Many decades of research confirm that we cannot equate sexual identity with sexual behaviour, because there is always a gap between who people say they are and what they say they do. This is true for straight people, some of whom report having same-sex partners, as well as for lesbian and gay people. Whereas some people claim a bisexual identity to signal that their partners are of either gender, others have similar behaviour while claiming a straight, lesbian, or gay identity.

Newly recognized sexual identities, such as asexual and pansexual, expand the possibilities for understanding ourselves. However, it remains to be seen whether they will become embedded in our social structure and culture in the way that LGB identities have. Perhaps as time marches on, the boundaries between straight and LGB identities will become less relevant to us. For now, however, there is abundant evidence that this system of sexuality is a key force that shapes our social world.

2
How Much Sex Are We Having?

When it comes to sex, we live in a universe of stereotypes and myths. Much of what we think we know comes from anecdotes and home-grown theories. We also get a lot of messages from the media, whether in Hollywood films, popular music, or streaming services. Do they have any connection with reality? We might speculate, for instance, that singles are having more sex than married people. That having children ruins a couple's sex life. That senior couples never have sex at all. Which of these stereotypes, if any, are true? Do they accurately describe, more or less, the sexual behaviour of adult Canadians?

This chapter explores how often Canadians have sex, partnered or alone. The Sex in Canada survey provides an excellent snapshot of sexual activity to help us confirm or challenge some common tropes around sexual behaviour. Instead of relying on media, myths, or assumptions about how much sex people were having, we relied on what they told us themselves. The survey also revealed the similarity or variety in their sexual activity. That is, was it mostly alike, or was there wide variation? With these data, we have a good view into what people are actually doing.

MASTURBATION

You don't need a partner to have a good time. Many of our participants reported that masturbation was a regular aspect of their lives. The majority had masturbated alone within the past month. Another 20 percent had done so at some point within the last year. It is very clear that most Canadians make masturbating a common feature of their sex lives. Although it was once a serious social taboo, today there is less stigma and shame surrounding it. We may not talk about it all the time, but most of us are enjoying regular sex on our own.

As Figure 2.1 shows, men masturbate more often than women: 64 percent of men, but only 45 percent of women, had done so in the past month. The cause of this discrepancy may be biological, if men have stronger sex drives than women. However, I think that sociological forces are also at play. For example, we know that the norms governing sexuality are different for men and women. Many gender scholars argue that women are subject to more restrictions on their sexuality and harsher judgments if they embrace their sexual desire.[1] This double standard means that men are socialized to see themselves as inherently filled with desire that must somehow be managed. Women, on the other hand, are constantly told that the female body is lacking in some way and that their own sexual desire is less natural than men's. These expectations for men and women may also affect the frequency of masturbation.

The gender difference in participants who had never masturbated persuades me that the sociological explanation has relevance. This relatively small group was dominated by women. Among our participants, 18 percent of women had never masturbated, whereas for men, the figure was 10 percent, almost half of that for women. Never once having

FIGURE 2.1 **Masturbation, by gender**

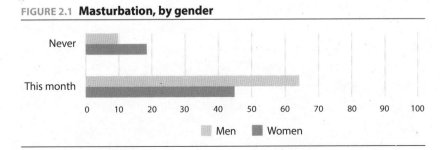

masturbated (or at least not admitting it) seems less an issue of sex drives and more of a thoughtful choice about acceptable behaviour. That women were so much more likely than men to make this choice (or, again, more likely to say so on a survey) suggests that they were responding to the restrictive norms that target them.

Only 14 percent of our survey respondents had never masturbated. This is strikingly different from a major US-based survey conducted during the 1990s, where the figure was 43 percent.[2] I used to teach this now outdated statistic to undergraduate students in my sociology of sexualities course. "They are lying!" my students would always say, one semester after the next. The eighteen- to twenty-one-year-olds in my class, who had come of age after the HIV crisis during an era of safer-sex education, could not imagine going a lifetime without masturbating. I used this example to teach them about the social organization of sexuality. I asked them to imagine their grandparents in their teenage years and young adulthood. What kinds of messages would they have received about masturbation? Perhaps they belonged to a church that saw it as a grave sin. Perhaps they married young and started having children right away, focusing on reproduction rather than sexual pleasure. Perhaps they believed the psychoanalytic perspective of the day that masturbation was a sign of sexual immaturity.

I remind my students of the powerful impact of the HIV crisis on public discourse about sex and sexuality. Confronted with a deadly sexually transmitted infection (STI) that had no cure, educators rejected the long-standing taboo on speaking frankly about sex. Many worked with activists to develop safer-sex education curriculums that included clear-eyed talk about the risks associated with the exchange of bodily fluids in partnered sex. Masturbation became widely understood as a healthy way to experience sexual satisfaction without the risk of catching an STI. Of course, the introduction of the internet made sexually explicit material widely available, continuing to smash taboos about masturbation. The result of all these changes is that the practice of masturbation is distributed unequally across the population. Older people are much more likely than younger generations never to have done it (Figure 2.2).

FIGURE 2.2 **Proportion of age group who never masturbate**

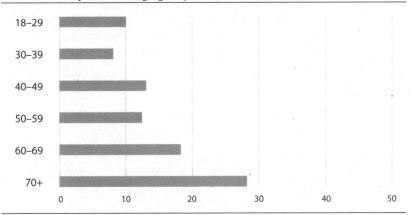

PARTNERED SEX

As enjoyable as sex with yourself can be, when we think of "having sex," we think of partnered sex. Sixty-eight percent of our participants told us that they had had sex with a partner in the past year. What qualifies as partnered sex? In this case, I am including any kind of sexual encounter that involves genitals. So, though kissing, cuddling, and intimate massages are important parts of our sexual lives (and I'll talk more about them in Chapter 4), these acts alone do not count as "having sex" for our purposes in this book. However, sex can encompass more than the most common understanding: penile-vaginal intercourse. Oral sex, anal sex, and genital touching are also included here.

Were you surprised to learn that a third of Canadians went without partnered sex during the past year? Going to bed with someone is a regular part of life, but there may be long periods when it doesn't occur. This might be due to a health problem, the difficulty of finding a partner, or it may just reflect a personal preference. In our survey, 21 percent, or about one in five, had not had sex with another person during the past year, even though they had engaged in it prior to that time and would otherwise be considered sexually active.

The remaining 11 percent had never had sex. There is a word to describe this group: virgins. Virginity has always been a loaded social identity. Judgments, disapproval, and stigma have been linked to one's status as a virgin or non-virgin, especially for women. However, the importance of virginity has changed drastically over the last century.[3] In the past, it was highly valued, particularly for young women. The loss of virginity outside of marriage was often accompanied by censure, not only for women, but also for their families. In a time when women were economically and socially dependent on men, first upon fathers and then upon husbands after getting married, retaining virginity was closely tied with their marriage prospects and economic security.

Today, the norms around virginity have changed. In some subcultures, such as in evangelical Christian traditions, chastity before marriage is still highly prized for both men and women.[4] However, for most Canadians, virginity has lost much of its significance. Prohibitions against sex before marriage have substantially diminished, and many young adults expect to have a sex life long before their wedding day. In fact, the stigma associated with virginity has reversed course, making it socially awkward to be a virgin past a certain age. Unless they have a staunch belief about refraining from partnered sex or they belong to a religious community that values virginity, young people can experience embarrassment if they haven't had sex yet.[5] Of course, gender plays an important role here. For young straight men, having sex with women is a way to establish both their heterosexuality and their masculinity,[6] two identities that are tightly coupled in our culture. Young women, however, still negotiate a sexual double standard. That is, whereas their male peers are lauded for having sex (and lots of it), they themselves can expect some level of disapproval if they follow suit. Accordingly, they describe their desire to have sex in both positive and negative terms.[7] Some see their sex lives as a project that needs to be managed so that they can lose their virginity while avoiding being labelled a "slut."[8]

You may have heard that young people are having less sex today than in previous generations. There is good evidence for this.[9] For example, data from the United States show that in the two decades prior to the COVID-19 pandemic, the proportion of sexually inactive young adults (aged eighteen to twenty-four) increased, with men more likely than women not to have been sexually active in the past year.[10] Similar patterns were found among teenagers as well.[11] Their decision to delay their first sexual encounter or to cut back on sex was aligned with a general avoidance of risky behaviour, such as substance use and hazardous driving. Many commentators welcomed this change as a positive development.[12] However, some are now characterizing these lower levels of sexual activity as a problem in itself, calling it a "sex drought."[13] And, of course, during the pandemic, young people had fewer opportunities for partnered sexual encounters than usual.[14]

In our pre-pandemic survey, we asked participants who had never had sex to give their reasons, allowing them to check all that applied. As Figure 2.3 shows, only 17 percent were saving themselves for marriage. Some hadn't found a partner yet, felt too shy to have sex, or wanted to wait until they fell in love.

Almost a quarter of these participants reported that they had never experienced sexual desire or attraction to others. Some people have low desire, others none at all. This can occur for a certain period or can persist throughout their lives. Sometimes, low desire might be associated with physical or mental illness, or it may be a side effect of a medication. In other cases, it is simply a part of natural human variation. As I mentioned in Chapter 1, sexual feelings are not the same as sexual identities, so we did not simply assume that participants who had no sexual desire would necessarily claim an asexual identity. Instead, we asked that

FIGURE 2.3 **Reasons for not having had partnered sex**

question directly. As it turned out, among participants who have not experienced sexual desire, 72 percent saw themselves as straight, and only 17 percent saw themselves as asexual. The asexual identity is still unfamiliar to many, but as it becomes better known, more people may adopt it in the future.

SEX OVER A LIFETIME

The sexual activity of Canadians varies across their life course. When we break down partnered sex by age group, it becomes clear that the amount of sex we have changes as we age. Figure 2.4 charts the proportion of people who had partnered sex in the past year. Even though it presents a cross-section of Canadians at one point in time, it suggests a pattern of sexual activity that alters throughout life. Seventy-eight percent of the youngest group, aged eighteen to twenty-nine, had sex with a partner during the past year. Then, sexual activity peaked for those in their thirties, with 83 percent of thirty-something participants reporting that they had sex this year. From age forty on, the percentage steadily declined.

It may seem self-evident that we'd have the most sex when we are young and fertile, establishing intimate relationships, and perhaps having children. As our bodies age and fertility declines, our sex drives slow

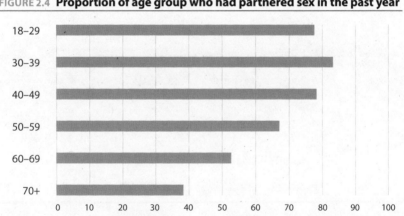

FIGURE 2.4 **Proportion of age group who had partnered sex in the past year**

down and we have less sex. Many elderly people do not have partners, so their sex lives, on average, decline. Those who do have partners might find themselves dealing with health troubles that reduce sexual activity.[15] Nevertheless, it is important to note that older Canadians do continue to have sex. Over one-third of those aged seventy and older (38 percent) had partnered sex during the past year. And 22 percent of them had it within the last month. This is an important reminder that fertility and sexuality are not the same thing. Sex remains a part of life for many Canadians well into their elder years.

SEXUAL IDENTITIES

Does sexual identity influence how often people have sex? That is, do lesbian, gay, and bisexual people have more sex than straight people? The subcultures that gay men and lesbian women developed in response to social exclusion, discrimination, and marginalization produced more than just gaybourhoods and fashion trends.[16] They created spaces where sexual norms could be reimagined, where the rules for regulating how much sex and with whom could differ from those of heteronormative social institutions. With this in mind, we might expect that the frequency of sex among lesbian and gay Canadians would differ from that of straight Canadians.

At first glance at the Sex in Canada data, however, there does not appear to be much difference. About 49 percent of straight Canadians and about 47 percent of gay/lesbian Canadians had sex in the last month. At about 60 percent, frequency was highest for bisexuals. Does this mean that they have more sex, but that there are no differences in frequency between straight, lesbian, and gay Canadians? No; it means that we must consider the important role of gender in organizing LGB and straight sexuality. When we split these groups by gender, a pattern of difference does emerge (Figure 2.5). The sexual frequency of gay men and lesbian women differs from that of straights, but in inverse proportion. That is, gay men have sex more frequently than straight men, and lesbian women have it less often than straight women. And there is a gender difference among bisexuals, too: 71 percent of bisexual men and 58 percent of bisexual women had sex in the last month.

FIGURE 2.5 **Partnered sex this month, by sexual identity and gender**

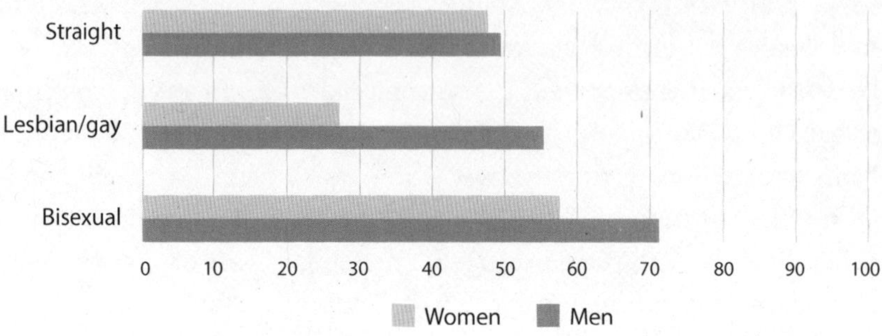

MARRIAGE AND PARENTING

Canadians are marrying less than ever before, and those who do tie the knot are delaying until they are older.[17] As a result, many are spending a longer period as singles. Adults commonly expect to be financially established in a career prior to getting married, and this means that into and through their twenties, and often well beyond, people are living as sexually active singles. Others never marry at all. What are the sex lives of these Canadians like?

Popular accounts typically imply that singles have more sex than married or common-law couples, but in fact the reverse is true. Married people have sex more frequently than their single counterparts. Over half of the married people in our survey (56 percent) had sex within the past month, compared to 35 percent of individuals who were unmarried and living alone. When we removed widowed, divorced, and separated participants from the picture, leaving only those who had never married, the proportion increased to 39 percent (Figure 2.6). This held true even when we controlled for age. The rumour that singles spend more time in the bedroom than married people is just not accurate, which makes sense. Finding a partner takes time and effort, and perhaps also some good luck. Couples have already overcome this hurdle.

Whether you're married or common-law, finding a sexual partner is easiest if you already live with one. In Canada, many couples are in long-term relationships that are not marriages, and others move in together as a temporary arrangement that may or may not lead to marriage.

FIGURE 2.6 **Partnered sex this month, by relationship status**

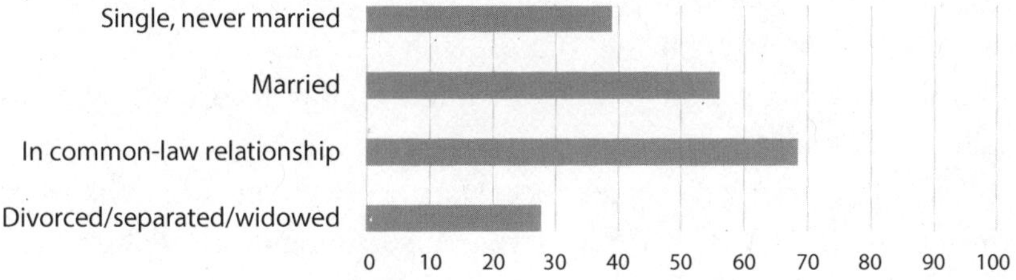

Couples who have cohabited for a certain period of time may be legally defined as "common-law." In our survey, participants in common-law relationships had more sex than those in any other type of relationship: 68 percent had sex within the past month, more than married couples or singles.

Regardless of whether a couple is married, the duration of their relationship has a slightly negative impact on the frequency of sex. That is, the longer they're together, the less often they have it. Part of this pattern has to do with age, as older couples are most likely to be in long relationships, and as mentioned above, they have less sex than younger couples. However, the link between duration and frequency held even when we controlled for age. As we all know, life gets busy, relationships can go through challenging times, and sexual attraction sometimes fades. There are many reasons why couples have the most sex when their relationship is new.

Having kids is thought to put a damper on the sex lives of couples. Parenthood is stereotyped as a humdrum aspect of life – or, at least, the sexual part of it. We imagine that having kids means having a diminished, routine, even boring sex life. The commonsense understanding is that parenting is exhausting and time consuming, and that parents just don't have the time or energy for sex. However, according to the Sex in Canada study, that's all wrong. The reality doesn't match the myth of parents who are too exhausted even to think about sex. In fact, 85 percent of parents with children under age eighteen living at home reported having active, satisfying sexual lives. They were just as happy with their sex lives as people who do not have kids, 83 percent of whom said they were satisfied.

Parents also had more sex, on average, than non-parents. Two-thirds (66 percent) had sex in the last month, compared to 43 percent of non-parents. This probably had less to do with children or parenting than with the fact that parents were more likely than non-parents to be co-habiting. Overall, Canadian parents were enjoying rich, varied sex lives. For example, among those under age sixty, parents were just as likely as anyone else to report that they gave oral sex to (and received oral sex from) their partner during the past month (Figure 2.7). They were more likely than those without kids to have used a sex toy in the past month as well. In other words, they were having fun in bed, where they engaged in lots of sexual play, and they reported high levels of good feelings about their sex lives.

FIGURE 2.7 **Parental status and sexual behaviour, 59 or younger**

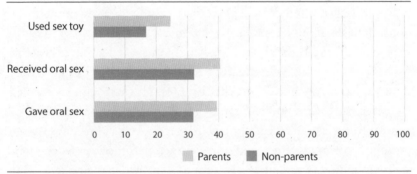

REPRODUCTION AND CONTRACEPTION

We may associate sex with making babies, but only a small proportion of the sex that Canadian adults have is oriented toward pregnancy. It should go without saying that not all sex is reproductive. There is no chance of pregnancy, for example, in same-sex sexual activity. Oral, anal, and manual genital stimulation, no matter the gender of participants, is not going to make a baby. And even among those engaging in penile-vaginal intercourse, most are trying to avoid pregnancy. Among women who had intercourse during the past year, only 7.6 percent hoped to become pregnant in the next six months (Figure 2.8). Another 20.0 percent were not trying to become pregnant, but thought it was okay if they did. For the majority of Canadians, sexual activity is not for

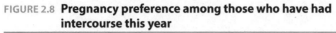

FIGURE 2.8 **Pregnancy preference among those who have had intercourse this year**

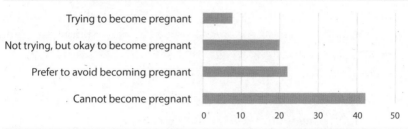

reproduction. They either cannot become pregnant or they take measures to avoid it.

CONTRACEPTIVE USE

Among those having penile-vaginal sex, 61 percent reported having used some form of birth control in the past six months. The most common choice was the condom, with 36 percent of participants opting for this method. Condoms are a particularly important type of contraception, as they also protect against many sexually transmitted infections (STIs), including HIV. Public health officials track condom use in various ways, sometimes across the entire population, but usually focusing on targeted groups where STIs are of particular concern, such as sex workers, undergraduate university students, or men who have sex with men.[18] The Sex in Canada survey examined the Canadian adult population at large, finding that, across all their sex encounters, about 25 to 30 percent involved condoms, with singles and young adults being the most active condom users.[19] In addition, visible minorities opted for condoms more often than other Canadians, men more than women, and those with higher levels of education more than everyone else.

"Female" condoms – barriers that are inserted into vaginas – are another method that combines birth control with protection against STIs. They can be inserted up to two hours before sex, and they consist of polyurethane rather than latex, which makes them compatible with a wider variety of lubricants. However, they are not nearly as popular as male condoms, with only 3 percent of our participants saying they had used one in the past six months.

Although condoms are not perfect, they are a highly effective barrier against STIs when used properly. As we will discuss in Chapter 5, their use is not consistent across social groups, as it is linked with differing estimates of personal risk for contracting STIs. For example, gay men used condoms much more frequently than straight men (Figure 2.9). Younger people used them more than older folks.

FIGURE 2.9 **Condom use, by sexual identity (men only)**

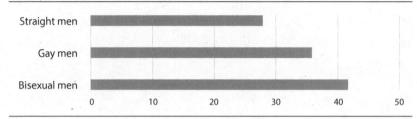

In terms of relationship type, singles (those who had never married) reported more condom use than participants in marital and common-law relationships. About half of singles had used a condom in their most recent sexual encounter, whereas only 15 percent of married people and 10 percent of those in common-law relationships had (Figure 2.10). Those who identified as "no longer married" fell between the singles and the married/common-law couples, with 24 percent reporting that they had recently used a condom. As a group, singles were younger than those who were no longer married, who may no longer be worried about

FIGURE 2.10 **Condom use, by relationship status**

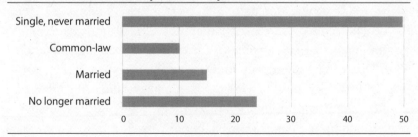

getting pregnant. Of course, age is no protection against an STI, and members of these two groups probably had similar risks of contracting one if they failed to use a condom.

BIRTH CONTROL PILLS AND OTHER CONTRACEPTIVES

We asked female participants to tell us what contraceptives they used besides condoms, allowing them to select as many as they had used in the past six months. Oral contraceptives, or birth control pills, were second, used by 20 percent of women. About 9 percent used hormone-delivering contraceptive devices such as patches, vaginal rings, under-skin implants, and injections, and 6 percent relied on intrauterine devices (IUDs) to prevent pregnancy. Barrier methods such as cervical caps, diaphragms, and spermicidal foams and gels were not very common, with fewer than 3 percent of women opting for any of them.

Just over 1 percent of participants used the rhythm method, in which they monitored their menstrual cycle and sometimes took their temperature to determine when they were fertile. Armed with this information, they could plan their sexual activities, having sex at low-fertility times if they wished to avoid pregnancy and having it at high-fertility times if pregnancy were the goal. This technique, also called sympto-thermal or natural family planning, has long been recognized by the Catholic Church as the only acceptable form of family planning. Over 10 percent of our participants reported using withdrawal – also called "pulling out" – as a birth control technique. This is when a man withdraws his penis from the woman's vagina before ejaculating. It can be somewhat effective at preventing pregnancy when accomplished correctly. However, choosing the opportune moment to disengage can be difficult, which means that withdrawal is not particularly reliable.[20]

Some Canadians undergo surgical procedures for a more permanent end to their fertility (although in some cases, these can be reversible with additional surgery). Such procedures are most common for Canadians in their middle years, who have had all the children they want or who decide they never want children. Among our participants, 21 percent of women reported having had a tubal ligation, and 20 percent of men had had a vasectomy.

UNPLANNED PREGNANCY

Despite the contraceptive efforts of sexual partners, unplanned pregnancies do occur. A 2010 research study estimated that 48 percent of pregnancies in North America were unintended.[21] In our survey, 5.5 percent of women said they had unexpectedly become pregnant in the previous six months. Among men, 7 percent thought they had unintentionally impregnated their partner during that period.

Some women try to end a pregnancy through "natural" means, such as by consuming certain teas, herbs, or plants that are traditionally said to cause an abortion or miscarriage. Some of these purported abortifacients may be safe, and others have unknown or even harmful effects for the woman who takes them. At best, they are unproven, at worst ineffective and dangerous. Of the women in our survey, 3.8 percent had tried to end a pregnancy via this means. However, other methods are safe and effective.

The emergency contraception pill known as Plan B, or the "morning-after pill," can significantly reduce the risk of pregnancy when taken within twenty-four hours after unprotected sex, with diminishing effectiveness up to five days afterward. Since 2005, it has been available in Canada to those over age seventeen without a prescription, as a pharmacist-delivered medication (as opposed to something anyone can grab from the shelf). Its repeated use has been shown to be safe.[22] Plan B is a popular form of backup contraception. Among the women in our survey, 21 percent said they had taken Plan B, about half of them more than once.

ABORTION

Abortions are relatively common, with about 100,000 pregnancies terminated by abortion in Canada each year. Among our survey participants, 17 percent of women had undergone at least one abortion, and of these, 37 percent had more than one. Although most surveys restrict abortion questions to women, we also asked men about their experience with abortions. Our question asked men to estimate how often a woman whom they had impregnated had an abortion. Their responses were strikingly similar to those of the women: just under 18 percent of them stated that women they had gotten pregnant had received abortions, and of those men, 29 percent said that it had occurred more than once. This parity between women's and men's responses suggests that many women who become pregnant communicate their abortion plans to their sexual partners.

Although abortion services are included in federally mandated medical care in Canada, the provinces are responsible for delivering health care, and some have failed to include abortion in their coverage. In 2019, Ontario and New Brunswick were found to have violated the Health Canada Act for forcing patients to pay private providers for an abortion.[23] Women also have trouble gaining access to health care providers who will perform the procedure, despite its status as a legal medical procedure covered in the Health Canada Act. This is a particular problem for women in remote or rural locations, where public transit is limited and health care facilities that do carry out abortions are a long drive away.[24]

In many cases, women can obtain an abortion that does not involve a surgical procedure. In medical (as opposed to surgical) abortions, women in the first nine weeks of a pregnancy can take a series of drugs called Mifegymiso. (Commonly known as "the abortion pill," Mifegymiso is actually a set of medications taken several days apart.) Abortion advocates hoped that the availability of medical abortions would improve access for these women. The Canadian government approved medical abortions only in 2016, decades later than in other countries. Although this was praised as a promising step to improve reproductive health care, it was accompanied by a burdensome stipulation that prompted criticism. Before Mifegymiso could be prescribed to them, women were required to receive an ultrasound, which meant that they had to access in-person treatment at a health care facility. For many, this proved just as difficult as obtaining a surgical abortion. Only since 2019 has Health Canada removed the ultrasound requirement, and it remains to be seen whether abortion access will improve in the future. In the Sex in Canada survey, 6 percent of women said they had sought an abortion but were unable to attain one.

SOCIAL PATTERNS IN SEXUALITY

Is everyone having more sex than me? Now you know! About 11 percent of Canadian adults have not yet had sex. About 49 percent had it during the past month, with the rest having engaged in it less recently than that, including 20 percent or so who'd been celibate in the past year. Many people make masturbation a regular part of their lives, with 55 percent enjoying the practice within the past month and over 75 percent in the past year. Although these figures tell us what the average Canadian does, there is also substantial variation across gender, age, and marital status. All the social forces that organize our world, sort us into families, and propel us into neighbourhoods give us shared experiences that make our lives a little different from others. These various locations intersect and combine to influence our sexual behaviour, just as they influence other behaviours. These patterns describe the social organization of sexuality in Canada today.

What do all these patterns mean? Although it's fun to discover how frequently various types of people have sex and to get a glimpse of their intimate lives, the inquiries of sociologists are guided by more than simple curiosity or prurient interest. The patterned differences in sexual behaviour begin to sketch out the way that social forces influence the sexual choices of individuals. They begin to reveal the ways that cultures and subcultures influence our lives as sexual beings, and they show that something as deeply personal and individual as sex is also part of the social fabric.

3
Commitment, Casual Sex, and Cheating

Historically, marriage has been the primary institution that regulates our sexuality. These days, with young adults waiting longer than ever to get married and increasing numbers of people choosing to remain single, marriage may not seem especially important. But a century ago, it was the only ticket to acceptable sexual behaviour. No one was supposed to have sex outside of wedlock, and husbands and wives were expected to remain faithful to each other throughout their lives. This idea may seem quaint today, but it is worth spending a moment on our culture's approach to sexuality, which has long emphasized constraining it by limiting sexual partners. As an institution, marriage has been enshrined in law by the state and has operated in concert with other social institutions such as religion, education, and family to shape our sexuality.

Parents and other family members regulate the behaviour of youth. Neighbours often keep a close eye on conduct, and gossip is a key tool to induce compliance with social norms. Even before sex education was part of the curriculum, schools passed on social values to children, including teaching them about marriage and family structures that rely on lifelong monogamy. Religious institutions of all kinds have played a central role in the marriages of their members. Most tie their understandings of sexual morality to marriage and monogamy, and then situate themselves as the gatekeepers for marital pairings, requiring couples to receive approval from a religious leader before agreeing to officiate at their weddings. The state also acts as a gatekeeper, issuing marriage licences to couples before they can be legally married. This bureaucratic intervention enforces norms of sexuality, ensuring that people who marry are, for example, old enough to be considered ready for sex. It has also been a key enforcer of monogamy, preventing people from marrying more than one person at a time.[1]

In practice, marriage has never entirely controlled sexual behaviour. Premarital sex and extramarital affairs have always existed, as have same-sex encounters and transactional sex of various sorts, including for money. However, in the past these were clear violations of the norm, which confined sex to the marital bed. People who flouted the rules could pay a high cost, ranging from social disapproval to incarceration. The consequences for transgressing the norms were delivered by social institutions that were closely aligned in their condemnation of sex outside of marriage. This tight link, especially between religion and the state, loosened considerably over time, creating a wider array of acceptable possibilities for organizing sexuality beyond the limits of a single, lifelong marital partner.

Even historically, the penalties for deviating from sexual norms were not evenly borne by all members of society. For example, male and female sexuality has been subject to differing degrees of social control. Men, especially those from wealthy and powerful families, could get away with much more libertarian approaches to sexuality than others, whereas women from all classes came under intense surveillance by their families and communities.[2] Indigenous people's sexuality was monitored and controlled by colonizing forces.[3] Individuals in marginalized positions – poor people, people with disabilities, immigrants, and members of racialized groups – were subject to greater control of their sexual behaviour than those in more powerful positions. But despite all this, in every time and every culture, at least some people managed to have sex outside of marriage. That they also managed to escape the associated penalties does not suggest that the norms did strongly influence the behaviour of most people. In fact, they have long been among our most central values, enmeshed with our understanding of people as good or evil, healthy or diseased, and moral or immoral.

Given that a century ago, so many social regulations were in place to ensure that young adults (especially women) had no sexual experience before their wedding night, and then had sex only their spouse for the rest of lives, you might be surprised that so much has changed. The sexual revolution represented a sea change, ushering in new ideas about sex and sexuality and new norms. For example, having sex as an unmarried person became acceptable. Divorce and remarriage became more common, and reproductive rights were recognized in our laws. Lesbian and gay sexuality, once mischaracterized as a mental illness, is now rightly understood as a normal variation of human sexuality. Living on one's own as a single person is no longer a reason to feel ashamed. Do all these developments mean that the constraints of marriage and other social institutions have disappeared? I don't think so, but they do seem to have changed substantially.

Although we now enjoy far more sexual freedom than we did in, say, 1950, we are nonetheless part of a social system that influences our sexuality. Our sex lives are still governed by norms, which are still enforced, if unevenly. The institution of marriage still plays a role in organizing our sexuality. This is true even though marriage is neither as constrictive nor as widespread as it once was. In this chapter, we take a closer look at marriage, monogamy, and emerging norms governing sexuality. We consider trends in marriage and non-marital sexuality, including cohabitation and common-law relationships, extended singlehood, monogamy and open relationships, and cheating.

MARRIAGE TRENDS IN CANADA

Some people worry that marriage is on the decline. Indeed, it is, with increasing numbers of people delaying it and even choosing to forego it. However, I'm not convinced that this trend is something to fear. Today, people have more options for their sexuality. Living independently as a single person or moving in with a partner are not nearly as scandalous as they used to be. And even though tying the knot is no longer an imperative, many Canadians find marriage appealing. In this chapter, I review trends on marriage, divorce, and common-law relationships, and then offer some insight from the Sex in Canada survey on the current association between marital status and sexual behaviour.

Marriage used to be nearly universal. Demographers track marriage rates, traditionally in terms of the proportion of women who have ever been married. Although this approach was developed before the legalization of same-sex marriage, it can be useful for understanding how things have changed over time. For example, back in 1970, over 90 percent of Canadian women had been married at some point in their lives. After that year, the number dropped steadily for two decades, until just over half of all Canadian women had been married.[4] Three changes are tied to this decline in matrimony: cohabitation without marriage, divorce, and extended singledom. Further, alternative configurations that don't follow the rules of traditional matrimony, such as polyamourous relationships, are becoming more visible these days. Of course, same-sex couples gained access to legal marriage only two decades ago, so you might think there would be more marriages now before that point. However, same-sex marriages are not numerous enough to reverse the overall trend.

COHABITATION AND COMMON-LAW RELATIONSHIPS

Since the 1970s, the proportion of Canadian couples who live together without getting married has steadily increased. In many instances, they intend eventually to marry, but others have no such plans. Much of this trend has been driven by Quebecers, whose marriage rates have declined the most. During the early 1970s, Quebec was much like the rest of Canada, in that over 90 percent of female Quebecers were married. In 2011, nearly 40 percent of Quebec couples were cohabiting but not married, whereas this was the case for 17 percent of couples outside the province.[5] When couples have lived together for a certain time, the government categorizes their association as a common-law relationship. Family law is both federal and provincial in Canada, and each level of government has its own definition of what constitutes a common-law couple. They also determine the legal similarities and differences between common-law relationships and marriages.

However, the federal government also has a definition of the common-law relationship: after cohabiting for one continuous year, a couple will automatically be classed as common-law. The partners must be having sex, as only "conjugal" relationships qualify as common-law. However, not all sexual relationships are categorized as conjugal: for example, those involving multiple partners, or with partners who cannot legally marry, such as close relatives or a person who is under age eighteen, are explicitly excluded. This approach, which is common in other countries as well, basically imposes the legal framework of marriage onto couples whether they get married or not. Ottawa applies its standard to areas that come under its jurisdiction, such as immigration and taxation, and it can also affect child support, the ownership of property, and inheritances.

DIVORCE

Although an increase in divorce is responsible for some decline in marriage, it gets more blame than it deserves. It is true that divorce has become more common since changes to the divorce laws made it easier to obtain. However, many divorced people remarry, and in doing so spend much of their adult lives in marriages. In addition, Canadians don't split up as often as we think. The well-quoted statistic that over half of all marriages now end in divorce is simply not true in Canada.[6] The endurance of this myth is probably due to the higher divorce rate of the United States. Up here, there are about seventy thousand divorces each year, which means that about 40 percent of all Canadian marriages end in divorce.[7]

In fact, marriages have become more stable over time. Statistics Canada has stopped measuring divorce rates, but experts estimate that they are on the decline.[8] It seems that people are being more selective about getting married, which improves their chances of staying with the same spouse throughout their lifetime.[9] On the other hand, demographers have consistently found that cohabiting relationships are not as stable as marriages, a tendency that increased as they became more common.[10] Researchers have found that, after a breakup, married women have lower incomes than their common-law counterparts but that this gap may be closing as time passes.[11]

EXTENDED SINGLEDOM

Many young people are deferring marriage, which is a much bigger contributor than divorce to the population of unmarried adults in Canada. Making a sharp break from the patterns of earlier generations, young people today expect to move out of the family home, establish an independent household of their own, have sexual partners without a marital commitment, and settle into a career before they think of venturing into matrimony. Others choose never to marry. Sociologists have detailed the rise of singledom among adults in general and young adults in particular. Economic considerations drive the decision for some. For example, many couples want to be on solid ground financially, saving up a nest egg before they marry.[12] Establishing a career and living independently are important goals for many young people, which distinguishes them from previous generations, for whom marriage was the very path through which youth achieved adult independence.

Living alone as a single person can be a preference or a product of circumstance, but it is more common than ever before. In the United States, about one in seven adults lives alone.[13] Pundits and conservative think-tanks may bemoan the decline in marriage and wring their hands over unmarried women in particular, but research shows that singles are as healthy and happy as anyone else, and some argue that single women are better off than their married counterparts.[14] Single adults are reshaping our culture, and new norms are emerging for sexuality and relationships (or the lack of relationships). Two competing sets of sexual expectations are prominent among twenty-something adults: serial monogamy and hooking up.

We can think of sexual culture as the set of social norms and collective meanings that governs our sexual lives. Serial monogamy has been an important part of sexual culture ever since attitudes toward "premarital" sex shifted in the 1960s. Even outside of marriage, monogamy has been a central tenet of most relationships. We may not expect a lifelong commitment, but many of us do expect sexual fidelity while the relationship lasts. Of course, this does not apply to all relationships, but it has been the unspoken rule for most. It is closely connected with our understandings of morality, of the right way to organize our lives, and of who is and isn't a good person. When we see an exception to this rule, such as the "one-night stand," which is not expected to be repeated, we note it as differing from the norm.[15]

Not everyone agrees, however, that monogamy is the best approach. People have been forming polyamorous relationships in greater numbers, it seems, in recent decades compared to previous generations. Polyamorous families, in which more than two people form a relationship and often share a household, have also been staking a claim for legal status and acceptance, fighting against the social constraints that require people to pair off. The vast set of federal and provincial family laws that grants legal standing to married and common-law couples hasn't yet fully opened up to the idea that a family might consist of three or more adult partners. However, family law in some provinces has made changes in one relevant area.[16] For example, Ontario's 2016 All Families Are Equal Act reflects that province's acceptance that relationships between parents and children are important regardless of whether the parents are married.[17] Because it recognizes that some children have more than two parents, the act has been embraced by same-sex parents who want to acknowledge both biological and non-biological parents, and some also see it as the first step toward more acceptance of polyamorous couples. However, others argue that even as Canadian law changes, it remains resistant to expansive family forms.[18]

SAME-SEX MARRIAGE

Bucking the trend of declining marriage, lesbian and gay couples can now legally marry, and an increasing number are taking this step. They were denied this right until 2003, when Ontario and British Columbia recognized same-sex unions, followed by the remaining provinces and territories in 2004 and 2005. In the summer of 2005, federal legislation legalized same-sex marriage throughout Canada. Many cohabiting couples took advantage of this change in the law from the beginning. The census started to record their numbers in 2006, finding that about 1 percent of all Canadian couples were same-sex pairings. As of 2016, there were roughly seventy-two thousand same-sex couples in Canada, about half of whom lived in a large city.[19] They don't marry nearly as much as different-sex couples. About one-third are married, but this proportion is increasing over time.

Some members of the 2SLGBTQ+ community remain critical of the institution of marriage. Some reject it as an instrument of patriarchy whose purpose is to control women's behaviour, and others see it as a measure of "normalcy" that offers inclusion and acceptance to some while excluding those whose romantic and sexual lives do not comply with the restrictive expectations of lifelong monogamy.[20] Of course, these criticisms are expressed by other Canadians as well, but they are more widespread in 2SLGBTQ+ communities, which have a broader acceptance of variation in family forms. For some, embracing marriage seems to jeopardize the important space that was created for those who had been rejected by their families or by mainstream society due to their sexuality. For others, marriage is a significant way to claim space that had been denied to same-sex couples. Those with children might see it as an essential legal foundation that secures their parental rights and legitimizes their families.

Despite concerns about the patriarchal nature of marriage, lesbian couples are much more likely than gay couples to get married. In the Sex in Canada survey, 55.0 percent of them were married, compared to 29.7 percent of the gay couples. This may be related to parenting responsibilities, as lesbian couples are more likely than gay couples to have children.[21] Many same-sex parents view marriage as an important way to define their family, seeing the legal status that it confers as vital in ensuring that they will retain custody of their children. In previous research with my colleague Melanie Heath, we asked recently married lesbian women about their weddings.[22] We found that they were deeply concerned with marriage as a heteronormative, patriarchal institution. However, they recognized that marriage did convey a certain legal status that had long been denied to same-sex couples. They took great care to organize their weddings, as well as their relationships, according to egalitarian norms. This helped them feel that they were changing the institution of marriage for the better rather than succumbing to outdated social expectations.

THE RISE OF HOOKUP CULTURE

The advent of "hookup culture" is tied to the expectation of delayed marriage and the resultant long period of single and childless adulthood.[23] Challenging the norms of serial monogamy, it centres on casual encounters, sexual interactions that are not accompanied by an anticipation that monogamy – or even a relationship at all – will result. In fact, scholars of hookup culture observe that avoiding emotional attachment between partners is paramount.[24] Hooking up can be thought of as a sexual project, one that differs from other sexual projects such as finding a long-term romantic partner.[25] Participants in hookup culture work hard to avoid "catching feelings" for each other so that they don't appear needy or desperate. There is no expectation of monogamy in this culture. Rather, its key value is sexual freedom.

It may seem that hookup culture is closely entangled with the rise of digital technologies, especially apps such as Tinder or Bumble. However, its emergence preceded the practice of swiping right on a phone app. Although pinpointing the beginning of cultural phenomena is always difficult, scholars began taking notice of its prevalence among university students and twenty-somethings in the early 2000s. Sexual subcultures whose practices resemble those of hookup culture have existed for some time. You might be reminded of the "free love" movement in the 1960s and 1970s. Sexual freedom has also been a long-standing component of the gay subculture. And opportunities to have sexual encounters that are not relationship-based, including with a sex worker, have been around forever. So, in what sense is hookup culture something new?

Scholars who study this subject argue that it reflects a shift in social expectations governing sexuality.[26] They find that especially among young adults, it is no longer that serial monogamy that is the taken-for-granted expectation. Rather, hookup culture has risen to a place of pre-eminence. The unspoken expectation is for one-time sexual encounters with no emotional attachments, and more relationship-based sex is becoming something that must be discussed and negotiated. This is as true for young people who dislike the practice of hooking up as it is for those who enjoy it. Whether or not they participate, most young adults must grapple with these realities.

Most of the literature on hookup culture focuses on university populations, but there is evidence that it is the dominant practice for a generation of young adults who are embracing extended singledom.[27] Hooking up allows them to be sexually active while also enabling them to postpone relationship formation and marriage as they set up their own households and establish their careers. This shift is not absolute, of course, and uncertainties regarding whether the sexual encounter signals a burgeoning romance or is just a one-time thing can cause confusion and pain.[28]

To better understand the current sexual expectations of Canadians, we asked the single people in our study what they thought others were looking for in sexual partners, as well as what they themselves were looking for. Asked whether they agreed with the statement "people my age just want to hook up or have casual sex," about half agreed and half disagreed. If we break down these responses by age group, however, we find that younger adults strongly endorsed the statement, whereas Canadians who were aged fifty and older were considerably less inclined to agree with it (Figure 3.1).

Yet hookup culture does not appear to be evenly distributed across Canada. For example, our survey suggested that it was more prominent among anglophones than francophones. Whereas 74 percent of anglophones between the ages of eighteen and twenty-nine said that people their age just wanted to hook up, only 57 percent of their francophone counterparts did. In addition, perceptions that others wanted to participate in hookup culture were weaker in Quebec than elsewhere in Canada (Figure 3.2).

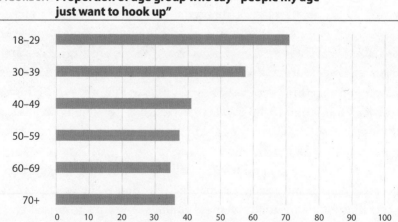

FIGURE 3.1 **Proportion of age group who say "people my age just want to hook up"**

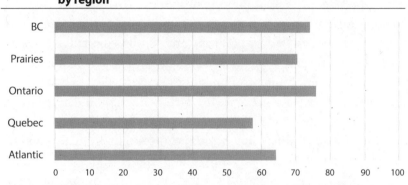

FIGURE 3.2 **Ages 18–29 who say "people my age just want to hook up," by region**

Further, though a majority of younger Canadians agreed that the expectations of "most people their age" were to hook up in casual encounters, this did not necessarily reflect their own preferences. We asked our single participants if they agreed with the statement "I would rather date someone I like or love than just hook up with someone casually." A large majority (87 percent) agreed. This may be interpreted as an indictment of hookup culture, which our participants saw as something that others favoured but not what they necessarily wanted for themselves. Indeed, most of our single participants (79 percent) hoped to be in love with someone during the next year.

That said, it is important not to draw too firm a boundary between casual hookups and the sexual connections that lead to romance and relationships, as most research shows that singles navigate both sets of expectations at the same time.[29] We also asked our single participants whether they agreed with the statement "people my age want to date someone and be in a real relationship." Given the findings presented above, one might assume that only a few would say yes, but that was not the case. Eighty percent of them agreed, including 72 percent of those between the ages of eighteen and twenty-nine.

Puzzled by the seeming contradiction between the claims that people wanted to hook up and to be in a real relationship, I looked at the overlap between the responses. As you can see in Figure 3.3, half of our respondents agreed with both statements: people their age wanted to hook up, and people their age wanted a real relationship. I think this points to the overlapping sexual projects of singles who, in many cases, are looking for both casual encounters and real relationships at the same time. This is supported by other research on hookup culture. For example, the university students whom Nicole Andrejek interviewed felt that it was imperative not to seem desperate or needy in a hookup, but they were also alert for signals that a partner might be interested in getting to know them or pursuing a relationship.[30] They reported not wanting to catch feelings, but they also confessed to being disappointed when someone didn't contact them after a hookup.

Our participants acknowledged these competing norms when they addressed the question of turning their hookups into relationships. Over

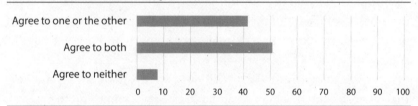

FIGURE 3.3   **Ages 18–29 who think others want to hook up or start a relationship**

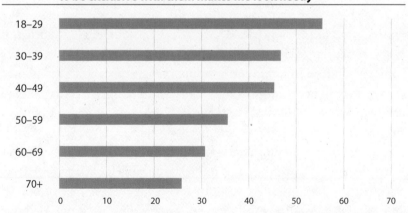

FIGURE 3.4   **Proportion who agree that "telling someone I want to be exclusive with them makes me look needy"**

three-quarters (76 percent) of the singles agreed with the statement "if I were hooking up casually with someone and wanted to turn it into a relationship, I feel confident that I could tell that person I wanted to be exclusive with them." Under half of them (43 percent) agreed with the statement "I am afraid that telling someone I want to be exclusive with them makes me look needy or clingy." However, more young adults (ages eighteen to twenty-nine) agreed with this statement than older age groups (Figure 3.4). Once again, high rates of agreement with both of these seemingly contradictory statements reveal the complexities of hookup culture. Sexual encounters today can be both casual and detached, and at the same time they can also be meaningful, romantic, and the start of a potential relationship.

NEW WAYS TO MEET PEOPLE

Digital technologies that enable potential partners to meet have evolved quickly during the last few decades. The digital world now includes subscription-based matching services, websites, and location-based apps in which one sifts through profiles to make matches with others who are nearby. In addition to accessing dating-specific apps such as Tinder, Grindr, and Bumble, people use other social media platforms such as Facebook, Instagram, and Snapchat to do a background check on someone they are interested in meeting, to carry on conversations, or to keep in touch casually. New apps and technologies are being introduced all the time, with features that attempt to improve the user experience.

Digital dating technologies have developed their own cultural norms for how to proceed.[31] Many users concentrate on impression management, crafting personas that will be attractive to others.[32] Some employ a strategy of contacting numerous potential partners, in hopes of winning a numbers game.[33] As many scholars note, online dating apps can often have an unappealing aspect for recipients, such as the unsolicited "dick pics" that men send to potential partners.[34] Users of dating apps must also assess the risks of contacting strangers for intimate encounters. Although many people have criticized digital dating technologies, they are widely used, especially by young adults. A 2020 Pew Research Center study found that 30 percent of adults in the United States, and almost half of young adults aged nineteen to twenty-nine, had used them.[35]

We were curious about how big a role online dating played in helping people form relationships, so we asked our participants how they met their current partner (Figure 3.5). Seventy-eight percent had met their partner in person, and only about 20 percent through a website, app, or other technology-mediated platform. Even among young adults aged eighteen to twenty-nine, face-to-face meetings were by far the most common: about 70 percent met their partner in person versus 30 percent through a dating app. Of course, we should keep in mind that these technologies are relatively recent inventions and that longer-term relationships would have started before many of them came on the market. I anticipate that online technologies will launch an increasing proportion of relationships as time passes.

Gay men in particular have been at the cutting edge of digital dating technologies. Location-based matching apps such as Grindr, which targets them, were among the first to gain sizable numbers of members. Given the special role of online dating for gay men, we might expect to

FIGURE 3.5 **How did you meet your partner?**

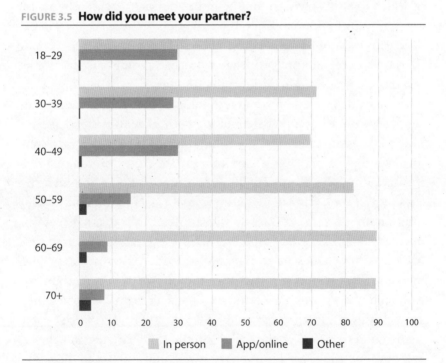

see some differences between how gay and straight men met their partners. As Figure 3.6 shows, 41 percent of gay men, compared with 19 percent of straight men, met their partners online. This discrepancy was similar for women as well. Among those in relationships, 30 percent of lesbian women, compared with 18 percent of straight women, reported that they met their partners via the internet.

FIGURE 3.6 **How did you meet your partner? by gender, sexual identity**

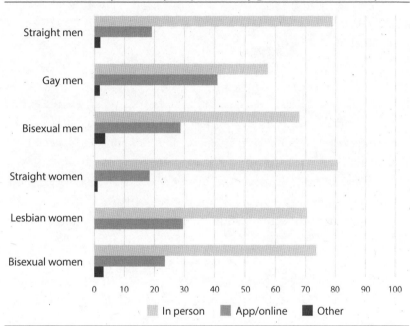

MONOGAMY, OPEN RELATIONSHIPS, AND CHEATING
With all the talk of hookup culture, it may seem that monogamy is waning in Canada. However, the Sex in Canada survey showed that it is still a central organizing principle in the vast majority of intimate relationships. Among our participants who were in a relationship, 89 percent characterized it as monogamous. Another 5 percent said they had not discussed the topic with their partner. Only 6 percent described their relationship as "open," meaning that they and their partner had agreed that one or both of them could have sex with other people.

Some types of relationships are more likely than others to be

FIGURE 3.7 **Monogamy, by relationship status**

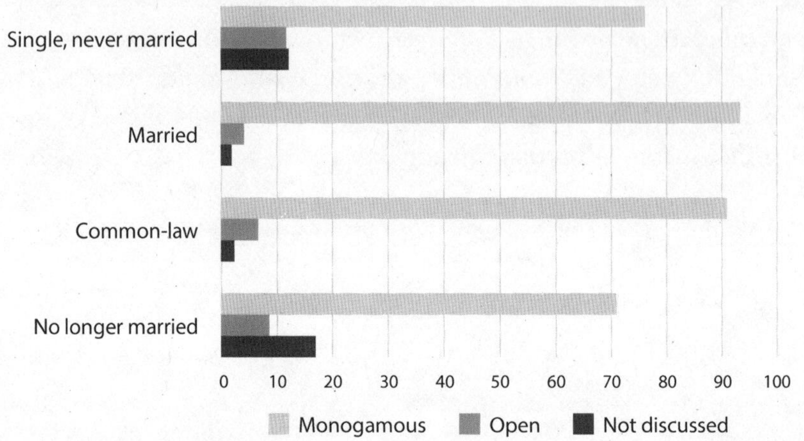

non-monogamous. For example, 7 percent of our common-law couples stated that their relationship was open, compared to only 4 percent of married participants (Figure 3.7). Eleven percent of unmarried, non-cohabiting couples were open, according to our participants. Age also had an impact, with younger adults a little more likely than older ones to be in open relationships.

The gay subculture has celebrated sexual freedom and open relationships since at least the 1960s.[36] Gay liberation activists sought freedom from restrictions on sexual expression, including homophobia as well as monogamy, arguing that limiting sexuality was harmful to individuals and to our culture.[37] Given this, it may not be surprising that gay and bisexual men are more likely than straight men to be in open relationships (Figure 3.8). Lesbian women are often held up in contrast to gay men and characterized as strongly committed to monogamy. However, though they had fewer open relationships than gay men, both they and bisexual women were more likely than straight women to be in open relationships. These findings are consistent with similar studies done in the United States.[38]

CHEATING: BREAKING THE MONOGAMOUS CONTRACT
A promise of monogamy does not always hold over the life of a relationship. Just how many involve episodes of sexual infidelity is very difficult

FIGURE 3.8 **Monogamy, by gender and sexual identity**

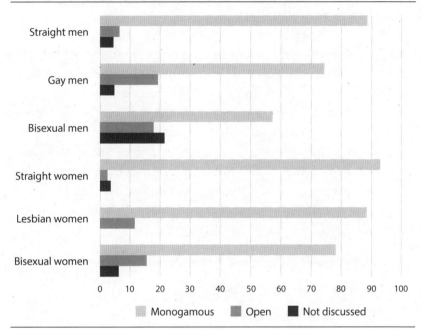

to assess, but we love to speculate about it. An affair often provides the drama in films and television shows. Dating websites such as Ashley Madison cater to married people who are looking for ways to cheat on their spouses.[39] How often does this happen among monogamous couples in Canada today?

When we asked participants if their relationship was monogamous or open, we included two options for monogamy: "entirely monogamous (meaning you and your partner have agreed to be sexual only with each other and have indeed only been sexual with each other to your knowledge)" and "supposedly monogamous (meaning you and your partner agreed to be sexual only with each other AND one or both of you have engaged in sexual activities with other people but didn't tell the other person or hid it from the other person; aka one of you 'cheated' or had an affair)." This distinction between "entirely monogamous" and "supposedly monogamous" enabled participants to distinguish between what their relationship was supposed to be and what it really was. It did not capture every instance of infidelity, as some cheating partners might never have been caught.

Plus, cheating relies on secrecy, and many people prefer to keep it dark. And even as social tolerance for a range of sexual activities grows over time, adultery is still censured, so guilt and shame may have discouraged our participants from divulging their dalliances. Nonetheless, a sizable number of them were willing to disclose that their relationship had endured some cheating. About 10 percent indicated that they were in a "supposedly" monogamous relationship. The type of relationship also mattered to infidelity (Figure 3.9). Married people were less likely to report cheating than cohabiting common-law individuals or people who were not living with their partners. Our findings are consistent with other social science on this topic.[40]

FIGURE 3.9 **Cheating in supposedly monogamous relationships**

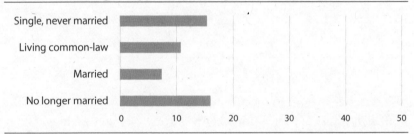

In addition, cheating had a gender dynamic, as more men than women reported that their relationship was "supposedly" monogamous. About 58 percent of our "supposedly" group were men, and only 41 percent were women. Does this mean that the men cheated more than the women? Such a conclusion would be consistent with the social science on the topic, which finds that they do.[41] This gender imbalance was the same when we restricted the sample to straight-identifying participants. If men are cheating more, the gender of their partner doesn't seem to make a difference.

WHAT ABOUT LOVE?

For many of us, love is a central part of our sexual experiences, and it is also the basis for marriage and common-law relationships. Much of the anxiety about hookup culture is grounded in the sense that sex without romance and love is unfulfilling in some way or even immoral. The Sex in Canada survey asked a few questions about the emotional connections between partners, which revealed that most sexual encounters also included feelings of love and intimacy. For example, 80 percent of participants said they loved their most recent partner (Figure 3.10). Only 16 percent said that in their most recent sexual encounter, neither partner loved the other.

FIGURE 3.10 **Love between sexual partners**

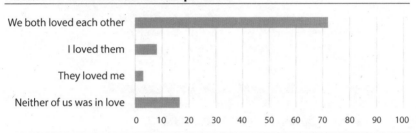

Canadian culture has many gendered stereotypes about love and sexuality. According to these cultural tropes, women are more emotionally attached to their partners, and men's approach to sexual encounters is more distant. Women are clingy and needy, men aloof and unattached. Our survey shed some light on the connection between gender and feelings of love and intimacy, but the responses of men and women didn't much resemble the stark gender differences of the traditional image. The clearest finding was that a large majority of both men and women had felt love and emotional closeness during their most recent sex. Sixty-nine percent of men and 71 percent of women said that it had been either "somewhat" or "very" emotionally intimate (Figure 3.11). So, though women may be a little more likely than men to report feelings of intimacy, there is much more gender similarity than difference on this account.

According to the stereotype, men typically prefer sex that has no emotional strings attached, regardless of whether they are gay or straight. However, our survey found that gay and bisexual men were much more likely than straight men to opt for this type of sex. Figure 3.12 charts participants' thoughts on the intimacy of their most recent encounter,

FIGURE 3.11 **Proportion saying most recent sexual encounter was emotionally intimate**

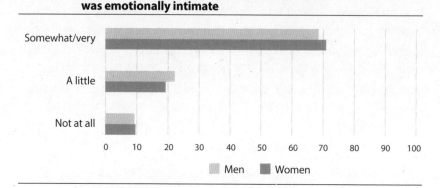

FIGURE 3.12 **Emotional intimacy, by gender and sexual identity**

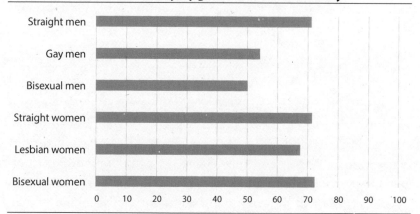

with 54 percent of gay men saying that it was emotionally intimate, compared to 71 percent of straight men. Among women, the pattern differed. There is not much difference between bisexual (72 percent), straight (71 percent), or lesbian women (68 percent).

It makes sense that feelings would differ according to type of relationship. Our single participants were much less likely than those in a long-term relationship to say that they loved their most recent partner (Figure 3.13). Married people and those living common-law were also most likely to characterize their last sexual encounter as "very emotionally intimate." Their relationships were grounded in expectations for love and intimacy. When sex occurs outside of a relationship, the rules are less clear, and there is more room for pleasure without intimacy.

FIGURE 3.13 **Love and intimacy, by relationship type**

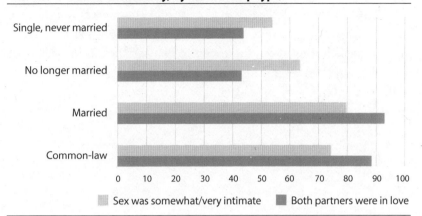

Single, never married

No longer married

Married

Common-law

0   10   20   30   40   50   60   70   80   90   100

▓ Sex was somewhat/very intimate   ■ Both partners were in love

MARRIAGE AND COMMITMENT ARE STILL IMPORTANT

Marriage may be on the decline in Canada, but it is still an important social institution that organizes our sexuality. Although Canadians are putting off their first marriage until later in life, and some are settling into relationships without getting married at all, the expectations that marriage represents – a lifelong, loving commitment to one partner – are central to how adult relationships should work, at least as an ideal. Monogamy, essential to marriage but extending into common-law and non-marital relationships, is still the taken-for-granted norm in many cases.

Canadians have a strongly negative opinion of adultery, but the Sex in Canada study showed that it did not always spell the end of a relationship. About 10 percent of our participants indicated that their relationship was only "supposedly" monogamous – that either they or their partner had been unfaithful at some point. Whether these affairs remained secret or whether the cheating partner was found out was not clear. Nor did we know whether the infidelity was a one-time fling or an entrenched pattern. Monogamy seems to be especially important to Canadians as they age, with younger ones being much more likely to feel that their peers are interested mostly in casual sex. The rise of hookup culture is a significant shift, representing a stage of life for young adults, who are more likely than previous generations to have an extended period of singledom.

Despite the emphasis on detached, casual sex that is central to hookup culture, our survey showed that most sexual encounters were loving and intimate. Women were a little more likely than men to say that they loved their most recent partner and that the sex was intimate, but the differences were small, and the bigger story is that large majorities of both men and women told us that their last sexual encounter felt intimate and was with someone they loved.

4

What Are We Doing in the Bedroom?

We all want to know: when Canadians have sex, what exactly are they doing? We are curious about what is common or rare and whether everyone else is having oral sex or using vibrators or inviting a third person (or a fourth) to join them. And we may also ponder whether the sex we have is "normal." This chapter doesn't make judgments about normal or abnormal – it's really none of my business! Instead, I focus on what is common or uncommon – for example, how behaviour varies across age groups, for men and women, or for same-sex and other-sex activity. If you have ever wondered what sorts of sexual activities people engage in, this chapter has the answers for you.

WHAT COUNTS AS A SEXUAL ENCOUNTER?
First, we asked our participants to think back to their most recent sexual encounter. The survey gave no indication as to what this might entail – we let people choose from a list of behaviours such as kissing and cuddling, penile-vaginal intercourse, and anal and oral sex. Their answers revealed what they defined as a sexual encounter. They strongly agreed that it had to happen in person, not online. Not even one of them chose

an online interaction, such as sex over a video or phone connection, as their most recent encounter. On the other hand, everyone indicated that it included more than one of the options on the list, such as kissing, breast touching, and penile-vaginal intercourse.

Our culture can influence our ideas of what counts as "real" sex. In the media, in our conversations with each other, the stories we tell about what sex is and what it means to us are important to our shared understanding of sexuality. Presently, the penis is the star of the show, whereas the clitoris and other pleasurable body parts are cast in supporting roles. In this heteronormative account, it is typical to define sex as penile-vaginal intercourse and other sexual activity as peripheral. When we say that all the kissing and licking and touching that happens during sex is "just" foreplay, we imply that it leads up to the main event, when the penis is inserted into the vagina. Foreplay, in this way of thinking, doesn't count as real sex.[1] The final curtain for a sexual encounter is also centred on the penis. Sex finishes when the man's orgasm happens. Anything that occurs after that, including a woman's orgasm, is considered extra – perhaps for a special occasion like a birthday or anniversary? Otherwise, if it doesn't happen for her while the penis is in the vagina – better luck next time!

Even though most people who have sex are not trying to become pregnant, our heteronormative ideas about what counts as sex are still very closely tied to reproduction. Sex education classes stress it, with detailed lessons on how sperm and egg combine and implant in the uterine lining. Of course, this is important information for everyone. However, an overemphasis on reproduction and pregnancy prevention, in schools as well as in larger cultural narratives, can limit our understanding of what sex can be. When I call this narrative heteronormative, I mean more than just the obvious assumption that sex involves a heterosexual pair, with one penis and one vagina. I also mean that it is embedded with traditional ideas about gender, assumptions of how men and women differ, and what their respective roles should be in giving each other pleasure. This phallocentric view tells a story about gender, relying on the stereotype that men's and women's bodies differ in fundamental ways. As the story goes, men have a strong need for sexual satisfaction, but women have lower sexual appetites and are perhaps more interested in the emotional connection that a sexual encounter brings. These expectations, in which men and women are captured as "opposite" genders that fit together perfectly as a heterosexual couple, are the building blocks of social inequality. They create a status hierarchy of sexuality and gender that situates heterosexuality over lesbian, gay, and bisexual forms of sexuality, and men over women. They also influence how we understand our sexual encounters.

Same-sex sexual activity can offer a different perception of what sex should be like and what counts as sex. Indeed, gay and lesbian cultures move away from narratives based in gender differences and from the reproductive aspects of sexuality. For example, women who have sex with women converge around the idea of genital stimulation – women's sexual pleasure – as what qualifies as sex.[2] In same-gender encounters, mutual pleasure and a wider variety of ways to enjoy sex are emphasized. Of course, you don't have to be lesbian or gay to adopt a more egalitarian or inclusive understanding of sexuality, and many straight people reject the narrow, restrictive heteronormative version.

Indeed, the heteronormative stereotypes may seem outdated or quaint, but many Canadians still subscribe to them. Although they affect what we think and what we do in the bedroom, it is also true that our sexual cultures – and with them our sexual behaviours – vary across the population. The social forces that determine our lives, such as where we live, whether we attend university, whether we are single or married, and so on, also shape our sexual cultures. These variations shape the setting in which our sexual activity takes place, and they influence how we understand our sexual selves and our partners. In doing so, they nudge our behaviour in ways that form measurable patterns by gender, age, education, and even region of the country. What kind of sex we have, at least in part, is a social process. Our cultural understandings of gender and sexuality affect sexual behaviour and sexual pleasure.

KISSING AND CUDDLES

Kissing and cuddling are acts of affection. They connote romance, caring, and love. Who doesn't love the thought of cuddling up with an intimate partner, feeling safe and warm? You may not see these as sexual behaviours, but they are an important part of sex for many Canadians.

No one who took our survey said that their most recent sexual encounter included only kissing and cuddling, but they were the most common behaviours mentioned. They are not enough to count as sex on their own, yet they are a very important part of Canadians' sex lives.

A large majority (80 percent) of participants included kissing along with other sexual behaviours, and 69 percent engaged in cuddling. Both acts were ubiquitous among all sorts of adults. In every age group, for instance, more than three-fourths of participants told us that there had been kissing and at least 60 percent that there had been cuddling when they last had sex. Cuddling was even more common for older groups: 75 percent of those fifty and older reported having done it, as did more than 80 percent of the oldest group (seventy and up).

Kissing and cuddling are commonly seen as gendered. Those myths of heterosexual sex tell us that women are passionate cuddlers and that men tend to put up with it. This is part of our cultural baggage that perceives the female sex as most dependent upon relationships, whereas men are understood to be more self-sufficient and oriented toward sex without a relationship. It also positions women as emotionally expressive and men as stoic and reserved. If, like me, you'd guess that this discrepancy would show up in our respondents' memories of their most recent sex, with straight women reporting more kissing and cuddling than straight men, you would be wrong (Figure 4.1). Among straight men and women, roughly equal proportions recalled kissing and cuddling.

However, we did see some gender differences in same-sex interactions. For example, 70 percent of gay men reported having kissed during their most recent sexual encounter, whereas 94 percent of lesbian women engaged in smooching. Gay men cuddled less than straight men (65 versus 71 percent) and lesbian women more than straight women (83 versus 69 percent). Are these differences due to gender? Do they reflect differing heterosexual, lesbian, and gay norms? If I had to guess, I would say that it's a little of both. Men and women respond to gender norms that shape their preferences in the bedroom, and lesbian and gay subcultures have developed their own norms that achieve the same end. Both lesbian and gay subcultures differ from the heterosexual patterns that govern straight sexuality, but they also differ from each other.

We also found regional variations in how much sex included kissing

FIGURE 4.1 **Kissing and cuddling in most recent sex, by gender and sexual identity**

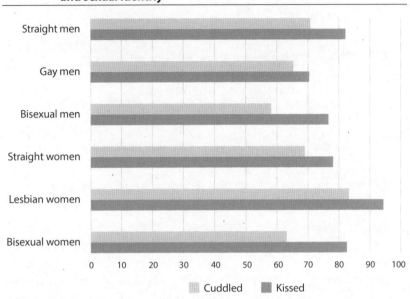

and cuddling. Even though both were quite common everywhere, they were a little more popular in some places than others. Knowing this, would you suspect that the weather might be at least partially responsible? Perhaps Canadians who live in the colder parts of the country have a more practical reason for snuggling under the covers than those on the relatively warmer West Coast. I wish I could offer some insights from the northern territories to test this idea properly, but because very few of our participants lived in the North, we can consider regional differences only among the provinces. And the data did not support the weather hypothesis. Those living in British Columbia (69 percent) cuddled just as much as those in the Atlantic provinces (68 percent) or in the Prairies (70 percent). As Figure 4.2 suggests, the tendency to cuddle appears more related to cultural differences than to the weather. Francophone Quebec stands out as the cuddliest province, and people in the Prairies and Atlantic Canada kiss just a bit more than other Canadians.

Sex without kisses and cuddles happens about 20 percent of the time, and it's fairly evenly distributed across relationship types, with just one

FIGURE 4.2 **Kissing and cuddling in most recent sex, by region**

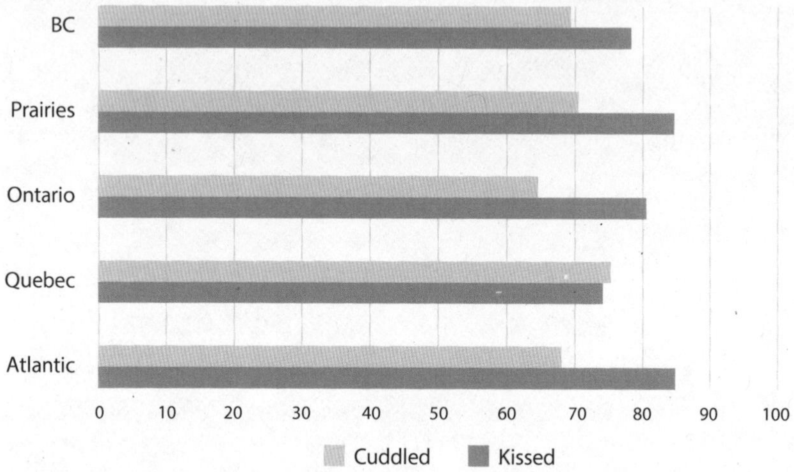

predictable exception. People having sex with someone outside a romantic context, such as with someone they'd just met or with a "friend," were
less kissy and cuddly than those having sex with a long-term partner or
a steady date (Figure 4.3). I imagine that the association of kissing and
snuggling with intimacy and love makes these behaviours a little awkward for those who are firmly in the friend zone.

PENILE-VAGINAL INTERCOURSE
Penile-vaginal intercourse gets top billing in our heteronormative culture, and as you might suspect, it was very common among our straight
participants. In this group, 62 percent reported having had intercourse
during the last year, and two-thirds had it in their most recent sexual
encounter. This was quite consistent across ages and relationship types.
Younger adults, aged eighteen to twenty-nine, were a little less likely
than all other straight participants to have included intercourse in their
most recent sexual experience, but all other straight respondents had
similar levels of intercourse. Similarly, single, common-law, and married
heterosexuals had consistently high rates of it.

Where do Canadians get the idea that real sex is penile-vaginal sex?
From many sources. For example, sex education curriculums in schools
can place a heavy emphasis on reproduction and the prevention of

FIGURE 4.3 **Kissing and cuddling in most recent sex, by relationship to partner**

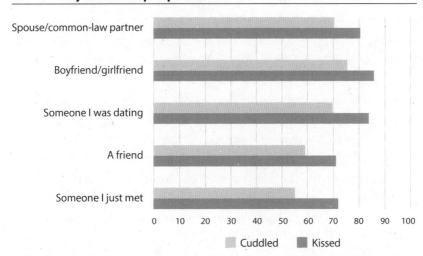

pregnancy. Although these lessons are necessary, they are often delivered to the exclusion of topics such as pleasure, communication between partners, and the development of sexual citizenship (that is, the sense of one's right to sexual self-determination).[3] In families, parents feel responsible for having "the talk" with their children. However, social norms dictate that it should be awkward and stressful, motivating both parents and teenagers to avoid deep and meaningful conversations about sex as pleasurable, intimate, and emotional, sticking to the basics of the birds and the bees.[4] And in both popular media and pornography, representations of men's orgasms are more plentiful than women's.[5] In many porn videos, women are portrayed as reaching orgasm without clitoral stimulation, penetration by a penis typically being sufficient to do the job.[6]

ORAL SEX
Has the stigma around oral sex – the stimulation of a partner's genitals with one's mouth – fallen away? Have we as a culture come to agree that this is a regular, normal part of a healthy sex life? Do some of us think it is icky and gross? Or does the fact that it is about pleasure rather than procreation still make it seem suspect to some? When I talk to my students about sexuality, we often measure our collective discomfort about

any given sex act by observing whether saying it out loud makes us giggle – that's one sure sign of a stigmatized topic of discussion. Then again, the official terms for oral sex, fellatio and cunnilingus, are just inherently funny words, so the giggle test may not be the best measure in this case. Whatever words we use, the Sex in Canada survey confirmed that oral sex is common among Canadians.

Just over half of our participants reported both giving (51 percent) and receiving oral sex (53 percent) in the past year (Figure 4.4). During the last month, 29 percent gave and received it. However, another 20 percent had never given or received it. This suggests that, at least among some, a distaste for oral sex is prevalent. Nonetheless, it is a common activity. When recalling their most recent sexual encounter, 36 percent of participants said they gave and 38 percent that they received it. There is no doubt that it is widely practised.

FIGURE 4.4   **How recently did you give/receive oral sex?**

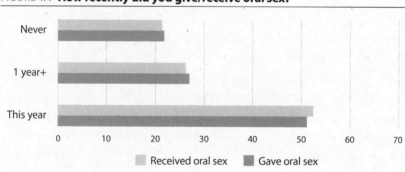

LGB AND STRAIGHT ORAL SEX

A lifelong avoidance of oral sex was much more common among straight participants than among gay men, lesbian women, or bisexuals. Among men, 22 percent of straight men reported never having received oral sex, whereas only 6 percent of gay/bisexual men said the same. The story was similar for women: a quarter of straight women had never given oral sex, but only 16 percent of lesbian and 8 percent of bisexual women had never given it to a partner.

As Figure 4.5 shows, when men had sex with men, they were much more likely to give oral sex than if their partner was a woman (51 percent versus 37 percent). Similarly, they received more oral sex from male partners than from female ones (59 percent versus 40 percent). Women also performed more oral sex with same-sex partners than with men, though the difference was smaller than among male respondents. In their most recent sex, they gave only slightly more oral sex to female partners (37 percent) than to male partners (34 percent). Likewise, 38 percent of women received oral sex from female partners, but only 32 percent of women with men partners said the same. Why might that be the case? I suspect that heteronormativity plays a role, with the emphasis on intercourse crowding out the possibility for oral sex among straight partners.

FIGURE 4.5 **Proportion giving oral sex in most recent sex, by gender**

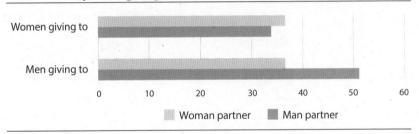

A straight cultural understanding of what counts as sex, what is normal, and what is expected matters to how we approach partners, what we communicate to them, and even to what we think is exciting or off-putting. Heteronormativity might prioritize vaginal penetration for male-female sex, but same-sex pairs are subject to a different set of expectations in 2SLGBTQ+ subcultures. However, it's important to note that multiple sexual subcultures exist within 2SLGBTQ+ communities. The striking differences between gay men's sex and that of lesbian women indicate that gay cultures prioritize oral sex to a greater extent than their lesbian counterparts. Bisexuals, both men and women, also engage in much more oral sex than lesbians or straight men and women.

AGE AND ORAL SEX
Another pattern in oral sex is generational. One way of determining how social norms change over time is to look for differences between

age groups. Just as we saw with masturbation in Chapter 2, people in older age cohorts are the least likely to have given or received oral sex in the past year. As Figure 4.6 reveals, adults between the ages of sixty and sixty-nine and those who were seventy and older were most likely never to have received oral sex, at 24 percent and 41 percent respectively, compared to 20 percent or less for each age group younger than sixty (a pattern that held for giving oral sex, too).

FIGURE 4.6 **Proportion of age group reporting no oral sex in lifetime**

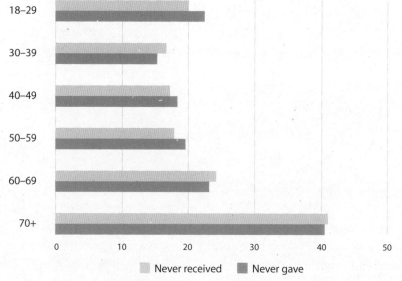

These measurable differences in the sexual practices of age groups or cohorts are an important example of the influence of social forces, not only on our thoughts about sexuality, but on our embrace of sexual behaviours. We know that older adults, on average, married at younger ages than more recent cohorts of Canadians, and a greater proportion were raised and remained in churches that deemed all non-procreative sexual activity, including oral sex, sinful. Those who are over seventy today reached adulthood before the widespread availability of oral contraceptives ("the pill"). This development contributed to the decoupling of sexual behaviour from reproduction and served as an important pillar of the sexual revolution in 1969–70, when attitudes liberalized quite suddenly and dramatically.[7] These septuagenarians – and those in their eighties and nineties – came of age prior to this shift in the meanings and morality of sex, which accounts for the stark differences in their reports of sexual behaviour relative to other generations.

TOUCHING AND MASSAGE

Sexual encounters involve a whole range of intimate touching and sensation, more than just penises, vaginas, and mouths. Our participants engaged in sensual touching, including massage, breast touching, genital touching with hands, and the use of hands, fingers, and their genitals to stimulate a partner's genitals and anus. These body experiences are a common part of sex.

SEXUAL MASSAGE

The pleasant feelings of being touched and caressed by a sexual partner are an important aspect of intimacy and sexuality. It's no surprise, then, that massage was a common feature in the sex lives of our participants. Just over half (52 percent) had received a body massage from a partner within the past year, and 54 percent had given one. Their reports were close to equal for men and women.

Incorporating massage into our sex lives is pretty common, but how likely was any given sexual encounter to include it? When survey participants reported on their most recent sex, almost one in five (19 percent) noted intimate massage. We might expect it to occur most often in committed relationships, as it is considered an expression of love and care, but there wasn't as much variation across partner types as you might think. How close you are to your partner doesn't seem related to whether you'll be getting a massage.

The experience of intimate massage is also common across sexual identities. Slightly more lesbian and gay participants had given a massage during the past year (56 percent versus just over 50 percent of straight participants), and 60 percent of bisexuals both gave and received them in the same period. Once again, a picture of sexual practices begins to take shape around gender and sexual identity. Whereas gay men were a little less likely than straight men to have given or received a massage,

FIGURE 4.7   **Intimate massage in most recent sex**

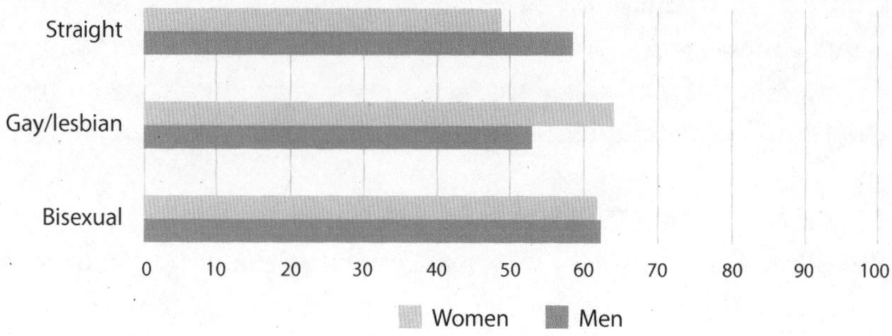

lesbian women were more likely than straight women to have engaged in it (Figure 4.7).

BREAST TOUCHING AND NIPPLE PLAY

Our culture is seemingly obsessed with sexualizing women's breasts. In almost every form of Canadian media, breasts are showcased as symbols of heterosexual desire, packaged for the male gaze. Yet in our social worlds, the fixation on breasts can also mean shaming women, such as when breastfeeding moms are made to feel unwelcome in public places. Decades of feminist theory have shown that these practices both objectify and devalue women. Yet it is also true that breasts, especially nipples, are sensitive to touch and are experienced as erogenous zones on both men's and women's bodies. So, between culture and biology, it should be no surprise that the majority of sexual encounters involve breast touching and nipple stimulation. Among our participants, 58 percent had included it in their most recent sex. This breaks down to equal proportions (60 percent) of encounters involving a man and a woman and those involving two women, but only 28 percent between two men (Figure 4.8).

HANDS AND FINGERS

The intimacy of touching genitals and causing sexual excitement is a special part of the connection between partners. It is also very common. Over half of our participants (57 percent) had engaged in it during their most recent sex. The gender of partners created some variation. In sex

FIGURE 4.8 **Breast/nipple play in most recent sex, by gender pairings**

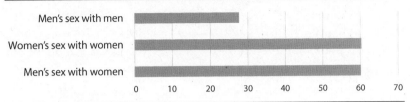

between men and women, 58 percent said that at least one partner had used their hands to touch genitals and 50 percent that fingers were inserted into the woman's vagina (Figure 4.9). For women having sex with women, 54 percent reported genital touching and 56 percent mentioned vaginal fingering. Men having sex with men did a little less genital touching (49 percent). The use of hands to bring pleasure was common across age groups. In every age cohort, at least half of respondents got handsy the last time they got it on.

FIGURE 4.9 **Genital stimulation with hands/fingers in most recent sex, by gender pairings**

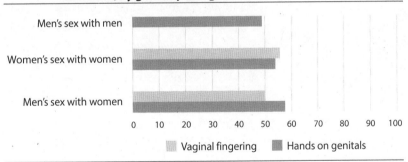

ANAL PLAY

If you were to guess at how many Canadians include anal play in their sex lives, what would you figure? On the one hand, Canadian culture has a long tradition of rejecting anal sex as beyond the pale. It has been characterized as unnatural, dirty, and sinful. Religious organizations have condemned it, and for generations, it was simply unmentionable. On the other hand, depictions of anal sex are now common in pornography, which is easier to access than ever before. They are increasingly mainstream, too, with passing references to anal sex on hit comedies such as *Schitt's Creek* and *The Mindy Project* and more serious discussions in the popular publications *Marie Claire* and *Men's Health*.[8]

Indeed, in the not-so-distant past, anal sex was a criminal offence in Canada. So was any other non-reproductive sex, such as oral sex, even among consenting adults. However, these laws were rarely enforced, with a key exception: the police used them as a tool in the persecution of gay men, entrapping and harassing them. This reinforced the belief that anal sex is what gay men do, and its close association with gay communities contributed to homophobic attitudes in many spheres. This narrative has been used to argue against rights for the 2SLGBTQ+ community, in both the courts and the public sphere, and public discomfort with the practice was an important factor in Canada's delay in removing discriminatory anti-gay sections from the Criminal Code.[9] The liberalization of Canadian sex laws in 1969 did not include the legalization of anal sex per se, and well after that date police continued to surveil and arrest men who had sex with other men. They used charges of indecency, vagrancy, and violation of the "bawdy house" rules for sex in bathhouses and other public places to criminalize same-sex behaviours.[10] In 2017, prompted by this record of violent persecution and imprisonment, the federal government apologized to the 2SLGBTQ+ community and passed legislation to facilitate the expungement of criminal records.[11]

As I discussed in Chapter 1, the attitudes of straight Canadians regarding the 2SLGBTQ+ community have improved dramatically in recent decades, and new legal rights have moved the country toward greater equality. Indeed, the young people in my university courses have trouble imagining, let alone remembering, a Canada in which 2SLGBTQ+ rights such as same-sex marriage did not have widespread approval. And though support for 2SLGBTQ+ communities is at an all-time high, the cultural link between anal sex and gay sexual identity has loosened significantly. Popular references to anal sex are often made in heterosexual contexts, and even some conservative religious communities are beginning to accept it under certain circumstances, such as evangelical Christian sex advice authors who argue that it can be an enjoyable part of Christian marriages.[12]

Between the disentanglement of anal sex with gay men's sexuality and the growing cultural openness to 2SLGBTQ+ sexuality, perhaps our taboos on anal sex have disappeared? Our data showed that quite a number of Canadians had tried it, though it was not a regular feature of their sex lives. Gay men were the most likely to have had it in their most recent sexual encounter, but even among this group, it was less than 40 percent. Overall, about 40 percent of men reported having given anal sex – that is, having put their penis into a partner's anus – at some point in their lives (Figure 4.10). That figure dropped to about 23 percent when we asked about the past year and to about 10 percent for the past month. About 20 percent of men had received it, with a decline to 14 percent in the past year and to 7 percent in the past month. Women had slightly less experience with anal sex – 37 percent had had it at some time, 15 percent in the last year, and 6 percent within the past month.

FIGURE 4.10 **Experience with anal sex, by gender**

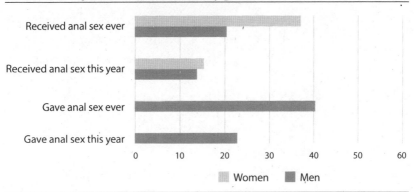

Large swaths of the Canadian population have some experience with anal sex, though it appears quite infrequent compared to oral sex, kissing, touching, and massage. Among our participants, just under 7 percent had had it during their last sexual encounter, either on the giving or receiving end (or both). Younger adults outreported older ones, with nearly 10 percent of those under thirty but less than 4 percent of those sixty and over having engaged in it (Figure 4.11). With regard to relationship type, married Canadians were less likely than separated or divorced ones to have included anal sex recently. Those who were single and had never been married were the most likely to try it.

FIGURE 4.11 **Anal sex in most recent sex, by age group**

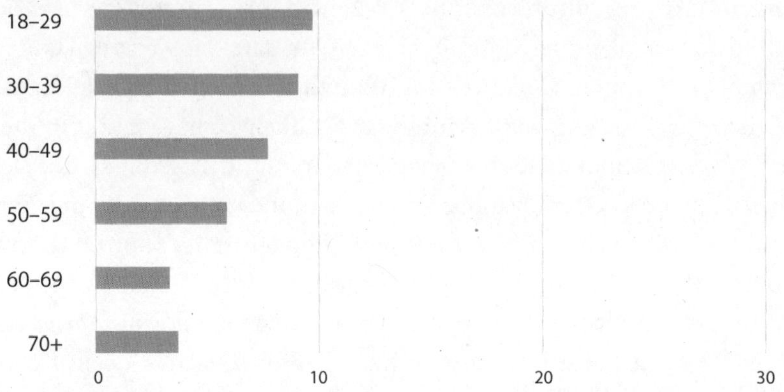

The Sex in Canada survey undermines the myth that anal sex is re-stricted to gay men. Although 79 percent of our gay participants had received anal sex at some point in their lives, so had 71 percent of bisexual men and 11 percent of straight men (Figure 4.12). When it came to giv-ing anal sex, 86 percent of gay men, 64 percent of bisexual men, and 34 percent of straight men had done so. About 38 percent of gay men had engaged in it during their last sexual encounter. For male-female sex, the figure was between 3 and 5 percent; women reported 3 percent and men reported 5 percent. Although anal sex was most common among gay and bisexual men, a significant number of straight men had also tried it.

Anal play can include fingering and penetration with dildos and other toys. Because we didn't ask about which body parts interacted with sex toys or dildos, our survey gave us little extra insight into this aspect of anal play, but we did ask whether partners used their fingers during their most recent sex. Men had done so about twice as often as women (11 percent versus 5 percent). When it came to gender, about a third of the men who had sex with men (31 percent) had done so during their last sex, but only about 7 percent of men who had sex with women said the same. About 4 percent of straight women had included anal finger-ing during their last sexual encounter, as had 6 percent of women who had sex with women. What conclusions can we draw from these data? Although men having sex with men were most likely to have anal sex,

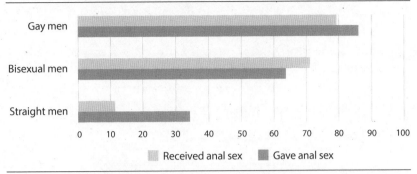

FIGURE 4.12 **Men's lifetime experience with anal sex, by sexual identity**

Received anal sex Gave anal sex

they were by no means the only group to do so. It is an occasional feature of many people's sex lives.

VIBRATORS AND TOYS

We don't necessarily need extra stuff to have sex; having it on your own or with a partner is easy enough without adding equipment to the equation. But sex toys can be fun accompaniments. Dildos and anal inserts, vibrators and feathers can stimulate, excite, and bring pleasure. Costumes, restraints, and blindfolds are commonly used in role play, and props and toys feature prominently in communities that share certain sexual practices, such as the BDSM (bondage, domination, sadism, and masochism) community. Even so, there are serious taboos around sex toys, and many people feel embarrassed about shopping for them. As with so many other topics related to sexuality, this shame may gradually be lifting.

There are many types of sex toys, but we grouped them into two: vibrators and non-vibrating toys. Vibrators can bring arousing feelings to many body parts, both male and female, but we mostly associate them with clitoral stimulation and women's pleasure. Women report more intense orgasms when using a vibrator, and doctors and clinicians sometimes prescribe them to female patients who are experiencing sexual dysfunction.[13] Studies in the United States have found that just over half of women use vibrators, most often in masturbation but also in partnered sex.[14] Researchers also note that women's vibrator use is associated with positive sexual function and health-promoting behaviours such as regular gynecological checkups.[15] How common are vibrators in Canada? It turns out that we are very similar to our American cousins. As Figure 4.13 shows, just over half of Canadian women (52 percent) had used a vibrator at some point, and about one-third (33 percent) had used one in the past year.

FIGURE 4.13 **Women's experience with vibrators**

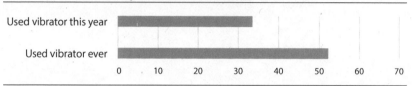

Vibrators are not only for masturbation; including them in partnered sex can also be pleasurable. Women were much more likely to use one during same-sex encounters than when having sex with men (Figure 4.14). Over 30 percent of them had used a vibrator in their most recent sex with another woman, whereas only 12 percent had done so when their partner was a man.

FIGURE 4.14 **Women's vibrator use in most recent sex, by gender of partner**

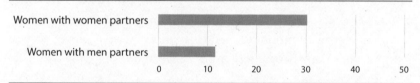

Vibrators were more popular than non-vibrating toys among our respondents. About 38 percent had used a non-vibrating toy at some point, about 22 percent in the past year (Figure 4.15). In partnered sex, about 5 percent had included one in their most recent encounter. Young adults used sex toys much more often than older ones. Almost half (46 percent) of those in their thirties (of all genders) had used a vibrator during the past year. Toys were considerably less popular among older participants, with less than 15 percent of those sixty and up having used any kind of toy during the past year.

FIGURE 4.15 **Experience with vibrators and non-vibrating sex toys**

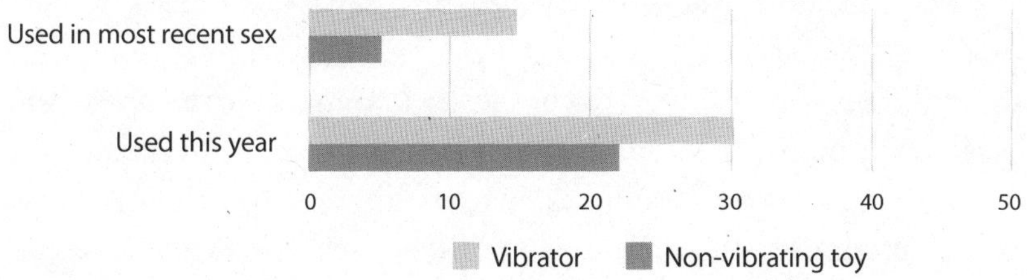

SEX WITH MULTIPLE PARTNERS

How common is sex between more than two people? We know that orgies, sex clubs, and parties to facilitate group sex have long existed. We know, too, that polyamorous relationships are becoming increasingly popular, but we should bear in mind that the term polyamory describes relationships, not sexual encounters. Group sex may be a part of some polyamorous relationships, but there are many configurations of poly-amory that does not include group sex.[16] Our participants had the option of choosing "multiple" when they told us about their most recent partner. This key insight gave us a little window into sex in groups of three or more, though it couldn't tell us, for example, what group sex meant to people or to their relationships. It indicated only how common the practice was. Among our participants, just a handful (less than 0.5 per-cent) said that their most recent encounter involved multiple partners. More research is required into the practice of group sex, but for now we know that it is a relatively uncommon part of Canadian lives.

PATTERNS OF SEXUAL BEHAVIOUR AND INTIMACY

Our survey revealed that Canadian adults enjoy varied types of sex and sexual behaviours. If you are a romantic, you might be heartened to learn that much of our sexual expression includes intimacies such as kissing, cuddling, and massage. If you are an advocate for expansive understandings of sexuality, you might feel reassured by the fact that many Canadians have engaged in oral and anal sex. If you are an advocate for women's orgasms, you might be encouraged by the apparent popu-larity of vibrators and sex toys (or think the numbers are still too low!). As a sociologist, I am interested in how gender, age, and sexual identity shape sexual practice. That is, how do social categories, identities, and locations determine our sexuality – What is the social organization of Canadian sexuality?

The differences we uncovered in the Sex in Canada survey reveal how social forces push our sexuality in various directions, clustering us into groups that behave a little differently from other groups. These patterns can be described as the social organization of sexuality. Gender, sexual identity, and age are prime examples of forces that structure our social lives (sexuality being just one domain). Although there is plenty of within-group variation, the choices that individuals make are constrained and enabled by their social locations, nudging them to conform to social expectations more often than not. I will take up that sociological lens again in Chapter 6, when I explore other ways that social orders influence sexual behaviour.

5

Pleasure, Pain, and Risk

Sex can be a source of both pleasure and pain, of discovery and danger. When we talk about it, we commonly split it into different conversations. We often refer to risk, perhaps not always in the most accurate way. Our talks about sexual violence are typically directed to young women as advice on how to avoid being attacked by a male stranger: don't go out alone at night; don't wear revealing clothing; never be alone with a man you don't know. However, both men and women can experience sexual assault, and the perpetrator is less likely to be a stranger than someone they know.[1] What we need is clear talk, based in solid evidence, about keeping ourselves safe from sexual pain, violence, unplanned pregnancy, and all the downsides of sex. We also need strategies to empower people of all genders to speak up for themselves about what they want or don't want in bed. And, as a society, we must insist that people listen and respect the wishes of others. This is why this chapter has started where sex always should: with a discussion of consent.

The next stop is pleasure. The ways we talk about pleasure are interesting, too. Depending on who our listeners are, we might avoid the topic altogether. Especially with young people, pleasure can get short shrift in such discussions, which rarely mention that sex can feel good, be emotionally fulfilling, and can enhance our connection with a partner. Setting aside our worries about the harmful aspects of sex to imagine the fun possibilities can be difficult. Our fears around teen sex are so acute that parents routinely imagine that only other people's kids – not their own – are interested in it. Often, in a misguided effort to prolong the innocence of childhood, they try to ensure that their kids don't learn about sex.[2] Despite all these efforts, every generation inevitably ends up becoming sexually active sooner or later.

And on to sexual pain and other negative aspects of sex. Frankly, I'm not convinced that the disappointing aspects of our sex lives are mentioned nearly often enough. Sex can be bad in many ways, yet these facets seem to remain taboo topics, even as discussing the pleasurable aspects becomes more and more acceptable. For instance, college students may assume that hooking up on campus is only about fun and friends and avoiding the responsibilities of a relationship.[3] They also need to be adequately prepared for the high rates of sexual violence that can occur in their social circles, the lasting harm of non-consensual experiences, how to get help with sexually transmitted infections (STIs), and even the mundane disappointments of lacklustre sex.[4]

Pleasure, pain, and risk are not equally distributed across all sexually active Canadians. In many cases, they map onto existing social inequalities such as gender, sexual identity, and age. The orgasm gap in heterosexual sex and the practice of faking it offer a glimpse into the gender inequalities of sexual pleasure. We seem to vary in our ability to communicate clearly what brings us pleasure and what is uncomfortable, scary, or painful. And it is obvious, too, that we do not always help each other to speak up, listen to each other, or respect the wishes of our partners. Some people feel entitled to whatever they want sexually, whereas others do not feel safe or confident in asserting their boundaries. The idea that each of us has the right to define good sex and to end a sexual situation that feels bad is known as "sexual citizenship."[5] Our social location – in terms of gender, race, sexual identity, and financial security – can affect both our ability to exercise sexual citizenship ourselves and to grant citizenship to others around us. There is a link between social inequalities the personal empowerment we feel to insist on healthy, happy sexual encounters.

CONSENT

Good sex, I'll say again, starts with consent that is given enthusiastically in an ongoing way throughout a sexual encounter. Indeed, our ideal of good sex involves adult partners who are fully informed about what they are doing, unimpaired in their decision making, and in eager agreement to all the aspects of the encounter. Unfortunately, as a society, we fall short of this ideal alarmingly often. Rape and sexual assault are crimes of sexual activity without consent. Despite low reporting and conviction rates for both, estimates show that 30 percent of Canadian women and 8 percent of Canadian men have been sexually assaulted at some point.[6] To put it another way, almost one in three women and one in ten men in your life, whether you know it or not, lives with such trauma. Many survivors state that the reporting process simply worsens the situation. They may not be believed. They may be asked to retell their story repeatedly. They may feel that their own actions are being questioned. Thus, one estimate suggests that only a small fraction of sexual assaults (about 5 percent) are reported to police.[7] The #MeToo movement, which amplified public discussion about sexual violence, was associated with a slight increase in reports starting in 2017, yet overall approximations still suggest that less than 10 percent of assaults are reported.[8]

Distinguishing good sex from bad has not always revolved around the issue of consent.[9] Historically, religious institutions relied on morality, marriage, and reproduction for their definitions. Good, moral sex happened between (heterosexual) spouses, with the goal of making a baby. Bad sex was everything else, including masturbation, premarital and extramarital sex, and violent acts such as rape and incest. Nonconsensual sex was definitely on the "bad" side of morality, but the line itself was less about consent and more about a narrow ideal in which the purpose of sex was to create babies within marriages.

Although rape has been criminalized for centuries, early forms of the law saw the woman as having been "spoiled" and thus assigned the role of victim, not to her, but to her husband or father, a point that many commentators used to highlight women's de facto legal standing as property, rather than as individuals with legal rights.[10] Later, rape laws carved out exceptions for unwanted sex within marriages, and they included the stipulation that women resist with "utmost force." Even as laws modernized through the twentieth century, consent was only one factor in adjudicating sexual assault crimes. Substantial public agitation for legal reform was required before consent became so fundamental to our sexual values.[11]

The changes owe much to feminist activism. Since the 1960s, feminists have asserted women's sexual agency, established support centres for sexual assault survivors, and rejected victim-blaming narratives of sexual assault. Women's rights activists fought to implement sexual harassment policies in workplaces and to revise rape laws to criminalize sexual assaults within marriage. And feminists shaped public discourse by trumpeting the right to say no to unwanted sex. These discussions, as well as important conversations about 2SLGBTQ+ rights that similarly asserted claims to sexual freedom, established a new cultural approach to the subject. In Canada today, wholehearted consent is the primary marker of good sex, and its absence is universally defined as bad, even as much sexual activity falls between these two ends of the spectrum.

Given that non-consensual sex is so common, we assumed that at least some of our participants would have experienced it. We knew that our questions might bring up a painful memory or cause stress, so everyone who took the survey was supplied with links to support resources. And when we asked about their most recent sexual encounter, we began by asking how much they had desired it. We offered a range of responses, from "I wanted this sexual experience very much" to "I was assaulted or raped; I said no." Less than 1 percent selected the latter. For them, we asked no further questions about the incident. Instead, we offered a link to support resources and directed them to skip to the next section of the survey. This means that our data in the previous chapter, for instance, included no information about episodes of sexual violence.

As you can see from Figure 5.1, a number of participants said that their most recent sex fell into the grey area of non-consent. If they said they hadn't wanted sex but agreed to it anyway, we asked a follow-up question: "There are many reasons why people agree to (or 'say yes to') sex they don't want. Which of the following were true for you? (Select all that apply)." The responses to this question are given in Figure 5.2. Open-ended answers included phrases such as "it just happened," "to keep the relationship strong," and "didn't want to hurt [a partner's] feelings."

FIGURE 5.1 **How much did you want your most recent sexual encounter?**

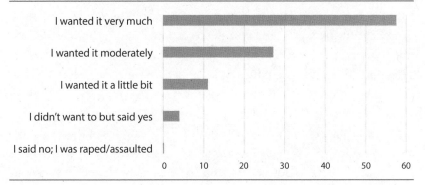

FIGURE 5.2 **Reasons to have sex by those who did not want to**

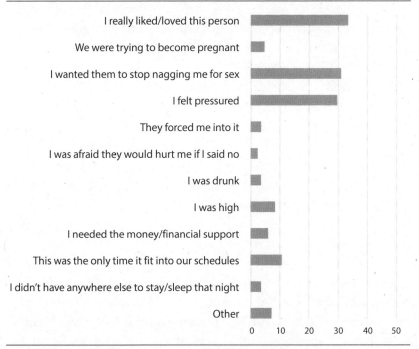

Figure 5.2 contains many heartbreaking reasons for agreeing to un-wanted sex, including poverty and having no place to stay. And yet, there is quite a range, from "he or she forced me into it," which corresponds to the definition of sexual assault, to "this was the only time it fit into our schedules," which suggests an otherwise consensual relationship with a busy partner. In assessing the encounters that were not coerced and could thus technically be defined as consensual, thinking of a spectrum between enthusiastic and unenthusiastic consent might be a useful approach. In my view, the latter deserves much more thoughtful consideration and research. Should we include discussions of unwanted-but-agreed-to sex in our sex education courses? If we continue to use the standard of wholehearted consent as the basis for good sex, "grey area" encounters would be classed as bad – but we don't know enough about the extent to which they may be harmful. The reality is that sex can also be unpleasant, painful, or emotionally unsatisfying even when both parties consent to it and even when it has enjoyable aspects. It's complicated. Still, joyful and fulfilling sex is possible. It is attainable for many Canadians. Consent is only the bare minimum. Good sex starts there, but we need to make space for psychological safety and easy communication between partners to lay a foundation for truly enjoyable sex.

PLEASURE

The good news is that when sex is consensual, most people find it pleasurable. Very pleasurable. In the Sex in Canada survey, we gave participants a range to capture how much they had enjoyed their most recent encounter, from "not at all pleasurable" to "extremely pleasurable" (recall that we asked these questions only if the experience was consensual). Figure 5.3 shows that over 97 percent enjoyed the sex at least "a little." Over half said it was "quite a bit pleasurable" or "extremely pleasurable." It lifts my spirits to think about all the enjoyable, good-feeling sex that Canadians are having across the country.

One important aspect of sexual pleasure is arousal – that familiar "is it getting warm in here?" feeling. Very few participants reported feeling "not at all" aroused during their most sexual encounter (about 3 percent), whereas about 30 percent said they were "a little" or "moderately" aroused, and about two-thirds stated that they were "quite a bit" or "ex-

FIGURE 5.3 **How pleasurable was your most recent sex?**

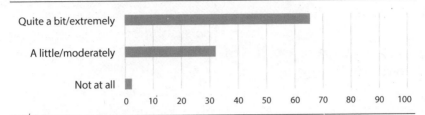

FIGURE 5.4 **Prior to your most recent sex, what was your level of desire?**

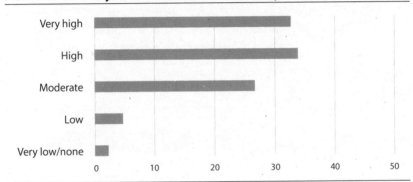

tremely" aroused. As Figure 5.4 indicates, we got similar numbers when we asked, "Prior to sex, what was your level of desire for your partner?" On the whole, our respondents were feeling the heat for their partners.

GENDER, SEXUAL IDENTITY, AND PLEASURE

Overall levels of sexual pleasure are high, but not all Canadians are having an equally good time in the bedroom. Gender is an important dividing line. On average, men enjoyed themselves more than women did during their last encounter and were less likely to say that it was "not at all" pleasurable. We might speculate that this discrepancy has to do with biological differences between male and female bodies. After all, our cultural myths suggest that men have a stronger sex drive than women. This may be the case, but I expect that the biological explanation would apply more to arousal than to pleasure. Being aroused might suggest a physical response to turn-ons, but pleasure seems to revolve around a subjective state: enjoyment. Nonetheless, the gender differences were very similar for both questions, with men reporting both greater feelings of arousal and more pleasure in their most recent sex (Figure 5.5).

A closer look suggests a more sociological reason for the gender difference in pleasure: the dynamics of heterosexual sex. Among men, straight men had the highest levels of enjoyment, with 71 percent saying that their most recent sex was either quite a bit or extremely pleasurable, with gay men (67 percent) and bisexual men (65 percent) at similarly high levels (Figure 5.6). Among women, bisexual (73 percent) and lesbian (69 percent) women reported high levels that were similar to men. However, only 60 percent of straight women said that their last sex was quite a bit or extremely pleasurable. Given this, the intersection of gender and heterosexuality rather than gender on its own would seem to produce an inequality in pleasure.

FIGURE 5.5   **How pleasurable was most recent sex? How aroused were you?**

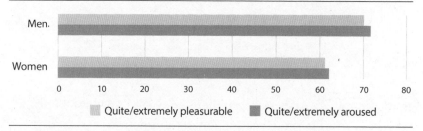

FIGURE 5.6   **Proportion reporting most recent sex was quite/extremely pleasurable, by gender and sexual identity**

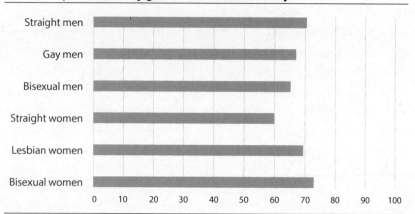

It becomes especially challenging to hold onto the long-debunked myths that women's bodies are less capable than men's of experiencing sexual pleasure in the face of these differences. The issue of physiology drops away when we consider the pleasure gap between straight and lesbian women, pointing us instead to possible variations in the quality of encounters, the development of skill in pleasing a partner, and the type and amount of communication between partners – all social dynamics. If straight women are not enjoying sex as much as lesbian women, the likeliest explanation is that the kind of sex that straight couples have, on average, is not as enjoyable for women as the kind of sex that lesbian couples have.

AGE AND PLEASURE

Age is another factor that may affect pleasure. Our culture tells us that desire wanes over time, that our most vibrant sexual selves exist in early adulthood, and that we then experience a slow decline until we die. A common narrative holds that men reach their magical period of "sexual prime" before women do, after which both sexes have nothing to look forward to but less of it (sub-prime, I suppose). If this were true, our survey results would be expected to confirm it. In other words, men's arousal would have reached its highest levels in young adulthood, whereas women's would start low, peak in middle age, and then decline. Although our female participants might seem to have followed this pattern, men's levels of arousal were steadily high at all ages (Figure 5.7). In fact, 72 percent of our oldest men, those who were seventy and older, reported that they were "quite a bit" or "extremely" aroused in their most recent sexual encounter.

Arousal and pleasure may describe differing aspects of sexual enjoyment. In terms of age, however, the patterns we see in the survey results for pleasure are similar to those for arousal. Men's pleasure was high across all age groups, with 65 to 75 percent of men at all ages reporting quite a bit or extreme pleasure. Older men, meanwhile, reported having slightly greater pleasure than younger ones. Women's pleasure was also high but not as high as men's. Between 52 and 66 percent of them experienced high degrees of it, and younger women had more pleasure than older women.

FIGURE 5.7 **Proportion feeling quite/extremely aroused in most recent sex, by age and gender**

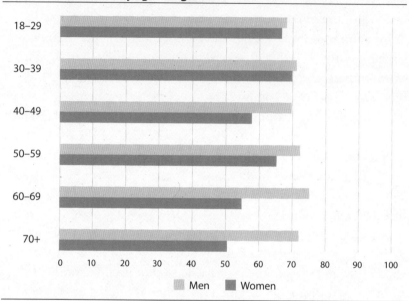

HEALTH AND PLEASURE

We might expect that poor health would disrupt sexual pleasure. After all, health problems can make every aspect of life miserable. In the Sex in Canada survey, we included three self-assessment measures of health: physical, mental, and sexual. Participants rated each one as poor, fair, good, very good, or excellent. Rather than defining physical, mental, and sexual health for them, we let them decide what counted in each category. Although this may produce an imprecise measure, participants turn out to be quite good at assessing their health, supplying results that are similar to other measures of health. Physical and mental dimensions of health can affect our enjoyment of sex.

Physical Health

Let's look at physical health and sexuality. Over three-fourths (78 percent) of our participants reported that their health was good, very good, or excellent, 17 percent that it was fair, and 5 percent that it was poor. Unsurprisingly, those who were in poor or fair health were least likely to have enjoyed themselves during their most recent sexual encounter.

Physical discomfort, low energy, and other illness-related issues probably diminish the ability to experience or enjoy the pleasurable aspects of sex. Among our participants, over 70 percent of those in very good or excellent health, but just over half of those in poor health (53 percent), said that their most recent sex was quite a bit or extremely pleasurable. Poor health also interfered with feelings of arousal: 75 percent of those in excellent health felt very aroused, versus 52 percent of those in poor health.

Poor health seemed to affect some people's enjoyment more than others. To a much greater extent than for men, it diminished pleasure for women (Figure 5.8). Women and men who were in excellent health had similarly high levels of pleasure in their most recent sex, 75 percent and 73 percent, respectively, but so, too, did most men in fair or poor health (59 and 69 percent). Women in fair (55 percent) or poor (42 percent) health were much less likely than those in excellent health to report high levels of pleasure.

Why might poor health reduce women's sexual pleasure more than men's? The answer is not obvious. It may be related to our discussion above, since health tends to decline as we age, and the relationship between age and pleasure is different for men than for women. Another

FIGURE 5.8 **Proportion reporting quite/extremely pleasurable most recent sex, by health and gender**

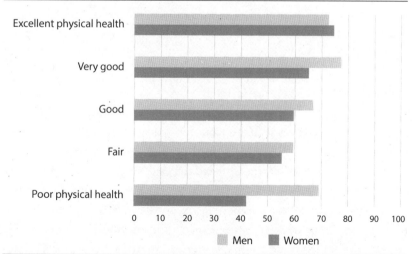

possibility is physiological. Perhaps feeling pleasure is more difficult in ailing female bodies than in male ones. Or perhaps – once again – we need to take a sociological view, suggesting that women in poor health are likelier than their male counterparts to have sex that they aren't particularly excited about. This may be especially true of straight women, who may be prioritizing the pleasure of their partners over their own.

Mental Health

Of course, mental health is also very important to well-being, and we can imagine that it, too, may affect the capacity for sexual pleasure. About 17 percent of our participants said that their mental health was fair or poor, 26 percent said good, and the rest said very good or excellent. Those who selected "very good" or "excellent" were most likely to say that their last sexual encounter was highly enjoyable. Likewise, those who rated their mental health as poor were most likely to report that it was "not at all" pleasurable.

Once again, we see a gender difference. Men's responses did not suggest a clear relationship between mental health and having a happy time in bed. Men whose mental health was poor were just as likely as those with very good mental health to feel that their last sex was very pleasurable (Figure 5.9). Those whose mental health was fair or good enjoyed themselves less than all other men. On the other hand, men in poor mental health were more likely than other men to report that their last sex was not at all pleasurable. The responses of women created a clearer pattern, which suggested that poorer mental health was associated with less sexual pleasure.

RELATIONSHIP TO SEXUAL PARTNER

Intimacy and the connection between partners might also affect the degree of pleasure in a sexual encounter. Some research links relationship status and sexual outcomes. For instance, in examining whether a long-term, committed partnership led to better sex, some studies suggest that the months and years of association foster a greater sense of intimacy, knowledge about what a partner enjoys, and/or particularly good communication about what brings pleasure.[12] This is especially the case for couples that take a practice-makes-perfect approach to sexual satisfac-

FIGURE 5.9 **Proportion reporting quite/extremely pleasurable most recent sex, by mental health and gender**

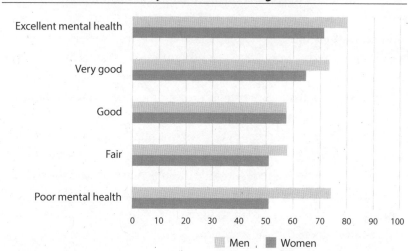

tion.[13] Other studies examine the quality of casual sexual encounters, such as hookups on college campuses, finding a significant orgasm gap between men and women.[14] Together, all these studies indicate that women in heterosexual contexts experience greater pleasure in committed, long-term partnerships than in casual sex. For this reason, we expected that participants who were married or who had a common-law partner would report the highest levels of pleasure.

Indeed, it seems that, though Canadians may find it exciting to meet someone new, having sex with the same person over time produces the most enjoyment. Our data showed that roughly two-thirds of participants whose last sexual encounter was with their spouse, common-law partner, or a boyfriend or girlfriend rated it "quite" or "extremely" pleasurable. The number dropped for participants in other relationship types that were probably of shorter duration, such as for those having sex with a steady date (63 percent), with a friend (58 percent), or with someone they had just met (52 percent).

Straight women are often singled out as a group whose sexual pleasure hinges on their relationship with their partner(s). On average, they have less pleasurable sex and fewer orgasms than straight men (or lesbian and bisexual women, for that matter), which has prompted researchers to ponder what might improve their situation. If we focus on the straight women in the Sex in Canada survey, we find that their reported pleasure followed the same pattern as for all Canadians, with those in more committed relationships expressing greater enjoyment. That said, there are two differences to note. First, the proportion of straight women who had highly pleasurable sex was consistently lower than the proportion of straight men who said the same, regardless of relationship status (Figure 5.10). Second, the pleasure discrepancy between having sex with a spouse versus someone they had just met was greater for straight women than for straight men. That is, they were almost twice as likely to have good sex with a spouse than with someone new, and the pleasure gap was much smaller among straight men. In casual hookups with a stranger, less than one-third of straight women but 62 percent of straight men enjoyed themselves a great deal.

FIGURE 5.10 **Relationship type and pleasure, straight men and women**

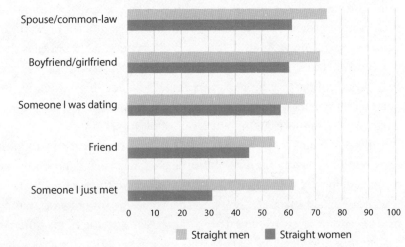

ORGASMS

Orgasms are a singularly agreeable aspect of sexuality. That sense of release is unlike any other physical sensation. It would be silly to think about sexual pleasure without considering orgasms. Still, some people warn against becoming too focused on whether they occur – that is, they argue against the "orgasm imperative," or the cultural idea that orgasm is the purpose of sex, as too pressure-filled and a distraction from all the other pleasant sensations of sexual activity.[15] Nonetheless, orgasms are central to sexual pleasure. Among our participants, about 73 percent had climaxed during their most recent sexual encounter. Not surprisingly, this group also had greater pleasure: 75 percent of those who had an orgasm rated their sex as highly pleasurable, compared to just about 40 percent of those who did not reach orgasm (Figure 5.11).

FIGURE 5.11 **Orgasm and pleasure in most recent sex**

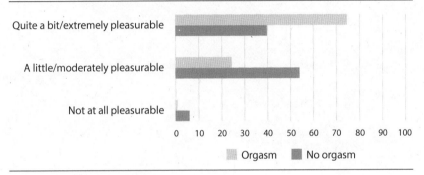

MULTIPLE ORGASMS

After an orgasmic release of sexual tension, a certain amount of time must elapse before the body can build arousal to the point of another orgasm. When two orgasms happen in the same sexual encounter, we count these as multiple orgasms. There is a lot of variation in the time it takes to recover from an orgasm and become turned on again. About 15 percent of our participants had multiple orgasms in their most recent sexual encounter. In general, the female body is thought to have the greatest capacity for multiple orgasms; in our survey, 13 percent of men and 18 percent of women had them during their most recent sex – a difference, though perhaps not as great as you might have guessed (Figure 5.12).

The gender of one's sexual partner matters when it comes to experiencing multiple orgasms. Those in same-gender encounters were most likely to have them. Figure 5.13 shows that men who had sex with men

FIGURE 5.12 **Multiple orgasms, by gender**

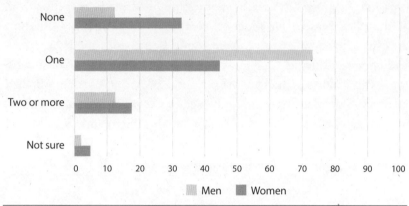

FIGURE 5.13 **Multiple orgasms, by gender of sexual partner**

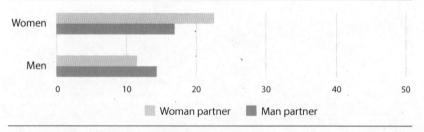

were a little more likely to have multiple orgasms than those who had sex with women (14 percent versus 11 percent). Women who had sex with women were more likely to have multiple orgasms than those who had sex with men (23 percent versus 17 percent).

HETEROSEXUALITY AND THE GENDER GAP IN ORGASMS

Not only did mixed-gender couples report fewer multiple orgasms in their sexual encounters, but there was also a significant gender gap in orgasms in heterosexual sex: men have more. Whereas 86 percent of men who had sex with women in their most recent encounter had an orgasm, only 62 percent of women with men sex partners said the same (Figure 5.14). Lots of myths and misinformation make claims about this gap and its cause, mostly chalking it up to women's challenging bodies or their excessive emotional needs. Some have suggested that, from an evolutionary perspective, men's orgasms are imperative for reproduction to a greater extent than those of women, but others have found that such assumptions are not supported by the evidence.[16] In fact, orgasm inequality is not adequately explained by female physiology or neediness. Rather, the main cause is social, linked to the gender dynamics in heterosexual relationships.

FIGURE 5.14 **Orgasm in most recent mixed-gender sex**

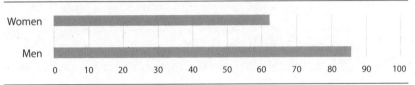

I have thought quite a bit about the gender gap in orgasms. My colleagues Nicole Andrejek, Melanie Heath, and I examined it through the data in the Sex in Canada survey in tandem with forty follow-up interviews.[17] We tested the claims that the gap may arise from women's lack of practice at bringing themselves to orgasm through masturbation or from their greater need for a long-term relationship to create a safe space for their orgasms. Neither of these claims were supported by the data. Rather, the correct explanation was the simplest one: women were most likely to climax when they or their partner stimulated their clitoris, often with oral sex. Our findings are quite clear: women have fewer orgasms than their male partners because what went on in bed typically concentrated on the penis rather than the clitoris.

However, our interviewees offered other explanations – ones that were rooted in myths about female sexuality. In a self-fulfilling prophesy, misguided ideas about women's bodies and their capacity to enjoy sex affected the type of sexual activities in which they and their partners engaged. Specifically, three myths – that women's bodies are inadequate, that their privates are yucky, and that they're not especially keen on orgasm anyway – combine in heterosexual sex, creating a dynamic in which partners simply don't do the behaviours that stimulate the woman's clitoris enough for her to climax. (I touch on "faking it" in the next section.)

The first myth, long proven false, is that female bodies are somehow more challenging to bring to orgasm than male bodies. We've known better for more than a half century: research by Alfred Kinsey and colleagues and by William Masters and Virginia Johnson found clear evidence that female physiology is not an impediment to orgasm, but a boon.[18] These scholars demonstrated that the female capacity for multiple orgasms exceeds that of the human male. And yet, this myth is prevalent throughout our culture, and women and men both referred to it during our interviews. Many implied or stated outright that women should reach orgasm during penile-vaginal intercourse, ignoring clitoral manipulation in favour of sex that directly stimulated the penis. This fit with our data, which showed that heterosexual understandings of what counted as sex determined what they and their partners did during their most recent sexual encounters. Additionally, when men reached orgasm, they felt that sex was over, expressing disappointment that women "took too long" to have their own orgasms.

Misogyny is clearer in the second myth: that women's genitalia are shameful, unappealing, or even repulsive. Some of us grew up during an era when the vulva and vagina were considered gross, smelly, and dirty. Women were made to feel ashamed of their genitals, discouraged from even looking at or knowing their own bodies. Men, too, were taught that the female body was unpleasant, nasty, or scary, rather than something they might enjoy exploring, touching, or tasting. Stigmatizing and shaming women's bodies while simultaneously casting women themselves as objects for male pleasure is a pernicious combination. Recent decades may have dimmed this second myth, yet comments from our interviewees confirmed that it has not yet been snuffed out. Some regarded oral sex or manual stimulation of the clitoris as "dirty," "kinky," or "not natural." Some of the women characterized their own bodies in this way, explaining that they discouraged their partners from engaging in these activities.

The third myth is that women don't "need" or enjoy orgasms as much as men. Our interviewees told us that, unlike men, who feel they must reach orgasm whenever they have sex, women partake in it more for the emotional connection than for the sexual release. In other words, the woman's job was to facilitate the man's pleasure, with her reward as the intimacy and closeness produced through heterosexual sex. This reasoning relies on myths of women's sexual passivity and men's aggression, along with the idea that male and female bodies differ in some fundamental way. It has proven difficult to shake. If our culture encourages men to express their sexuality while simultaneously disparaging female sexuality as shameful, and if we retain a lingering sense that women's bodies are kind of gross but also extremely enticing for men, we probably shouldn't be surprised that men's feelings of entitlement to sexual pleasure remain a little more straightforward than women's.

If there is any good news here, it came from the older straight women who told us that they overcame their shameful feelings as they aged. Some also said they had found a new partner who was more invested than previous ones in their orgasms. Individuals do resist these cultural myths, and there are some excellent books out now that encourage women to embrace their bodies and nurture their sense of entitlement to good sexual feelings.[19] Until we address the social stigma and shame around women's sexuality, sexual desires, and bodies, and until men shift their attitudes and behaviour, the gender gap in heterosexual orgasms will persist.

FAKING IT

The mythology around orgasms holds that women regularly fake them, perhaps to conclude a bout of mediocre sex or to spare the feelings of an unskilled lover. Men, according to the myth, are unable to feign orgasm because the absence of ejaculate would give them away (in fact, male orgasm without ejaculation does sometimes occur). Although we didn't have a survey question on why men and women faked an orgasm, we did ask whether they had done so. If participants had not had an orgasm in their most recent sexual encounter, we asked whether they pretended to have one. Just under one-quarter of women (23 percent) who did not have an orgasm faked one. A few men also told us they faked an orgasm: about 12 percent of those who did not experience an orgasm pretended to have one. However, most of our participants did report having an orgasm in their most recent encounter, so faking it is the exception, not the rule. Among all participants recalling their most recent sexual encounter, between 1 and 2 percent of men and about 7 percent of women reported faking it.

PAIN

How often do we experience pain during sex? How severe is it, and how long does it last? Painful sex is fairly common, though it is not often mentioned. Before getting down to the numbers, can we address the myth that losing one's virginity is necessarily painful for women? This is a harmful fallacy whose message is that women must just grin and bear the discomfort, when the truth is that first penetration does not need to be painful and in fact can feel very pleasurable. And greater experience should increase the probability of avoiding unwanted sexual pain.

In the Sex in Canada survey, just under a quarter of our participants (23 percent) reported that their most recent sexual experience was painful in some way. Most said that it was "a little" (14 percent) or "moderately" (5 percent) painful, though a few reported that it was "quite" (2 percent) or "extremely" (1 percent) painful. About half of those who experienced pain told us that it was brief – five minutes or less. For another 28 percent, it lasted an hour; for 8 percent, it persisted for a day or more. Please recall that these figures do not include any non-consensual sexual experiences. We asked these questions only of those whose sex was consensual.

FIGURE 5.15 **Experienced pain in most recent sex**

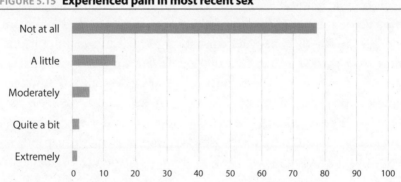

Again, we see women at a disadvantage. They were twice as likely as men to say that their most recent sex was painful (30 percent versus 15 percent). The largest gender differences were in the lowest levels of discomfort; 19 percent of women had experienced "a little" pain in their most recent sex, compared with only 8 percent of men. As the level of pain increased, the gender disparities decreased (similar proportions of men and women reported quite or extremely painful sex). This trend was similar with regard to the duration of the pain, too: among those who felt pain, men were more likely than women to say that it lasted for a day or more.

FIGURE 5.16   **Pain in most recent sex, by gender**

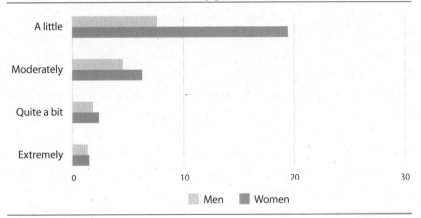

This is one area where both biological and social factors combine to produce a gender disparity. Being penetrated is more likely to be painful than the act of penetrating, and women who participate in penile-vaginal intercourse may experience discomfort for a variety of reasons that range from mild vaginal dryness to medical issues such as vulval skin conditions, vaginal or urinary tract infections, or a tissue injury (whether caused by the penetration itself or something else).[20] In addition, sociocultural factors may prevent women from voicing concerns about penetrative pain, and our cultural narratives sometimes present pain as something that women are expected to tolerate during sex. However, treatments for chronic painful sex are available, and partners can change their sexual activities to minimize pain.

You might imagine that we would experience more painful sex as we get older; however, this pattern did not appear in our survey responses. Forty percent of young adults, aged eighteen to twenty-nine, had felt some pain in their most recent sex, a higher number than for any other age group. Among those in their thirties, 28 percent felt some pain, and for older groups, between 12 percent and 19 percent did. I wonder if those who are older have learned from experience, planning ahead for pleasure, making sure that lubricant was on hand, etcetera, to better fend off any potential discomfort.

PLEASURE AND PAIN

Pain can be a serious problem that interferes with the enjoyment of sex, but in some cases, it can coexist with pleasure. Some people feel that the combination is exciting and gratifying. Given this, we expected that at least some of our participants would connect pain with pleasure, but how many? And would enjoyment diminish as pain intensified, or would it increase? Although much sexual pain is unpleasant and unwanted, not all of it is.

The integration of pleasure and pain is no surprise to the subcultural communities involved in BDSM, in which the intentional giving and receiving of pain during sex is understood to be enjoyable and stimulating.[21] They have developed rigorous systems of rules to ensure the safety of participants while introducing stress and pain into sexual pleasure.[22] However, you don't need to belong to a BDSM community to combine pain and pleasure. One estimate suggests that about a third of Canadians have participated in sexual behaviour they define as "kink."[23] We didn't ask about the intentionality of inflicting or receiving pain in sex, but we did ask about pain and pleasure. Among our participants, between one-third and one-half of those who had pain in their most recent encounter found it to be either quite a bit or extremely pleasurable. Figure 5.17 displays, for each level of pain experienced, the proportion of participants who enjoyed it.

It is important to acknowledge those who feel pleasure during painful sex, whether because of the discomfort or despite it, but we also need to keep in mind that we can't (and shouldn't) extrapolate from their experience to a general population trend. First, only a few of our par-

FIGURE 5.17 **Pleasure and pain in most recent sex**

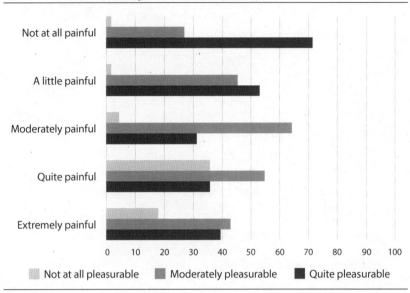

Not at all pleasurable   Moderately pleasurable   Quite pleasurable

ticipants had uncomfortable sex. Second, in instances of non-consensual sex, we did not ask about pleasure or pain. What we do know is that pain and pleasure are not incompatible and that some people enjoy the mix under certain circumstances, such as when both parties give their full consent.

SEXUAL HEALTH, PAIN, AND RISK

Poor sexual health is another negative aspect of sexuality. Among the various ailments that hinder enjoyment of sex, erectile dysfunction has received significant attention. Since the discovery of erection-producing medications such as Viagra and Cialis, having fewer or softer erections than desired can be readily treated with a number of common prescription medications. Just over 10 percent of our men participants had used a prescription medication designed to help them attain or maintain an erection in their most recent sexual encounter.[24] Another 4 percent had used a non-prescription herb or supplement (products that have not been proven effective and that can be harmful, I should note).

Vaginal dryness is also a common problem. Natural vaginal wetness can be a sign of arousal, but dryness does not always mean that a woman is not turned on. It can reflect dehydration or be the side effect of another ailment. And it can result from diminished levels of estrogen, which often makes it a chronic problem for post-menopausal women. Whatever the cause, it can make sex quite painful, involving irritation and even tearing of the vaginal tissue. Figure 5.18 shows that many of our women participants had found it slightly difficult (23 percent) or difficult (9 percent) to become naturally lubricated in their most recent sex; fewer reported that they found it either very difficult (4 percent) or extremely difficult (4 percent).

FIGURE 5.18 **How difficult was it to become naturally lubricated in most recent sex? (women only)**

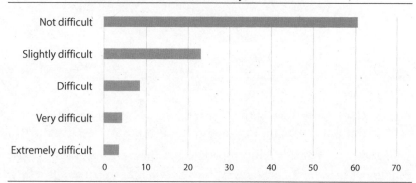

When chronic vaginal dryness is due to the low estrogen levels of menopause, doctors can prescribe treatments, including hormone therapy. For situational dryness, the most common remedy is an over-the-counter lubricant. Sometimes, partners get creative in using the solutions at hand, from lotion to saliva (Figure 5.19). Our participants turned to a variety of slippery substances: in their last sex, over 20 percent used an over-the-counter sex lubricant, almost as many (17 percent) opted for saliva, and others relied on a variety of oils and lotions. Petroleum-based oils, I should add, are not compatible with latex condoms, as they increase the likelihood of breakage.

SEXUALLY TRANSMITTED INFECTIONS

The skin-to-skin contact of sex and the exchange of bodily fluids can sometimes lead to sexually transmitted infections, or STIs. These have

FIGURE 5.19 **Types of lubricant used in most recent sex**

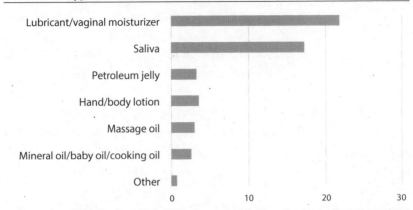

been considered critical public health problems for over a century. As far back as the Second World War, the Canadian government distributed condoms to soldiers so that they wouldn't get sidelined by STIs.[25] Accordingly, we have a great deal of rigorous data on STIs. We know, for example, that over 100,000 Canadians get chlamydia each year, over 30,000 are diagnosed with gonorrhea, and over 6,000 with syphilis.[26] We also know that the rates for these STIs are on the rise, with cases of gonorrhea having nearly doubled in the last five years. And although many STIs can be treated with antibiotics, antibiotic-resistant strains of gonorrhea are becoming increasingly prevalent.

In sex education courses, we teach young people that the only sure way to avoid STIs is not to have sex, and that safer-sex tools, such as condoms and dental dams, should always be used to reduce the risk of catching an STI. Our public health agencies also relay these messages to the public, focusing mostly on youth, people with multiple partners, and those who are especially at risk, such as sex workers and men who have sex with men. But, of course, anyone who is sexually active has some chance of contracting an STI. However, the risk is not distributed equally. The danger of transmission is lowest in monogamous relationships (that is, until someone transgresses and has sex with a new person).

HIV is a tragic example of the way that social inequalities can shape the trajectory of an STI. Globally, the ability to limit its spread has been a success story in wealthy North American and European countries, whereas African countries that lack the same resources have been devastated by the virus. In Canada, it has disproportionately affected gay men, Indigenous peoples, and immigrants from countries with high infection rates.[27] Since HIV emerged in the 1980s, it has killed millions of people, with most cases occurring in low- and middle-income countries with fewer resources to address the crisis.[28] Here in Canada, tens of thousands of HIV cases have been reported since the Public Health Agency of Canada began collecting statistics in 1985.[29] Currently, just over half of new HIV infections are among men who have sex with men.[30]

Antiretroviral treatments can keep the infection at bay, help HIV-positive people to live longer, healthier lives, and reduce the risk of transmission to others. Pre-exposure prophylaxis treatments are also available to individuals who are at high risk of HIV exposure, such as through sex with an HIV-positive person or the use of injected drugs, but they can also be prescribed to "at risk" gay men who do not have HIV-positive partners.[31] Emergency post-exposure prophylaxis treatment can prevent infection within seventy-two hours of exposure to the virus, though it is not 100 percent effective.[32]

THE UNEQUAL DISTRIBUTION OF PLEASURE, PAIN, AND RISK

Sex is about pleasure. It is also about pain and the risk of harm. It is both at the same time. However, who has access to the most pleasure and who bears the most risk is determined, in part, by social inequality. The organization of the social world, especially the way that gender and heterosexuality make rules for how we should behave and produce unequal power relations, seeps into every aspect of our lives, including the intimate moments we share in the bedroom.

For example, age affects the risk of sexual harm. In Canada, nearly half of sexual assaults target women between age fifteen and twenty-four.[33] Of course, no age group (or gender) is safe from sexual assault, but young adults have the highest risk. Our data showed that gender and sexual identity are associated with our perception of risk. Our assessments of risk are informed by the reality that straight women and 2SLGBTQ+ individuals are at the highest risk of sexual and gender violence by far. Gay men, potentially because HIV has a disproportionate impact on their community, have the highest risk of contracting STIs. These differences are social facts.

As a society, we don't often talk about how gender and sexual identity map onto differences in our access to sexual pleasure. This is probably because social scientists rarely ask people about how enjoyable their sex lives are. Well, we asked. Now we need to come to terms with the way that gender and sexual identity combine to diminish the pleasure of straight women relative to lesbian women and gay men, but especially relative to straight men. On the whole, when women have sex with women, or men with men, pleasure is equally distributed among the partners (by degree and by orgasm count), but the picture changes when we look at heterosexual encounters. The self-reports of our survey participants suggest that heterosexuality encourages both women and men to concentrate on men's pleasure more than on women's.

Some might imagine that this pleasure gap can be remedied simply by encouraging straight women to stand up for themselves and demand improvement. Although that approach may work for some, I see the pattern as connected to unequal social institutions – the problem is far bigger than any one individual, no matter how empowered she may be. For example, the gap fit with other inequalities between the sexes, such as the higher number of hours that mothers spend on childcare or that women in heterosexual marriages devote to housework.[34] It is also consistent with the enduring gender gap in wages for paid employment.[35] To be sure, some progress can be made by individual women who find their voices and ask for more attention to their sexual needs. I think it's also important to see that patterns in the bedroom are connected to patterns throughout society. We have to ask, Why do heterosexual pairs find themselves in this unequal place, whereas lesbian women and gay men do not? My guess is that the expectations embedded in the institutions of gender and heterosexuality are inherently unequal. If we want to make sexual pleasure an egalitarian domain, it's probably best to start by examining our cultural expectations and social inequalities.

6

The Social Organization of Sexuality

If sex is a taboo topic, just imagine adding religion and politics to the discussion! But both of these subjects matter to our sexual behaviour, as do our social locations along several vectors of inequality. That means Canadians' sexuality and sexual behaviours vary in a patterned way, along with other aspects of their lives. Age, education, religion, political inclinations, and many other characteristics map onto sexual activity, a fact that becomes visible when we take a bird's-eye view of sexuality, as we did with the Sex in Canada survey. For instance, we've seen that sexual identities such as straight, gay, lesbian, and bisexual influence – but do not always determine – the gender of our partners. In many cases, sexual identity also influences sexual behaviours, as discussed in Chapter 4, where we saw that women use vibrators and other sex toys more often with women sexual partners than with men. And, of course, gender affects our sexual choices in all sorts of ways, some of which are obvious and others surprising. We also found correlations between age and sexual behaviour, which revealed varied approaches to sexuality across the life course: older and younger adults might want to do different things or do the same things in different amounts. The correlations also demonstrate how sexual norms have changed over time, such that growing up in a more recent era creates new possibilities relative to previous generations. Through a sociological lens, we see how circumstance places us in social locations that influence our lives in many ways. In this chapter, we'll consider the ways that mundane aspects of our lives, such as our education, where we live, or how we worship, sort us into social contexts that shape our sexual behaviour.

POSTSECONDARY EDUCATION

Sociologists have spent a lot of time examining the sexuality of university students. In fact, many insights developed in the sociology of sexuality stem from studies that concentrated on this group. Campuses can be regarded as microcosms of the larger world, and they are unique settings in which young adults encounter sexual opportunities with little parental oversight. From such studies, we know, for instance, that particular institutions, such as the hypermasculine spaces in fraternity houses, increase the potential for sexual violence.[1] We also know that social class and gender can produce stigma for some sexually active students, while creating shame-free possibilities for others.[2] There's a scholarly consensus that university students have now embraced hookups, casual encounters with no romantic expectations, as the expected mode of interaction – and that they've done so for a variety of reasons.[3] Even the gender gap in orgasms largely revealed itself in university data.[4]

All these insights are vital to helping us understand the role of social institutions and local sexual cultures in shaping our sexual behaviour, yet we cannot assume that what we learn on a university campus can be generalized to the rest of the world. When we looked at the 253 full-time students who participated in our survey, we found that their sex lives differed from those of non-students in a number of ways. For example, 52 percent of students used a condom in their most recent sexual encounter, whereas only 22 percent of non-students did so. Students also masturbated more often than anyone else, with about 64 percent of them reporting they had done so alone in the past month versus 54 percent of non-students (Figure 6.1).

FIGURE 6.1 **Proportion masturbating this month, by student status**

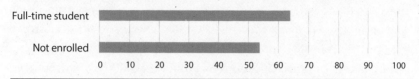

Oral sex, vibrators and sex toys, and a greater variety of sexual behaviours were more prevalent among students, too (Figure 6.2). We imagine that their social context – filled with many sexually available peers in a marked departure from most of non-student adult life – may give them leeway to explore. Variety, it seems, is the spice of student life, which may explain why our university respondents were a little more likely than non-students to be contented with their sex lives. Eighty-eight percent of them were happy, compared to 83 percent of non-students.

FIGURE 6.2 **Proportion using sex toy/having oral sex this month, by student status**

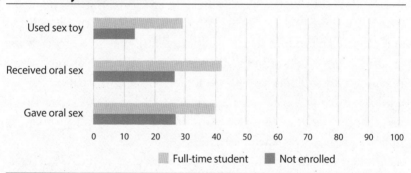

Some (but not all) of these differences can be attributed to age. Whereas some undergraduates are parents or full-time workers who have gone back to school, many more are just exiting adolescence. For them, college may prolong the time before the onset of adult responsibilities such as establishing a career or a family. As mentioned earlier, this extended period is relatively new in Canada. In the past, marriage was the primary path into adulthood, the moment when young people moved out of their parents' home and set up on their own. In other words, sexual coming of age and social coming of age occurred simultaneously. Since the 1960s, increasing numbers of young people have delayed marriage or have chosen to forego it.[5] However, for sociological reasons, this relatively new life stage is not accessible to everyone. Compared with residents of many other countries, more Canadians will pursue higher education, but not all of them can do so. Attaining a university degree is an expensive proposition, one that typically requires a deferral of earning power, and is thus most accessible to children of middle-class and high-income families with the resources to support their educational preparation for lucrative professional careers and class replication.[6] Children from families with lower incomes are less likely to attend college or university.[7] For them, adulthood often means stepping directly from high school into full-time employment.

What's at play here is not so much that students and non-students make different choices, but that not everyone has the same menu of options to choose from. Our sexual opportunities are shaped by our entry into the workplace or into education, our earnings, and our life stage. And the differences will last far beyond the few years that some young adults spend in university and others do not. For example, masturbation is more common among students than non-students, and it is also more common among adults who had ever attended any college or university than among those with a high school diploma or less. In addition, during the last year, those with more education reported more frequent oral sex and use of vibrators and other sex toys, too, regardless of their age (Figure 6.3).

FIGURE 6.3 **Education level and sexual behaviour**

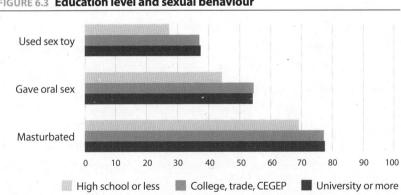

Note: CEGEP is a Quebec postsecondary education that features training opportunities and three-year degrees.

Some observers connect these differences with the liberal education offered at university, claiming that it expands both the minds and the sexual sensibilities of students. At most, that is a partial explanation. I think that living for some years as an unmarried adult increases sexual opportunities and broadens perspectives, regardless of whether students receive a liberal education or work-related training. For those who move out of their parents' homes to complete their studies, time living on or near campus increases their proximity to potential partners. These aspects of higher education are at least as important as any classroom material. In many ways, the sex lives of people who attended career- and trade-related colleges had more in common with those of university alumni than with those whose formal education ended with high school graduation. It appears the curriculum is less relevant than the shared experience of continuing one's education into adulthood.

LANGUAGE AND CULTURE

Bilingualism is a defining feature of Canadian society, and the language differences between anglophone and francophone Canadians represent differences in culture. In our multicultural society, language barriers produce specific folkways. That is, special foods, holiday celebrations, music, and art are shared to a greater degree within than across languages, and these differences shape people's understanding of the world around them. Approaches to sexuality and sexual behaviour are also culturally inflected. The Sex in Canada survey did uncover some differences in sexual behaviour between anglophones and francophones, suggesting that language influences the social context for our sex lives in key ways. The differences weren't as large as the stereotypes about English and French Canadians might have us believe. Still, if you imagine that French-speaking Canadians "do it" more often, more casually, and perhaps in more varied and interesting ways than their English-speaking counterparts, you are probably correct.

To distinguish the preferred languages of our participants, we had only to look at whether they completed their surveys in English or French. But we also need to consider the ways that language differences are geographic differences, at least to some degree. The province of Quebec is the regional home for the francophone nation within Canada, and its many French-speakers have a strong influence on statistics for the whole country's francophone population. For example, this is observable when it comes to marriage – anglophone couples are much more likely to get married than francophones, who have higher rates of common-law relationships. This, however, may have as much to do with the bureaucratic regimes of Quebec, which are sometimes seen as benefiting unmarried couples, as it does with cultural preferences among language groups.[8] According to Statistics Canada, 40 percent of Quebec's cohabiting couples are unmarried, compared to 16 percent in the rest of Canada.[9]

Other departures between the groups are more open to interpretation. We found that French-speaking Canadians had more sex than English-speaking ones. The former were more likely than the latter to have had sex in the past year (77 percent versus 66 percent), and 53 percent of francophones had it during the last month, compared to 48 percent of anglophones. In terms of sexual behaviours, the groups were similar in their use of vibrators and other sex toys during partnered sex – 17 percent in each group reported that their most recent sex included toys (Figure 6.4). Francophones gave a little more oral sex than anglophones in their last sexual encounters (42 percent compared to 35 percent), and they were more likely to cuddle, but the English group (81 percent) was more likely than the French (75 percent) to include kissing. These differences may be grounded in slightly differing values, a different way of understanding the meaning of a given sexual activity, or a general outlook on

FIGURE 6.4 **Language and sexual behaviours**

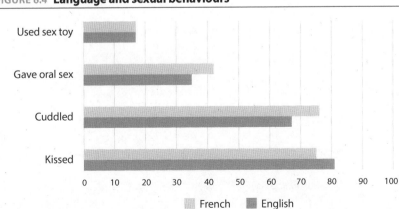

sex, but it seems that our sexuality is influenced by the culture – and language groups – in which we are embedded. We are all influenced by social forces, and the sexual choices we make will be influenced by the social contexts in which we live.

REGION

Why might living in one part of the country versus another shape our sexual behaviour? As we discovered in Chapter 4, we can't blame the weather. And policy differences probably don't play much of a role either, as policies governing sexuality and family formation are pretty similar across Canada. What about unique regional cultures? Imagine how these might affect the way that people see the world at a collective level: perhaps, for instance, the West Coast's reputation for a laid-back attitude or the Atlantic provinces' for a practical and sensible approach to life might be replicated in their varying approaches to sex. The Sex in Canada survey did reveal some interesting, if slight, divergences between the provinces. (Unfortunately, we didn't have enough participants from the northern territories to know how they might compare to the rest of the country.)

Our data showed that masturbation, for one, was more frequent in Quebec than in the rest of the country (this result was also reflected in the language group data). Residents on the Prairies and in the Atlantic provinces joined Ontario at the "average" on this measure (between 53 and 55 percent). British Columbians were at the low end (51 percent), and

FIGURE 6.5 **Proportion masturbating this month, by region**

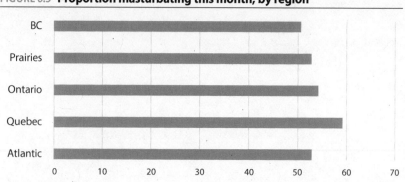

FIGURE 6.6 **Proportion engaging in partnered sex this month, by region**

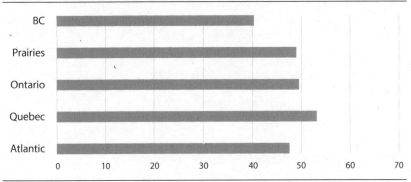

Quebec took the lead (59 percent) when it came to solo sex during the last month. Figure 6.5 lets you peek into this usually private endeavour.

Partnered sex followed a similar pattern (Figure 6.6). The Prairie provinces, Ontario, and Atlantic Canada were all near the national average (49 percent) in having partnered sex during the past month. A slightly higher proportion of Quebecers, 53 percent, had it, whereas just 40 percent of British Columbians said the same.

And the pattern held for several sexual behaviours (Figure 6.7). When asked whether they'd given oral sex during the last month, 32 percent of Quebec respondents said they had. This is just slightly more than the Prairies, with 30 percent, Ontarians at 29 percent, or those in the Atlantic provinces at 28 percent, and quite a bit more than in British Columbia, where 20 percent of participants said they had given oral sex this month. The patterns for receiving oral sex during the past month were similar as well. However, for sex toy use, there were only statistically insignificant differences across regions. Here, Quebec was on the low end, with only 13 percent having used one in the past month. British Columbia, Ontario, and the Atlantic provinces were near the average, with about 15 to 16 percent, and the Prairie provinces had above average use of vibrators and other sex toys, at 20 percent. There are any number of possible explanations for these differences, including many that we've already discussed in this book. For example, demographic variation means that Atlantic Canadians are slightly older, on average, than other Canadians. Cultural differences, such as those captured by the francophone/anglophone divide, are also tied to region of residence.

FIGURE 6.7 **Proportion using sex toy/giving oral sex this month, by region**

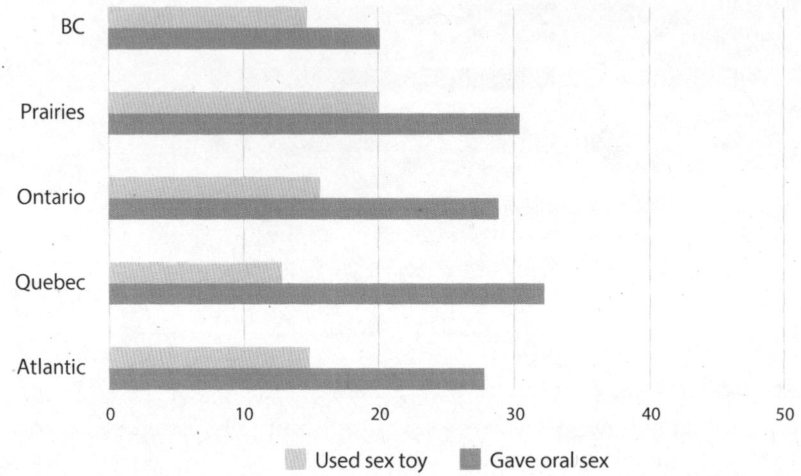

Used sex toy   Gave oral sex

The urban/rural divide is one regional difference that we might want to scrutinize. In some provinces, such as Ontario and Quebec, a large section of the population clusters in several large cities, whereas in other provinces that are more rural, such as Saskatchewan and Manitoba, people live in smaller towns or out in the country. Could these differences in population density affect their chances of finding a partner? Although we could speculate that, say, someone who lives in downtown Montreal would be more successful in this respect than a resident of a tiny farming community on the prairies, we saw only small differences in sexual frequency. Singles who lived in rural areas were a bit less likely than urbanites to have had partnered sex during the last month (36 percent versus 39 percent).

You might suppose that masturbation would be most popular in the countryside, where partners could be difficult to find. Instead, urban/rural differences were small and statistically insignificant. For example, 56 percent of city dwellers and 49 percent of rural residents said they had masturbated this month. Sex toy and vibrator use was also similar: between 14 and 16 percent of Canadians had used a toy in the past month, regardless of how much they might need to worry about a neighbour overhearing (Figure 6.8).

When urban and rural partners did connect, their sexual activities

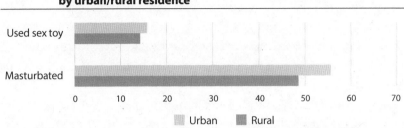

FIGURE 6.8 **Proportion using sex toy/masturbating this month, by urban/rural residence**

differed slightly. For example, urbanites were a little more keen on oral sex. Specifically, 37 percent of them and 32 percent of rural dwellers had given oral sex in their most recent encounter, and 39 percent versus 30 percent had received it. Urbanites reported more use of vibrators and other toys in their partnered sex as well, with 17 percent of them having done so, compared to 13 percent of rural residents. These variations may seem big, but they are not statistically significant, which means we can't be sure that future studies will find the same differences.

The patterns in the sexual behaviours of urban and rural Canadians all flow in the same direction, with urbanites having slightly more and more varied sex than rural dwellers, but keep in mind that the differences are small and often not statistically significant. They may be due to population density or to some cultural and demographic differences between Canadians who live in the city and those who live in the country. People in Canada's rural areas tend to be more religious than those in its cities, or that thinking of oneself as liberal or conservative is correlated with living in more or less densely populated areas. Let's consider those social dimensions next.

RELIGIOUS AFFILIATION

Religious affiliation is vital to our sense of self and our sexual morality. The religious institutions to which we belong, whether they are churches, synagogues, mosques, or temples, have moral codes that govern sexuality. They teach followers how to behave in ways that conform to their understanding of morality. There is a lot of consistency across the various religions. For example, many emphasize marriage and monogamy as central to sexual morality. But there is substantial variation as well, both in what sexual behaviours are considered moral and immoral and in how deeply sexuality is stressed as essential to moral character.[10] That is, some religions may countenance only very strict and narrow sexual choices but will nonetheless welcome and value constituents who fail to comply. In others, adherence to sexual norms is a condition of belonging.

It used to be that nearly all Canadians belonged to a church or other religious institution, but this has changed since the 1960s. Currently, about a quarter of Canadians now claim no religious affiliation. The diversity of affiliations has also broadened, as immigration patterns bring a wider variety of religious identities into the country. All this demographic change both loosened the cultural influence of religion and increased the number of ways that Canadians can experience it and engage with religious institutions. Some commentators argue that these trends have had a major impact on sexual morality, worrying that the waning influence of religion has diminished our capacity to make positive moral choices around our sexuality. Others celebrate the changes, tying the liberalization to positive social developments, such as the legal recognition of same-sex marriage. The decline of religious influence on the state has opened new possibilities.

According to the 2016 census, two-thirds of Canadians are affiliated with a Christian church: 39 percent are Catholics and 27 percent are Protestants. Among the Protestants, an important division is between "mainline" churches, such as the Presbyterian and United Churches, and "evangelical" denominations, such as Pentecostal.[11] About 24 percent of Canadians have no association with a religion. Under 3 percent belong to churches that are neither mainline nor evangelical, such as Orthodox, Jehovah's Witness, and Latter-Day Saints. In Figure 6.9, we included them in the "other religion" category, a diverse mix that reflects the full spectrum of Canadian spirituality: Muslim, Jewish, Sikh, Hindu, Buddhist, and other Eastern faiths, as well as traditional Indigenous beliefs. In total, about 11 percent of Canadians fall into this category, but because each of these traditions represents such a small proportion of the population, limitations of the data prevented us from considering them separately.

FIGURE 6.9 **Proportion engaging in oral sex in most recent sex, by religious affiliation**

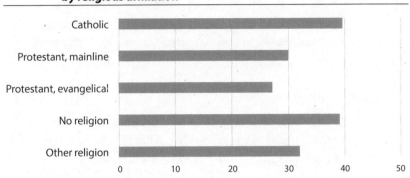

Some people argue that as Canada becomes increasingly secular overall, even those who maintain ties to a religious institution will feel less compelled to follow its teachings on sexuality and sexual behaviour. However, a general decline in the influence of religion will not necessarily affect individual behaviour. The Sex in Canada project confirmed that people with certain religious affiliations (but not others) organized their sexual behaviour differently from those who had none. Our data on oral sex enabled us to explore the link between religion and sexual behaviour. Some religious institutions reject oral sex as immoral, believing that any form of non-procreative sex is wrong. Others encourage it, as long as it occurs within marriage.[12] Many avoid the topic altogether – perhaps their silence communicates stigma and shame as effectively as any condemnation.

According to the Sex in Canada data, both evangelical and mainstream Protestants were less likely than Catholics and religiously unaffiliated Canadians to have given or received oral sex during the past year.[13] Whereas 57 percent of Catholics and 53 percent of those with no religion gave oral sex this year, only 37 percent of Protestants had. When we asked if they gave oral sex to their most recent partner, the pattern was similar: 39 percent of those with no religious affiliation and 40 percent of Catholics said yes, compared to 30 percent of mainline Protestants and 37 percent of evangelicals. When it came to oral sex during the most recent encounter, more details revealed themselves: evangelicals were

less likely than mainline Protestants to have given or received it. Masturbation, similarly, was lowest among Protestants, with just 65 percent of
mainline Protestants and 60 percent of evangelicals having done it within
the year, compared to 75 percent of Catholics and 83 percent of those
with no religion.

POLITICAL LEANINGS

Why would our political opinions have anything to do with our sexual
behaviour? In theory, maybe they shouldn't. After all, pleasure is pleasure,
and what feels good to someone on the right wing of the political spectrum will feel just as good to someone on the left, correct? Maybe not.
Our political opinions, like our religious affiliations, are parts of our
identity, and they can be an important way that we understand ourselves.
To the extent that this is the case, sexual behaviour may become a cultural
signifier of group membership on the right, in the middle, or on the left
– and a way to distinguish ourselves from groups that we dislike. Many
people claim that Canada is becoming more politically polarized by the
minute. Given that some sexual behaviours are also politicized, we might
expect our political identities to align with our sexual activity.

The Canadian political landscape is sometimes captured by affiliation
with one of the major parties, such as the Liberals, Conservatives, New
Democrats, and the Bloc Québécois. However, many Canadians consider
themselves to be independent of parties, and the complexities of party
platforms make it difficult to place people on a spectrum of political
leanings. Instead, we asked our participants to situate themselves on a
scale from "very conservative" to "very liberal," relying on their own
perceptions of how they compared to other Canadians. Interestingly,
the sexual behaviours of those who identified as liberal differed from
those of conservatives. The former were more likely to have masturbated
this year (82 percent) than moderates (71 percent) or those on the right
(66 percent). If you think that perhaps conservatives are more religious
than liberals (they are), and that this might explain the differences in
masturbation, that would be a good guess. However, even when we
controlled for attendance at religious services, it turned out that conservatives were still the least interested in solo sex.

Those who saw themselves as politically liberal also engaged in a wider variety of partnered sexual behaviours. Although liberals and conservatives reported similar amounts of penile-vaginal intercourse, they differed in other sexual activities. Liberals were a lot more likely than moderates or conservatives to have given or received oral sex or to have used a vibrator or sex toy in their most recent sexual encounter (Figure 6.10). It looks like liberal politics are associated with an expansive sensibility around sexuality, whereas conservatism prefers a more traditional approach that focuses on intercourse.

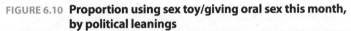

FIGURE 6.10 **Proportion using sex toy/giving oral sex this month, by political leanings**

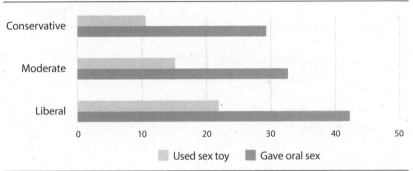

Like religious identities, political identities appear to be an important part of how we understand ourselves as people; therefore, they influence even our most intimate choices and behaviours. The old feminist saying asserts that the personal is political,[14] and our data seemed to show that the political is also very personal. This came into sharp focus when we asked participants about their understanding of themselves as feminists. Only about 39 percent of women and 24 percent of men told us they would call themselves a feminist. Be it small, this group was distinctive in its sexual behaviour. For example, feminist women masturbated more often than non-feminist women, and non-feminists were more likely never to have done it.[15]

Feminist claims for gender parity extend into the bedroom, where the sexual behaviour of feminist women and men differed from that of non-feminists. For example, in sex between men and women, feminists were more likely than non-feminists to have kissed and cuddled during their most recent encounter. Their most recent partnered sex was more likely to have included vibrating toys: 11 percent of feminists, compared to 8 percent of non-feminists. Feminists were also more enthusiastic about oral sex on women. For example, feminist men having sex with women are more likely to say that their most recent sexual encounter included going down on their partner.[16] In addition, feminist women were more likely than other women to say that their partner performed oral sex on them (Figure 6.11). Feminist sexual behaviour centres women's pleasure.

FIGURE 6.11   **Proportion receiving oral sex in most recent sex, by feminist identity (women only)**

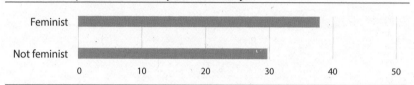

Perhaps this shouldn't be surprising. Feminism stresses self-empowerment for women and gender equality, sentiments that go beyond the demand for equal pay for equal work. In other aspects of our lives, however, a feminist sensibility doesn't actually manifest in more equality, as in the equal distribution of childcare and household chores.[17] Believing in gender equality doesn't automatically translate to parity in practice. Still, feminism seems to facilitate sexual behaviour that prioritizes warmth and love, as well as women's pleasure.

LEGACIES OF RACISM

The Sex in Canada survey is also useful to show that some social divisions do not necessarily map onto differences in sexual behaviour. For example, we can begin to debunk some racist stereotypes that suggest that white Canadians have different sexual inclinations than members of racialized groups. In general, there is no truth to the idea that members of racialized groups might have more or different types of sex in comparison to those who are classified as white. In many aspects of sexuality, as Figure 6.12 reveals, Canadians who identified as members of racialized groups were indistinguishable from those who identified as white, and any small differences are statistically insignificant. The false narratives that have, historically or in the current day, marked members of racialized groups as hypersexual, exotic, or morally questionable have caused – and continue to cause – significant harms. They put members of racialized communities at higher risk of negative sexual outcomes and sexual assault.[18] They also heighten the risk of sexually transmitted infections, including HIV.[19]

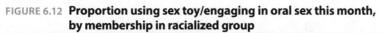

FIGURE 6.12 **Proportion using sex toy/engaging in oral sex this month, by membership in racialized group**

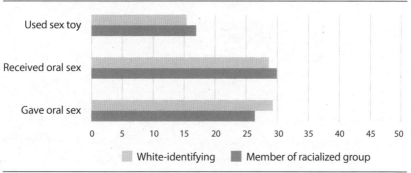

Racist tropes about sexuality can be traced to Canada's colonialist history, in which colonial forces justified their rule in part by stressing differences between their own sexual practices and those of Indigenous peoples. Wherever they observed a difference, they deemed it evidence of moral inferiority. The emphasis on supposed deviations from Christian norms was a part of the racialization process that "othered" Indigenous peoples and justified the supposed "civilizing" project of colonial governance.[20] Sexuality has similarly been harnessed for the purpose of producing racial differences, for maintaining a racial hierarchy that was nothing more than a fiction to support inequality, oppression, and harm. Immigration policy justified excluding people based on invented myths of sexual impurity.[21] However, despite our history of creating and maintaining racial divisions and producing inequalities, there is little difference to see when it comes to sexual activity.

Condom use proved the exception to this rule. Members of racialized groups used condoms more often than those who identified as white (Figure 6.13). The higher prevalence of STIs in their communities may be at play here. Or perhaps those who are subject to racist stereotypes take greater care to use condoms than those who are not, whose sexuality is treated as normal and unproblematic. Among our participants, 53 percent of those who identified as members of racialized groups had used condoms during the past six months, compared to 32 percent of those who identified as white.

FIGURE 6.13 **Condom use, by membership in racialized group**

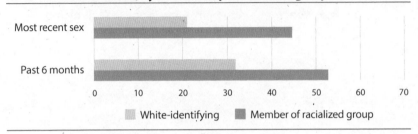

The sexual dimensions of racialization constitute an important sociological topic, which deserves far greater attention than I can offer here. An overview of the Canadian population, such as the one in our survey, allows only for broad, homogenizing categories such as "members of racialized groups," although this category obviously contains so much diversity and variation of experiences. Ideally, an analysis of sexual behaviour would consider each separate group on its own. The data in the Sex in Canada survey design were limited, however, and wouldn't allow for such a fine-grained analysis. Studies that offer a greater depth of focus are much needed, and I hope that scholars will soon undertake this work.

SOCIAL PATTERNS IN SEXUAL BEHAVIOUR

The social organization of sexuality refers to the ways that sexuality differs across social locations. Sexual behaviour is articulated in patterns, as revealed in our survey responses, which clustered along the lines of age, gender, and region, as well as across shared experiences and identities, such as belonging to a religious community. The patterns of our social choices map onto the structure of the social world: cultural differences, inequalities, identities, and other groupings. These differences in location sometimes create differing opportunities, constraining and enabling sexuality in ways that both limit our behaviour and generate possibilities for sexual expression – and that's the sociology of sexual behaviour.

To be clear, this is not a deterministic relationship. Social location does not force us to behave in one way or another. Indeed, this is observably false. There are always exceptions, even to the most prominent rules. However, when we step back from examining personal choices and instead look at patterns of sexual behaviour, as we can with survey data, the strong connection between social locations and sexual behaviour becomes obvious.

This view is key to thinking about sexuality from a sociological perspective, rather than the highly individualized lens of personal choice that we've all been taught is the best way to understand sexuality. That is, the sociology of sexualities, though not denying that personal choices are important, tries to situate them in the social contexts that forge our reality. Our cultural emphasis on taking personal responsibility for our sexual choices and condemning those whose choices we dislike overlooks the social and institutional world in which those choices are made. It overlooks the influences of peer groups and families, the inequalities all around us, and our interactions with institutions such as universities and religious denominations. The broader view lets us see how our social differences lay out a menu of sexual choices, influencing the sexual behaviours that we engage in as individuals.

Conclusion:
Sex in Canada

In 1967, while speaking with news reporters on Parliament Hill, then Justice Minister Pierre Elliott Trudeau famously declared, "There's no place for the state in the bedrooms of the nation." He was referring to his controversial new bill – the Criminal Law Amendment Act, 1968–69.[1] It was passed in 1969, the Criminal Code was duly revised, and Trudeau's comment went down in history. As the national myth goes, 1969 was a turning point in the liberalization of Canadian law, when activists won the day and the nation rejected outdated proscriptions against gay sex and abortion.[2] No doubt, the legislation was a signature achievement and recognition of the country's advance into a new era of cosmopolitan tolerance. Gay liberationists heralded freedom from state oppression, women's liberationists cheered freedom from patriarchal forms of marriage and the end of state control over reproductive choices. At least, that is what we tell ourselves.

As it happens, the rhetoric surrounding these policy shifts was far greater than the change on the ground. Neither homosexuality nor abortion were fully legalized.[3] Even as the bill decriminalized consensual same-sex sexual activity within the privacy of one's own home, it was full of loopholes and caveats. Critics correctly point out that anal sex specifically was still classed as a crime long after the bill became law, and the state actually used its stipulations to increase its persecution of gay men through bathhouse raids, police surveillance of public spaces, and entrapment for crimes related to sex in public.[4] Nor were abortion rights secured in 1969. In fact, an abortion could not proceed unless it was approved by a committee consisting of at least three doctors.[5] Nonetheless, when the Canadian state acknowledged the cultural shifts of the 1960s and enshrined some new sexual freedoms in law, public opinion perceived the change as historic.

Social change had been on the horizon for many years. The economic prosperity of the post–Second World War period created new possibilities for baby boomers to begin their independent lives as single adults. The Veterans' Land Act and the Veterans' Rehabilitation Act of 1945 helped more Canadians than ever to purchase a home and further their education.[6] During the war, many women had joined the labour force, a trend that continued after hostilities ended; making their own money allowed them to become independent adults without marriage. And soon enough, urban gay neighbourhoods blossomed, forming foundational communities in which the 2SLGBTQ+ social movement would coalesce.[7] Through the 1950s and 1960s, a desire for sexual freedom – freedom from judgment and the constraints of traditional moralism – fuelled growing fights for women's liberation, gay liberation, and collective resistance to authority of all kinds. And Canadians showed widespread support for changes to gender relations, for women's self-determination, and for reproductive rights. Paired with the new possibility of life as a single, sexually active adult without becoming a parent, which many young adults now enjoy, these shifts set the stage for social and legal change.

To be clear, the sexual revolution did not achieve liberation. With the benefit of hindsight, we can see that these changes were part of a whole slew of cultural, political, and social shifts in our sexuality and sexual behaviour, rather than an eradication of societal constraints. In other words, the rules changed, but there were still rules. Sexual activity has always been constrained by social systems and cultural values, as well as by institutions and structures that encourage and support certain forms of sexual behaviour more than others. The sexual revolution did open up spaces for new norms to take hold. Still, far from disappearing, the older norms remain influential today. For instance, our dominant culture highly values the sexual morality embodied in the traditions of marriage, monogamy, and parenthood. This persists alongside more expansive understandings of good, moral, healthy sexuality – ones that include 2SLGBTQ+ lives, respect reproductive choices, and do not connect sexual pleasure with shame.

In other words, Canada today is a land of multicultural sexualities. The Sex in Canada survey is the first large-scale study of just what Canadians do with these more expansive menus of sexual mores. The data in this book provide a snapshot of Canadian sexuality, revealing that the social patterns that shape our lives in general – the inequalities, the divisions between us, and the institutions to which we belong – are also influencing our sexual behaviour.

MULTICULTURAL SEXUALITIES

The change embodied in the sexual revolution is best captured as a shift to multiplicity. In the past, Canada had a single set of rules, produced in large part by the Catholic and Protestant churches to which the vast majority of Canadians belonged. These norms were supported by the legal system and upheld by a patriarchal social order that limited women's options, including marginalizing those who did not marry and have children, and stigmatizing those who became pregnant out of wedlock. These rules were ferociously heteronormative, with harsh punishments for anyone with same-sex desires or insufficient adherence to binary gender norms. Members of the 2SLGBTQ+ community endured legal discrimination in connection with employment and housing, forced institutionalization, expulsions from families, and arrest. Medicine and psychology aligned with the state and the church on these matters. Working in tandem, they bent sexual culture into a single value-laden structure.

But laws and social standards be damned – exerting total control over the sexuality of Canadians proved impossible. In fact, brave souls who refuse to follow the rules and who live in ways that feel true to them have always existed, despite the consequences. They sought out like-minded communities, located sexual partners, and formed activist movements to demand social change, and in doing so they expanded sexual possibilities for others.

Even so, the traditional institutions remain influential today, and their expectations regarding sexuality still matter in the lives of many Canadians. However, these norms have been forced to share the stage with new ideas, creating a more pluralistic social world. There are now more and larger spaces with alternative norms. Many are far more expansive and inclusive. These clearly resonate with a wide swath of Canadians, who began to share values and live by expectations that centred reproductive rights, sexual pleasure, and following one's own truth.

THE GROWTH OF 2SLGBTQ+ COMMUNITIES

Canada's 2SLGBTQ+ communities are an important engine of social change. Their activism began well before 1969, though since that pivotal date, the growth of 2SLGBTQ+ neighbourhoods in many cities, student groups on college and university campuses, and community institutions such as cultural centres, bookstores, and small businesses of all kinds has been profound.[8] Queer communities have become more visible in smaller towns and rural areas, too.[9] More Canadians are now aware and accepting of same-sex sexual desire because a strong social movement has both changed public opinion and secured new rights for 2SLGBTQ+ people. Thus, 2SLGBTQ+ communities are no longer inextricably tied to urban neighbourhoods and instead have become more integrated into an array of social spaces.[10]

The flourishing of 2SLGBTQ+ communities has been essential to the creation of Canada's multicultural sexual reality. It has produced many subcultures with differing sets of sexual norms, providing alternative ways to organize our sexual lives.[11] This diversity can be easy to overlook because 2SLGBTQ+ communities have operated in a coalition model of activism that combines the political and social interests of people with many sexual and gender identities. Under this one umbrella are numerous diverse, overlapping communities. In many cases, gay subcultures differ from those of lesbian women, and both differ from Indigenous two-spirit traditions. Some queer, trans, and bisexual Canadians have criticized the gay subculture as "homonormative," suggesting that it simply mimics the norms of heterosexuality, which should remind us that even pioneering forms of non-straight sexualities are options among many ways of living and loving.[12] Indeed, 2SLGBTQ+ communities are not immune from the inequalities that exist throughout Canada, and members of immigrant groups, religious minorities, and people with disabilities have offered sharp critiques of the barriers and social exclusions in queer communities.[13]

The sexual fields produced by 2SLGBTQ+ communities are spaces in which sexual freedoms are embraced and celebrated. They haven't achieved full equity and inclusion, but the social and political changes that have transpired since the 1970s brought a greater appreciation for sexual diversity and a belief in 2SLGBTQ+ rights. What was once a community of outcasts, bravely banding together for protection in a hostile – violent, punitive, and exclusionary – heterosexual world, is now a prime site of sexual multiculturalism. Heteronormativity still prevails, but the consequences for deviating from it have loosened sufficiently to allow more and more people to organize their sexual lives in ways that feel true to themselves.

A MULTITUDE OF SEXUALITIES

The work that 2SLGBTQ+ communities have done to uplift those who have been marginalized and excluded by heteronormative sexual cultures has also served as a model for other communities that may or may not emphasize same-sex sexualities. Spaces that differ from the heteronormative standard, and those that welcome all sexual identities, have also become more visible. These include polyamorous practices and relationships built on consensual non-monogamy.[14] Asexual people are also working to build communities and to establish norms for relationships that include no (or less, or particular kinds of) sexual activity, mostly through online forums and social media.[15] Other groups cluster around particular tastes and practices, including BDSM communities, spanking clubs, clubs for swapping partners, and groups fostering anonymous sexual encounters.

The rules that govern sexuality vary widely, even in the straight world. In some straight cultures, frank talk about desire is considered normal and expected, but in others, saying the word "pubic" out loud would make people want to die of embarrassment! In fact, the prevailing form of heteronormativity, which is okay with sex before marriage, masturbation, oral sex, and the use of toys, would seem far too permissive to many straight individuals. For example, some may refrain from certain sexual behaviours because their church prohibits them. Some may be drawn to restrictive sexual cultures because they fit with their own views on morality. And others, though perhaps secretly wishing to be more adventurous, see complying with the rules as a trade-off for the benefits of inclusion in the community.

Some of the variations in straight culture were apparent in the Sex in Canada survey. For example, we found that in sex between men and women, those who saw themselves as feminists were more likely than those who did not to engage in oral sex and masturbation. In addition, they paid more attention to women's pleasure.[16] On university campuses, straight norms include hookups as a defining feature of student life, as well as an understanding that they are not necessarily as acceptable in older adulthood.[17] The sexual cultures that all of us encounter are varied, and both they and our allegiances to them change over the life course.

NOSTALGIA FOR TRADITIONAL NORMS

Not everyone is happy about Canada's shift to multicultural sexualities. The changes that have opened up new sexual possibilities have been, and continue to be, contentious. For some, membership in a community that values restrictive sexual norms is not enough. They want everyone to obey the same rules, as we did in the past. As I write, conservative movements are trying to retract legal supports for expansive sexual norms and reproductive rights. In the United States, for instance, abortion is being limited and criminalized, and many jurisdictions are attacking lesbian, gay, and transgender rights. Some states have introduced laws that restrict teachers' ability to discuss same-sex family forms and 2SLGBTQ+ sexualities in the classroom and have banned gender-affirming treatments for trans youth.

These aren't just examples of American exceptionalism. Canadian conservatives are calling for similar legal retrenchments, as they maintain that inclusive approaches to sexuality and gender are harmful to children. Their views are most likely to be shared by Canadians who have ties to religion, both Christian and non-Christian. Many Canadian families, faiths, and communities hew to a sexual morality that fits better with the first half of the twentieth century than with the twenty-first. Therefore, it would be wrong to think that all Canadians have access to every sexual possibility, especially when they are young, or that harsh consequences for flouting the older, traditional norms have disappeared. They have not.

Even so, I don't see Canadians ever returning to a singular set of sexual norms. Our patchwork of possibilities, combined with social mobility for many Canadians, means that more and more people can arrange their adult sexual lives in a variety of ways. They have a wider set of choices for expressing their true selves and finding partners who share their desires. This actuality has also become institutionalized in ways that will be difficult to undo. Public opinion has shifted, and a large majority of Canadians support equal rights for members of the 2SLGBTQ+ community. And historically, socially conservative movements have not been as powerful in Canada as those in the United States.[18] My best guess is that the multiplicity of Canadian sexualities is here to stay.

SEX IN CANADA TODAY
So, how do we make sense of Canadian sexuality? The social organization of sexuality is usefully, if incompletely, laid out in the Sex in Canada survey. In these data, we find patterns of sexual behaviour that are shared across groups, as well as divisions between groups. By providing an overview of what sex is like in Canada, these patterns help us understand our country's numerous coexisting sexualities. Here is a quick review of some of the highlights in this groundbreaking survey's results.

SEXUAL RELATIONSHIPS
The Canadian sexual landscape is full of diversity. On average, though, the sex we're having fits well with traditional, restrictive morals: with a monogamous, long-term partner. Alongside this steady trend, the culture shifts and policy changes since the sexual revolution have produced new possibilities. For example, in previous generations, almost everyone got

married – more than 90 percent of adults – but this has dropped to a fairly level rate, with just over 50 percent of adults now expected to marry at least once. In Quebec, less than 40 percent will ever marry.[19] This trend has more to do with legality than with a change in relationships; we find that common-law couples are just as happy as their married counterparts (about 85 percent).

As much as Canadians continue to value long-term relationships, they generally don't mind if singles have hookups. The media may be perennially abuzz with handwringing over sex without romance or commitment, but hookup culture is now dominant among university students and single young adults.[20] Sexuality with no strings attached has also been a feature in gay culture for some time. Thus, though 90 percent of our participants' sexual encounters occurred within relationships (spouses, significant others, and dating partners), about 6 percent of their most recent sex involved a "friend with benefits," leaving around 4 percent having pleasurable commitment-free sexual connections. Sex with a stranger is a real possibility, especially if you are young or in a subculture that values sexual freedom, but we shouldn't assume that every Canadian adult is eager to hook up.

Of those who were in relationships, monogamy was still highly valued, but possibilities for polyamorous connections and other forms of consensual non-monogamy were also evident. About 6 percent of our participants were in an "open" or explicitly non-monogamous relationship. Another 5 percent had not discussed monogamy with their partners – which could mean that it was assumed, that the relationship was open, or that the rules were unclear. The rest, a full 89 percent of those in relationships, were committed to monogamy.

The legal recognition of same-sex marriage, which came in 2005, is regarded as another landmark moment in the liberalization of Canada. The 2016 census recorded that over seventy-two thousand same-sex couples shared a home, or almost 1 percent of all Canadian couples. About one-third of them were married.[21] This aspect of domestic life is one factor that contributed to an exodus from urban "gaybourhoods" and a deeper integration into areas that were once more exclusively heterosexual, such as the suburbs and small towns. Members of

2SLGBTQ+ communities probably lived in these places all along, but social change over the past several decades has fostered the conditions for increased (if still attenuated) visibility and inclusion.

SEXUAL ACTIVITY OVER THE LIFE COURSE

Sexual activity changes as we age. The freewheeling approach of our teens and twenties turns into a search for romance and partnership as we move into our thirties. Despite our cultural mythology, sharing a home with a partner increases the frequency of sex. People in their twenties, then, have less access to sex because they are less likely to live with a partner. Those in their thirties report the most frequent partnered activity. From the forties on, it declines, on average, a little bit each decade. But only a little bit: over 75 percent of those in their forties, just over half of those in their fifties and sixties, and almost 40 percent of those who were seventy and over had partnered sex in the past year. Those in the seventy-plus group who were sexually active reported positive feelings about their sex lives.

Before the sexual revolution, Canadians married relatively young. Women, on average, tied the knot for the first time at age 22.5 in 1960, a number that would edge closer to 30.0 by 2008.[22] We are also older when we begin having children. Back then, women's average age of first birth was just twenty-four, and now it is twenty-nine.[23] For many young Canadians, a period of adult singledom before marriage and parenthood has become the norm. This time of independence is an important stage in which they complete their education, establish careers, and connect with communities. They also explore sexually during these years, and new ways of finding sexual connections have emerged in the form of dating apps and similar technologies.[24] Sometimes, the sexuality of young adulthood is casual, with no expectation of a relationship; in other cases, it occurs in the context of dating and trying to find romance or in the context of a romantic relationship. But regardless of whether they live in the country or the city, this variety of sexual possibilities is similar for young singles.

In and among our data were a number of other notable findings, each deserving inquiry: younger adults were the most likely age group to use condoms. Canadians between the ages of eighteen and twenty-nine also reported the most frequent masturbation and use of vibrators and other toys in partnered sex. Those in the middle years were most likely to be parents (no real surprise there), and mixed-gender couples aged thirty to thirty-nine were the most likely to be trying for pregnancy when they went to bed together. Older Canadians cuddled more than others. And, thankfully, three in every four Canadians, across all age groups, were happy with their sex lives.

KEY SOCIAL INSTITUTIONS: RELIGION AND EDUCATION

Religion and education greatly affect sexual behaviour. They, too, have changed since the sexual revolution. Christianity, including the Catholic church and several Protestant denominations, were highly influential before the 1960s, counting the large majority of Canadians among their congregations. Since then, church attendance and affiliations have shrunk, with the result that many Canadians now have little to no connection with religion. Immigration patterns have also changed the picture by bringing growing numbers of non-Christian newcomers into the scene. In other words, Christianity still holds a prominent place, but it has much more company than it did generations ago. Religious institutions that remain stolid in their support for traditional sexuality are now one choice among many, as others grapple with questions of inclusion of 2SLGBTQ+ parishioners and whether to perform same-sex wedding rituals. Options for worship have expanded right alongside (and in tandem with) all Canadians' menus of sexualities.

Just as religion separates the social world into groups of people who engage in different cultural practices, education sorts Canadians into clusters of people who have different types of jobs and who often live in different neighbourhoods. Completing high school or not and then having access to college, university, and tertiary degrees such as law and medicine are markers of divisions that can serve as a proxy for social class, as they roughly correlate with job type and income level. Because education commonly sifts people into groups, sexual attitudes and activities differ somewhat according to educational attainment.

The Sex in Canada survey demonstrated that those with postsecondary education engaged in more expansive sexual behaviour than those who completed their education with high school (including more frequent masturbation, oral sex, and sex toy use). Although the types of activity may have differed by education level, happiness did not. Regardless of what they did under the covers, people in each of these educational groups were equally content with their sex lives.

GAY SEXUALITIES, LESBIAN SEXUALITIES, BISEXUALITIES

The multiple cultures produced by 2SLGBTQ+ communities have been instrumental in expanding sexual possibilities for all Canadians. Today, rich and varied subcultures are built around 2SLGBTQ+ identities, and sexual identity helps to cluster people into groups with their own sexual norms and styles. Although there are many diverse subgroups and sexual fields within 2SLGBTQ+ communities, survey analysis requires large numbers to offer an accurate picture, so we had to stick with the most numerous groups: gay men and lesbian women. Gender and sexual identity are social forces that influence their sexual behaviour, sometimes in opposite directions. For example, in Chapter 2, we discussed the link between sexual frequency, gender, and sexual identity, with gay men reporting more frequent partnered sex than straight men and women, who, in turn, had sex more often than lesbian women.

The types of sexual behaviours in which these groups engaged also differed. Gay men were more likely than lesbian women or straight men and women to have anal sex. They also gave more oral sex to their partners than straight men did, and lesbian women followed suit more than straight women did. Gay men were by far the most likely to report that their most recent partner was a friend or someone they had just met. By contrast, heterosexuals and lesbians more often reported that they were in a romantic relationship. Lesbian women were more likely than anyone else to have used a sex toy in their most recent sexual encounter. These discrepancies are products of the cultures that gay men and lesbian women developed to create new possibilities in the face of heteronormativity, but they are also grounded in the differences between the lesbian and gay communities.

CONSENT IS SEXY

Consent has emerged as an indispensable value that governs Canadian sexuality. The idea that we should not have to engage in sex unless we willingly and enthusiastically choose it is hard to argue against. And yet, non-consensual sex is a serious problem for Canadians, with hundreds of thousands experiencing sexual assault each year.[25] In many instances, perpetrators are not brought to justice, and victims often receive inadequate care. We still have much ground to cover before we achieve the ideal that all sex is consensual. Holding transgressors accountable must be among our first steps.

Social inequalities are important predictors of who is likely to be sexually assaulted.[26] Although no one is immune, the truth of the matter is that our entitlement to consent – or not – is shaped by inequality. For instance, men are most likely to commit sexual assault and women most likely to experience it, a fact that points to the ongoing processes of gendered power imbalances. The gender division in establishing who feels entitled to sexual access to other bodies, and whose bodily autonomy is violated, is foundational to understanding why this problem is so difficult to solve. Other inequalities are also relevant, with members of 2SLGBTQ+ communities, those who are racialized, and those who are cash-poor experiencing disproportionate rates of assault. Those who are multiply marginalized have an even greater risk. Decades of activism have helped establish a social norm of wholehearted consent for all sexual interactions, but the overall rates of sexual assault in Canada have not diminished.

This book is unable to address sexual assault, because the Sex in Canada survey did not ask participants about their experiences with it (see Chapter 5). What it can do, however, is shine a light on the pleasure of consensual sex between adults. When people are able to engage in the sexual behaviour that they freely choose, either alone or with equally enthusiastic partners, they create good feelings, including love, pleasure, and joy. When sex is consensual, Canadians are quite satisfied with their sex lives – as we learned, more than 80 percent of participants were happy with their sex lives and their relationships. In the past, we've been a bit shy about asking people about their sexual satisfaction here in Canada, so I can't tell you much about whether this level of contentment is greater, lesser, or about the same as before the sexual revolution. But as the news so often gives us reasons to be concerned about sexuality – whether it is teen pregnancy or hookup culture or online pornography

– there is something comforting about knowing that most people feel good in their sex lives.

SEEING THE SOCIAL PATTERNS OF SEXUALITY

The Sex in Canada survey revealed how social forces nudge our sexuality in differing directions, bunching us into groups that behave a little differently from each other. It uncovered patterns that describe the social organization of sexuality. Gender, sexual identity, age, religion, and education are prime examples of forces that structure our lives (sexuality being just one domain). Although there was plenty of within-group variation, these forces sort people into groups with more or less shared views on sexuality, and they nudge individuals toward some choices and away from others.

Sociology is rife with examples of how social institutions influence our everyday lives. However, when it comes to sexuality, we often imagine that our own behaviour is purely the result of our individual choices, preferences, and morality. Certainly, these play a key role in determining what kind of sexuality, what kinds of sexual behaviour, and how much sex we engage in. A sociological approach to sexuality, like the one in this book, simply reminds us that our choices are made within social contexts. Even as it is intimate, private, and personal, sexuality is also social.

The last takeaway here is perhaps an obvious one: social contexts change over time. Just as we have seen substantial change in the social organization of sexuality since 1969, we can expect to see much more in the future. We have learned that change happens when people band together in demanding that their voices be heard, their true selves acknowledged and celebrated. The forces that organize sexuality are constantly shifting, expanding, and reconfiguring. The Sex in Canada survey offers a baseline to which we can compare the sexual landscapes and behaviours of future generations.

Appendix:
Research Methods and Limitations

The Sex in Canada survey was awarded a certificate of clearance from the McMaster University Research Ethics Board (#2017-113). We used the questionnaire from the National Survey of Health and Sexual Behavior, a research survey administered by Debby Herbenick at Indiana University. However, we made slight modifications to adapt it for use in Canada. We had it translated into French so that we could administer it in Canada's two official languages. Participants were allowed to select the language they preferred.

We partnered with Environics Canada to administer the survey in 2018. Environics Canada is a research firm with a proprietary panel of 400,000 research participants, a large pool of volunteers who receive rewards for completing surveys of all kinds. Environics selected individuals from its pool and screened them with demographic questions to produce a sample that proportionally matched the demographics of Canadians, as given in the 2016 census. Through this screening process, we recruited participants in proportion to gender, age groups, self-identification as a "visible minority," primary language (English or French), highest level of education, and region of residence. We also screened for sexual identity at the recruitment stage. This allowed us to produce two pools of respondents: those who identified as straight and those who identified as lesbian, gay, or bisexual (LGB). Our purpose was to create an oversample of LGB-identifying Canadians so that we could have confidence in our analyses of lesbian, gay, and bisexual adults.

This quota-based sampling technique produced a total of 2,303 completed surveys: 2,003 straight-identifying and 300 LGB-identifying, each of which matched the Canadian population's demographics. Whereas the quality of probability samples is in part judged by their response rates, for nonprobability sampling like ours, a traditional response rate was not available. I can offer information only about the completion rate of those who volunteered to do the survey. A total of 6,685 people answered our screening questions and were either deemed eligible or were rejected because their demographic profile had already been filled. Of the 3,368 eligible participants who started the survey, 2,303 completed it, or about 68 percent.

As they engaged with the online tool, they were advised to find a private space to complete the survey. We asked a series of multiple choice questions, all of which included a "prefer not to answer" option, and many of which included an open-ended option for participant to offer an answer in their own words. No names or identifying information were collected. Upon completing the survey, they were thanked for their time with a reward from Environics. They were asked if they were willing to be contacted by researchers for a follow-up interview, and those who said yes gave us an email address. However, those addresses were not tied to their survey responses and were stored separately. This book relies on the survey data, not the follow-up interviews, though its section on the gender gap in orgasms does refer to our interview research.

Gathering online samples such as these is increasingly common in the social sciences, as conducting a survey through the traditional recruitment methods of randomly selecting telephone numbers becomes ever more difficult. Such surveys are so cumbersome in the new era of cell phones and spam. And, as so many of us don't pick up the phone if we don't recognize the caller's number, only dedicated agencies such as Statistics Canada have the resources and expertise to conduct them properly. Social science researchers who are interested in questions that Statistics Canada has not asked have been expanding their repertoire of data collection techniques to include a variety of non-random sampling methods. Although more and more studies are employing the quota-based recruitment that we used, it has some limitations that should be kept in mind.

For instance, our sample was demographically proportional to the Canadian population, but it may have differed from the population in other respects. Because our survey was administered online, those without access to the internet, or who lacked a cell phone or computer, were unlikely to be included in the sample, which meant that Canadians in the lowest-income groups had a greater barrier to participation than others. Respondents received small rewards from Environics Canada, which may be a stronger incentive for some than for others. It is difficult to know whether the sample was representative of the Canadian population in terms of socioeconomic status. Whenever a sample differs from the population you are trying to describe, the most important thing to understand is whether the difference is also related to the questions you are asking. So, for example, if you think that the sexual behaviour of people who lack internet access could potentially differ from that of everyone else, you could see our sample as biased toward the internet-enabled and might be skeptical about the claims in this book. If, however, you feel that internet access is unrelated to sexual behaviour, you might be more convinced.

One limitation with sampling is worth considering in greater detail. Our sample of three hundred LGB participants was matched to the Canadian population at large, rather than to a census of all LGB residents in Canada. This is because Canada doesn't have a census of LGB residents to tell us what the targets of that population should be (see Chapter 1 for a longer discussion of this important topic). If the demographics for people with LGB identities differ from those of the general population, our quota-based sampling strategy will have used the wrong quotas. For example, if younger people are more likely than older people to adopt an LGB identity, the LGB population at large is probably a bit younger, on average, than straight-identifying Canadians. If LGB-identifying people are more likely than straight Canadians to live in cities, our sample of LGB participants may slightly overrepresent LGB folk who live in the country. To the extent that either age or living in a city is associated with sexual behaviour, the claims in this book will be less accurate than if the LGB population matches the straight population exactly. We won't know how far off our sample is, if at all, until we have a census of the LGB-identifying population.

Because we were asking for such intimate information, it is possible that those who are more comfortable answering such questions are overrepresented in the sample, and their answers may paint a picture of sexuality that is a little more liberal and sex-positive than that of the general population. In addition, they might not always have given honest answers or have enjoyed perfect recall regarding their sexual experiences. Any of these factors would produce a gap between what their responses tell us and what the reality of Canadian sexuality is. The best way to determine the reliability of our findings is to do more research, collecting more data with a variety of sampling strategies. When we have done enough research that many approaches begin to converge around a common set of findings, we will feel more confident that we have a strong understanding of sexual behaviour patterns.

In terms of data analysis, the approach of this book is simple. As an introduction to the social organization of sexual behaviour in Canada, this volume offers basic descriptive statistics and crosstabs of associations between variables to provide an overview. On the occasion where more sophisticated analyses are described, it cites peer-reviewed research from the Sex in Canada project. As an open-science project, the anonymous data from the Sex in Canada research project have been made publicly available via Borealis: The Canadian Dataverse Repository.

Notes

Introduction: The Social Science of Sexuality

1 Julia Serano, *Sexed Up: How Society Sexualizes Us, and How We Can Fight Back* (New York: Seal Press, 2022).

2 Laura M. Carpenter, *Virginity Lost: An Intimate Portrait of First Sexual Experiences* (New York: NYU Press, 2005).

3 Arne Dekker and Gunter Schmidt, "Patterns of Masturbatory Behaviour," *Journal of Psychology and Human Sexuality* 14, 2–3 (2003): 35–48.

4 Robert Andersen and Tina Fetner, "Cohort Differences in Tolerance of Homosexuality: Attitudinal Change in Canada and the United States, 1981–2000," *Public Opinion Quarterly* 72, 2 (2008): 311–30; J. Scott Matthews, "The Political Foundations of Support for Same-Sex Marriage in Canada," *Canadian Journal of Political Science* 38, 4 (2005): 841–66; Lorne Bozinoff, "US Court Ruling Boosts Approval of Same Sex Marriage in Canada," *Forum Research*, news release, June 29, 2015.

5 Eric D. Widmer, Judith Treas, and Robert Newcomb, "Attitudes toward Nonmarital Sex in 24 Countries," *Journal of Sex Research* 35, 4 (1998): 349–58.

6 Sean Simpson, "Majority Continue to Support (77%) Abortion in Canada, but behind Sweden (87%), Belgium (87%) and France (86%)," Calgary, IPSOS, May 1, 2017, https://www.ipsos.com/en-ca/news-polls/majority-continue-support-abortion-canada.

7 Alexander McKay, Mary-Anne Pietrusiak, and Philippa Holowaty, "Parents' Opinions and Attitudes towards Sexuality Education in the Schools," *Canadian Journal of Human Sexuality* 7, 2 (1998): 139–45; Pamela Dickey Young, Heather

Shipley, and Tracy J. Trothen, *Religion and Sexuality: Diversity and the Limits of Tolerance* (Vancouver: UBC Press, 2015).

8 Gayle Rubin, "Thinking Sex: Notes for a Radical Theory of the Politics of Sexuality," in *Pleasure and Danger: Exploring Female Sexuality*, ed. Carole S. Vance (Boston: Routledge, 1984), 143–78.

9 Emily Weinstein and Carrie James, *Behind Their Screens: What Teens Are Facing (and Adults Are Missing)* (Cambridge, MA: MIT Press, 2022); Angela Jones, *Camming: Money, Power, and Pleasure in the Sex Work Industry* (New York: NYU Press, 2019).

10 Sean Waite and Nicole Denier, "A Research Note on Canada's LGBT Data Landscape: Where We Are and What the Future Holds: Canada's LGBT Data Landscape," *Canadian Review of Sociology* 56, 1 (February 2019): 93–117.

11 Howard Snyder, "Arrest in the United States, 1990–2010," Washington, DC, Bureau of Justice Statistics, 2012, https://bjs.ojp.gov/content/pub/pdf/aus9010.pdf.

12 Cristine Rotenberg, "Prostitution Offences in Canada: Statistical Trends," *Juristat* 36, 1 (November 10, 2016), https://www150.statcan.gc.ca/n1/pub/85-002-x/2016001/article/14670-eng.htm.

13 Miriam Smith, *Political Institutions and Lesbian and Gay Rights in the United States and Canada* (New York: Routledge, 2008).

14 Priya Krishnakumar, "This Record-Breaking Year for Anti-Transgender Legislation Would Affect Minors the Most," CNN.com, April 15, 2021, https://www.cnn.com/2021/04/15/politics/anti-transgender-legislation-2021/index.html.

15 Government of Canada, "Bill C-16: An Act to Amend the *Canadian Human Rights Act* and the *Criminal Code*," Justice.gc.ca, September 1, 2021, https://justice.gc.ca/eng/csj-sjc/pl/identity-identite/statement-enonce.html.

16 Jennifer K. Cano and Angel M. Foster, "'They Made Me Go through Like Weeks of Appointments and Everything': Documenting Women's Experiences Seeking Abortion Care in Yukon Territory, Canada," *Contraception* 94, 5 (November 1, 2016): 489–95; Mark Gollom, "Abortion Barriers in Canada Are Back in Spotlight Following Passage of Abortion Bans in U.S.," *CBC News*, May 18, 2019, https://www.cbc.ca/news/health/abortion-access-canada-us-bans-1.5140345.

17 Deana A. Rohlinger, "Framing the Abortion Debate: Organizational Resources, Media Strategies, and Movement-Countermovement Dynamics," *Sociological Quarterly* 43, 4 (2002): 479–507.

18 Jonathan Marc Bearak et al., "Country-Specific Estimates of Unintended Pregnancy and Abortion Incidence: A Global Comparative Analysis of Levels in 2015–2019," *BMJ Global Health* 7, 3 (2022): e007151.

19 Céline Le Bourdais and Évelyne Lapierre-Adamcyk, "Changes in Conjugal Life in Canada: Is Cohabitation Progressively Replacing Marriage?" *Journal of Marriage and Family* 66, 4 (2004): 929–42.

20 Doug Baer, Edward Grabb, and William A. Johnston, "The Values of Canadians and Americans: A Critical Analysis and Reassessment," *Social Forces* 68, 3 (1990): 693–713.

21 Laurel Westbrook, Jamie Budnick, and Aliya Saperstein, "Dangerous Data: Seeing Social Surveys through the Sexuality Prism," *Sexualities* 25, 5–6 (2022): 717–49.

22 Jessica Fields, *Risky Lessons: Sex Education and Social Inequality*, Rutgers Series in Childhood Studies (New Brunswick, NJ: Rutgers University Press, 2008).

23 Jamie Budnick, "The New Gay Science: Sexuality Knowledge, Demography, and the Politics of Population Measurement" (PhD diss., University of Michigan, 2020).

24 Laurel Westbrook and Aliya Saperstein, "New Categories Are Not Enough: Rethinking the Measurement of Sex and Gender in Social Surveys," *Gender & Society* 29, 4 (2015): 534–60.

25 Statistics Canada, "Canada Is the First Country to Provide Census Data on Transgender and Non-Binary People," The Daily, Ottawa, Statistics Canada, April 24, 2022, https://www150.statcan.gc.ca/n1/en/daily-quotidien/220427/dq220427b-eng.pdf?st=la_O8FPf.

26 Alfred C. Kinsey, Wardell B. Pomeroy, and Clyde E. Martin, *Sexual Behavior in the Human Male* (Philadelphia: Saunders, 1948).

27 Edward O. Laumann et al., *The Social Organization of Sexuality: Sexual Practices in the United States* (Chicago: University of Chicago Press, 1994).

Chapter 1: Thinking about Sexual Identity

1 Peter L. Berger and Thomas Luckmann, *The Social Construction of Reality: A Treatise in the Sociology of Knowledge* (New York: Anchor Books, 1990).

2 David F. Greenberg, *The Construction of Homosexuality* (Chicago: University of Chicago Press, 1988).

3 Jonathan Ned Katz, *The Invention of Heterosexuality* (New York: Penguin Group, 1995).

4 Michel Foucault, *The History of Sexuality*, vol. 1 (New York: Random House, 1978).

5 Lutz D.H. Sauerteig, "Loss of Innocence: Albert Moll, Sigmund Freud and the Invention of Childhood Sexuality around 1900," *Medical History* 56, 2 (2012): 156–83.

6 Katz, *The Invention of Heterosexuality*.

7 Jack Drescher, "I'm Your Handyman: A History of Reparative Therapies," *Journal of Homosexuality* 36, 1 (1998): 19–42.

8 Evelyn Hooker, "The Adjustment of the Male Overt Homosexual," *Journal of Projective Techniques* 21, 1 (1957): 18–31.

9 Abram J. Lewis, "'We Are Certain of Our Own Insanity': Antipsychiatry and the Gay Liberation Movement, 1968–1980," *Journal of the History of Sexuality* 25, 1 (2016): 83–113.

10 Foucault, *The History of Sexuality*.

11 Judith Butler, *Gender Trouble: Feminism and the Subversion of Identity*, 2nd ed. (New York: Routledge, 1990); Judith Butler, *Undoing Gender* (New York: Routledge, 2004).

12 Michael Warner, "Introduction: Fear of a Queer Planet," *Social Text* 29 (1991): 3–17.

13 J.E. Sumerau, Lain A.B. Mathers, and Dawne Moon, "Foreclosing Fluidity at the

Intersection of Gender and Sexual Normativities," *Symbolic Interaction* 43, 2 (2020): 205–34.

14   Michael D. Martinez, Kenneth D. Wald, and Stephen C. Craig, "Homophobic Innumeracy? Estimating the Size of the Gay and Lesbian Population," *Public Opinion Quarterly* 72, 4 (2008): 753–67.

15   Statistics Canada, "A Statistical Portrait of Canada's Diverse LGBTQ2+ Communities," The Daily, Ottawa, Statistics Canada, June 15, 2021, https://www150. statcan.gc.ca/n1/en/daily-quotidien/210615/dq210615a-eng.pdf?st=FTVsCzDb.

16   Statistics Canada, "Portrait of Families and Living Arrangements in Canada." Ottawa, Minister of Industry, 2012. https://www12.statcan.gc.ca/ccnsus-recensement/2011/as-sa/98-312-x/2011001/mi-rs-eng.cfm.

17   Statistics Canada, "A Statistical Portrait."

18   Gary J. Gates, "LGBT Demographics: Comparisons among Population-Based Surveys," Los Angeles, Williams Institute, UCLA, 2014, https://escholarship.org/uc/item/0kr784fx.

19   Statistics Canada, "Canada Is the First Country to Provide Census Data on Transgender and Non-Binary People," *The Daily*, Ottawa, Statistics Canada, April 24, 2022, https://www150.statcan.gc.ca/n1/en/daily-quotidien/220427/dq220427b-eng.pdf?st=la_O8FPf.

20   Jamie Budnick, "The New Gay Science: Sexuality Knowledge, Demography, and the Politics of Population Measurement" (PhD diss., University of Michigan, 2020).

21   Sari M. van Anders, "Beyond Sexual Orientation: Integrating Gender/Sex and Diverse Sexualities via Sexual Configurations Theory," *Archives of Sexual Behavior* 44, 5 (2015): 1177–1213, Kari Lerum and Shari L. Dworkin, "The Power of (But Not In?) Sexual Configurations Theory," *Archives of Sexual Behavior* 45, 3 (2016): 495–99; Patrick R. Grzanka, "Intersections and Configurations," *Archives of Sexual Behavior* 45, 3 (2016): 501–3.

22   Emma Mishel, "Intersections between Sexual Identity, Sexual Attraction, and Sexual Behavior among a Nationally Representative Sample of American Men and Women," *Journal of Official Statistics* 35, 4 (2019): 859–84.

23   Tony Silva and Tina Fetner, "Sexual Identity-Behavior Discordance in Canada," *Canadian Review of Sociology* 59, 2 (2022): 156–80.

24   Tony Silva, "Straight Identity and Same-Sex Desire: Conservatism, Homophobia, and Straight Culture," *Social Forces* 97, 3 (2019): 1067–94.

25   Brandon Andrew Robinson and Salvador Vidal-Ortiz, "Displacing the Dominant 'Down Low' Discourse: Deviance, Same-Sex Desire, and Craigslist.org," *Deviant Behavior* 34, 3 (2013): 224–41.

26   Tony Silva, *Still Straight: Sexual Flexibility among White Men in Rural America* (New York: NYU Press, 2021).

27   Brian Dodge et al., "Sexual Behaviors of U.S. Men by Self-Identified Sexual Orientation: Results from the 2012 National Survey of Sexual Health and Behavior," *Journal of Sexual Medicine* 13, 4 (2016): 637–49.

28　Paula C. Rust, "'Coming Out' in the Age of Social Constructionism: Sexual Identity Formation among Lesbian and Bisexual Women," *Gender & Society* 7, 1 (1993): 50–77.

29　Ritch C. Savin-Williams, *The New Gay Teenager* (Cambridge, MA: Harvard University Press, 2005).

30　Kristen Schilt, "The Unfinished Business of Sexuality: Comment on Andersen," *Gender & Society* 22, 1 (2008): 109–14.

31　Stefan Vogler, *Sorting Sexualities: Expertise and the Politics of Legal Classification* (Chicago: University of Chicago Press, 2021).

32　Amin Ghaziani, *There Goes the Gayborhood?* (Princeton, NJ: Princeton University Press, 2014).

33　Elizabeth A. Armstrong, *Forging Gay Identities: Organizing Sexuality in San Francisco, 1950–1994* (Chicago: University of Chicago Press, 2002).

34　Arlene Stein, "Sisters and Queers: The Decentering of Lesbian Feminism," In *Cultural Politics and Social Movements*, ed. Marcy Darnovsky, Barbara Epstein, and Richard Flacks (Philadelphia, PA: Temple University Press, 1995), 133–53.

35　Katherine McFarland Bruce, *Pride Parades: How a Parade Changed the World* (New York: NYU Press, 2016).

36　Amy L. Stone, "The Geography of Research on LGBTQ Life: Why Sociologists Should Study the South, Rural Queers, and Ordinary Cities," *Sociology Compass* 12, 11 (2018): e12638.

37　Warner, "Introduction: Fear of a Queer Planet."

38　Kristen Schilt and Laurel Westbrook, "Doing Gender, Doing Heteronormativity: 'Gender Normals,' Transgender People, and the Social Maintenance of Heterosexuality," *Gender & Society* 23, 4 (2009): 440–64.

39　Steven Seidman, "Deconstructing Queer Theory, or the Under-Theorization of the Social and the Ethical," in *Social Postmodernism: Beyond Identity Politics*, ed. Linda Nicholson and Steven Seidman, Cambridge Cultural Social Studies (Cambridge: Cambridge University Press, 1995), 116–41.

40　C.J. Pascoe, *Dude, You're a Fag: Masculinity and Sexuality in High School* (Berkeley: University of California Press, 2012).

41　Leila J. Rupp and Verta A. Taylor, *Drag Queens at the 801 Cabaret* (Chicago: University of Chicago Press, 2003); Vito Russo, *The Celluloid Closet: Homosexuality in the Movies*, rev. ed. (New York: Harper and Row, 1987).

42　Surya Monro, *Bisexuality: Identities, Politics, and Theories*, Genders and Sexualities in the Social Sciences (Houndmills, UK: Palgrave Macmillan, 2015).

43　Paula C. Rodríguez Rust, "Bisexuality: The State of the Union," *Annual Review of Sex Research* 13, 1 (2002): 180–240.

44　Corey E. Flanders, Cheryl Dobinson, and Carmen Logie, "'I'm Never Really My Full Self': Young Bisexual Women's Perceptions of Their Mental Health," *Journal of Bisexuality* 15, 4 (October 2, 2015): 454–80.

45 Casey E. Copen, Anjani Chandra, and Isaedmarie Febo-Vazquez, "Sexual Behavior, Sexual Attraction, and Sexual Orientation among Adults Aged 18–44 in the United States: Data from the 2011–2013 National Survey of Family Growth," *National Health Statistics Reports* 88 (January 7, 2016): 1–14.

46 Statistics Canada, "A Statistical Portrait."

47 Brenda Cossman, "Fifty Years Later: The Legacy of the 1969 Criminal Reforms," *University of Toronto Law Journal* 70, 3 (2020): 223–24.

48 Russo, *The Celluloid Closet.*

49 Gary William Kinsman, *The Regulation of Desire: Sexuality in Canada* (Montreal: Black Rose Books, 1987).

50 Sean Waite and Nicole Denier, "Gay Pay for Straight Work: Mechanisms Generating Disadvantage," *Gender & Society* 29, 4 (2015): 561–88.

51 Diane L. Beauchamp, "Sexual Orientation and Victimization," Ottawa, Statistics Canada, 2004, https://www.tandis.odihr.pl/retrieve/22973.

52 Greta R. Bauer and Ayden I. Scheim, "Transgender People in Ontario, Canada: Statistics from the Trans PULSE Project to Inform Human Rights Policy," London, ON, Trans PULSE Project, 2015, transpulseproject.ca/wp-content/uploads/2015/06/Trans-PULSE-Statistics-Relevant-for-Human-Rights-Policy-June-2015.pdf.

53 Amy Adamczyk, *Cross-National Public Opinion about Homosexuality* (Berkeley: University of California Press, 2017).

54 Robert Andersen and Tina Fetner, "Cohort Differences in Tolerance of Homosexuality: Attitudinal Change in Canada and the United States, 1981–2000," *Public Opinion Quarterly* 72 (2008): 311–30.

55 Emilie D'amico et al., "Gay, Lesbian, and Bisexual Youths Coming Out to Their Parents: Parental Reactions and Youths' Outcomes," *Journal of GLBT Family Studies* 11, 5 (2015): 411–37.

56 Schilt, "The Unfinished Business."

57 Landon Schnabel, "Sexual Orientation and Social Attitudes," *Socius* 4 (2018): 237802311876955.

58 Sarah Hunt, "An Introduction to the Health of Two-Spirit People: Historical, Contemporary and Emergent Issues," Prince George, BC, National Collaborating Centre for Aboriginal Health, 2016, https://www.ccnsa-nccah.ca/docs/emerging/RPT-HealthTwoSpirit-Hunt-EN.pdf; Sue-Ellen Jacobs, Wesley Thomas, and Sabine Lang, eds., *Two-Spirit People: Native American Gender Identity, Sexuality, and Spirituality* (Urbana: University of Illinois Press, 1997); Aren Aizura et al., eds., "Decolonizing the Transgender Imaginary," special issue, *TSQ* 1, 3 (2014); Jyoti Puri, *Sexual States: Governance and the Struggle over the Antisodomy Law in India* (Durham: Duke University Press, 2016); Day Wong, "Hybridization and the Emergence of 'Gay' Identities in Hong Kong and in China," in *Hybrid Hong Kong*, ed. Kwok-bun Chan (New York: Routledge, 2012), 199–217.

59 Alex Wilson, "How We Find Ourselves: Identity Development and Two Spirit People," *Harvard Educational Review* 66, 2 (1996): 303–18.

60 Robin Jarvis Brownlie, "Intimate Surveillance: Indian Affairs, Colonization, and the Regulation of Aboriginal Women's Sexuality," in *Contact Zones: Aboriginal and Settler Women in Canada's Colonial Past*, ed. Katie Pickles and Myra Rutherdale (Vancouver: UBC Press, 2005), 160–78.

61 Vanessa Watts, "Indigenous Place-Thought and Agency amongst Humans and Non Humans (First Woman and Sky Woman Go on a European World Tour!)," *Decolonization: Indigeneity, Education and Society* 2, 1 (2013): 20–34.

62 Sue-Ellen Jacobs, "Is the 'North American Berdache' Merely a Phantom in the Imaginations of Western Social Scientists?" in Jacobs, Thomas, and Lang, *Two-Spirit People*, 21–44.

63 Margaret Robinson, "Two-Spirit Identity in a Time of Gender Fluidity," *Journal of Homosexuality* 67, 12 (October 14, 2020): 1675–90; Wilson, "How We Find Ourselves."

64 Seidman, "Deconstructing Queer Theory"; Warner, "Introduction: Fear of a Queer Planet."

65 Lauren Berlant and Michael Warner, "Sex in Public," *Critical Inquiry* 24, 2 (1998): 547–66.

66 Laurel Westbrook, "Trans Categories and the Sex/Gender/Sexuality System," in *Introducing the New Sexuality Studies*, 4th ed., ed. Nancy L. Fischer, Laurel Westbrook, and Steven Seidman (New York: Routledge, 2022), 33–42.

67 Laurel Westbrook and Kristen Schilt, "Doing Gender, Determining Gender: Transgender People, Gender Panics, and the Maintenance of the Sex/Gender/Sexuality System," *Gender & Society* 28, 1 (2014): 32–57.

68 Celeste Mora, "What Is the Singular They, and Why Should I Use It?" *Grammarly Blog* (blog), June 1, 2018, https://www.grammarly.com/blog/use-the-singular-they/.

69 Sharon E. Preves, *Intersex and Identity: The Contested Self* (New Brunswick, NJ: Rutgers University Press, 2003).

70 Georgiann Davis, *Contesting Intersex: The Dubious Diagnosis* (New York: NYU Press, 2015).

71 C.J. DeLuzio Chasin, "Theoretical Issues in the Study of Asexuality," *Archives of Sexual Behavior* 40, 4 (2011): 713–23; Ellen Van Houdenhove et al., "Asexuality: A Multidimensional Approach," *Journal of Sex Research* 52, 6 (2015): 669–78.

72 Kristin S. Scherrer, "Coming to an Asexual Identity: Negotiating Identity, Negotiating Desire," *Sexualities* 11, 5 (2008): 621–41; Susie Scott, Liz McDonnell, and Matt Dawson, "Stories of Non-Becoming: Non-Issues, Non-Events and Non-Identities in Asexual Lives," *Symbolic Interaction* 39, 2 (2016): 268–86.

73 Canton Winer et al., "'I Didn't Know Ace Was a Thing': Bisexuality and Pansexuality as Identity Pathways in Asexual Identity Formation," *Sexualities* (forthcoming): https://doi.org/10.31235/osf.io/agnd8.

74 Autumn Elizabeth, "Challenging the Binary: Sexual Identity That Is Not Duality," *Journal of Bisexuality* 13, 3 (2013): 329–37.

75 M. Paz Galupo, Johanna L. Ramirez, and Lex Pulice-Farrow, "'Regardless of Their Gender': Descriptions of Sexual Identity among Bisexual, Pansexual, and Queer Identified Individuals," *Journal of Bisexuality* 17, 1 (2017): 108–24.

76 Adam Isaiah Green, "Queer Unions: Same-Sex Spouses Marrying Tradition and Innovation," *Canadian Journal of Sociology* 35, 3 (2010): 399–436.

Chapter 2: How Much Sex Are We Having?

1 Laura Hamilton and Elizabeth A. Armstrong, "Gendered Sexuality in Young Adulthood: Double Binds and Flawed Options," *Gender & Society* 23, 5 (2009): 589–616.

2 Edward O. Laumann et al., *The Social Organization of Sexuality: Sexual Practices in the United States* (Chicago: University of Chicago Press, 1994).

3 Laura M. Carpenter, *Virginity Lost: An Intimate Portrait of First Sexual Experiences* (New York: NYU Press, 2005).

4 Sarah Diefendorf, "After the Wedding Night: Sexual Abstinence and Masculinities over the Life Course," *Gender & Society* 29, 5 (2015): 647–69.

5 Hamilton and Armstrong, "Gendered Sexuality."

6 C.J. Pascoe, *Dude, You're a Fag: Masculinity and Sexuality in High School* (Berkeley: University of California Press, 2012).

7 Deborah L. Tolman, *Dilemmas of Desire: Teenage Girls Talk about Sexuality* (Cambridge: Harvard University Press, 2009).

8 Sharon Thompson, *Going All the Way: Teenage Girls' Tales of Sex, Romance, and Pregnancy* (New York: Hill and Wang, 1996).

9 Scott J. South and Lei Lei, "Why Are Fewer Young Adults Having Casual Sex?" *Socius* 7 (2021): 2378023121996854.

10 Peter Ueda et al., "Trends in Frequency of Sexual Activity and Number of Sexual Partners among Adults Aged 18 to 44 Years in the US, 2000–2018," *JAMA Network Open* 3, 6 (2020): e203833.

11 Gladys M. Martinez and Joyce C. Abma, "Sexual Activity and Contraceptive Use among Teenagers Aged 15–19 in the United States, 2015–2017," NCHS Data Brief, Data Briefs, Washington, DC, National Center for Health Statistics, May 2020, https://www.cdc.gov/nchs/data/databriefs/db366-h.pdf; Laura D. Lindberg, Lauren Firestein, and Cynthia Beavin, "Trends in U.S. Adolescent Sexual Behavior and Contraceptive Use, 2006–2019," *Contraception: X* 3 (2021): 100064.

12 Jeffrey J. Arnett, "Getting Better All the Time: Trends in Risk Behavior among American Adolescents since 1990," *Archives of Scientific Psychology* 6, 1 (2018): 87–95, https://doi.org/10.1037/arc0000046.

13 Kate Julian, "Why Are Young People Having So Little Sex?" *The Atlantic*, December 13, 2018, https://www.theatlantic.com/magazine/archive/2018/12/the-sex-recession/573949/.

14 Justin J. Lehmiller et al., "Less Sex, but More Sexual Diversity: Changes in Sexual

Behavior during the COVID-19 Coronavirus Pandemic," *Leisure Sciences* 43, 1–2 (2021): 295–304.

15 Helena Harder et al., "Sexual Functioning in 4,418 Postmenopausal Women Participating in UKCTOCS: A Qualitative Free-Text Analysis," *Menopause* 26, 10 (2019): 1100–9.

16 Amin Ghaziani, *The Dividends of Dissent: How Conflict and Culture Work in Lesbian and Gay Marches on Washington* (Chicago: University of Chicago Press, 2008); Victoria Clarke and Kevin Turner, "V. Clothes Maketh the Queer? Dress, Appearance and the Construction of Lesbian, Gay and Bisexual Identities," *Feminism and Psychology* 17, 2 (2007): 267–76.

17 Céline Le Bourdais and Évelyne Lapierre-Adamcyk, "Changes in Conjugal Life in Canada: Is Cohabitation Progressively Replacing Marriage?" *Journal of Marriage and Family* 66, 4 (2004): 929–42.

18 Melissa Bolton, Alexander McKay, and Margaret Schneider, "Relational Influences on Condom Use Discontinuation: A Qualitative Study of Young Adult Women in Dating Relationships," *Canadian Journal of Human Sexuality* 19, 3 (2010): 91–104; Larry K. Brown et al., "Condom Use among High-Risk Adolescents: Anticipation of Partner Disapproval and Less Pleasure Associated with Not Using Condoms," *Public Health Reports* 123, 5 (2008): 601–7; Shira M. Goldenberg et al., "International Migration from Non-endemic Settings as a Protective Factor for HIV/STI Risk among Female Sex Workers in Vancouver, Canada," *Journal of Immigrant and Minority Health* 17, 1 (2015): 21–28; Alexander McKay, Christopher Quinn-Nilas, and Robin Milhausen, "Prevalence and Correlates of Condom Use among Single Midlife Canadian Women and Men Aged 40 to 59," *Canadian Journal of Human Sexuality* 26, 1 (2017): 38 47; Michelle Rotermann and Alexander McKay, "Condom Use at Last Sexual Intercourse among Unmarried, Not Living Common-Law 20- to 34-Year-Old Canadian Young Adults," *Canadian Journal of Human Sexuality* 18, 3 (2009): 75–87; Joanne Otis et al., "Beyond Condoms: Risk Reduction Strategies among Gay, Bisexual, and Other Men Who Have Sex with Men Receiving Rapid HIV Testing in Montreal, Canada," *AIDS and Behavior* 20, 12 (2016): 2812–26.

19 Tina Fetner et al., "Condom Use in Penile-Vaginal Intercourse among Canadian Adults: Results from the Sex in Canada Survey," *PLOS ONE* 15, 2 (2020): e0228981.

20 Megan L. Kavanaugh and Jenna Jerman, "Contraceptive Method Use in the United States: Trends and Characteristics between 2008, 2012 and 2014," *Contraception* 97, 1 (2018): 14–21.

21 Susheela Singh, Gilda Sedgh, and Rubina Hussain, "Unintended Pregnancy: Worldwide Levels, Trends, and Outcomes," *Studies in Family Planning* 41, 4 (2010): 241–50.

22 Anna Pancham and Sheila Dunn, "Emergency Contraception in Canada: An Overview and Recent Developments," *Canadian Journal of Human Sexuality* 16, 3/4 (2007): 129–33.

23 Carly Weeks, "Ontario, New Brunswick Violating Canada Health Act by Forcing Patients to Pay for Abortions: National Abortion Federation," *Globe and Mail*, July 16, 2019, accessed Aug. 28, 2023, https://www.theglobeandmail.com/canada/article-ontario-new-brunswick-violating-canada-health-act-by-forcing-patients/.

24 Mark Gollom, "Abortion Barriers in Canada Are Back in Spotlight Following Passage of Abortion Bans in U.S.," *CBC News*, May 18, 2019, https://www.cbc.ca/news/health/abortion-access-canada-us-bans-1.5140345.

Chapter 3: Commitment, Casual Sex, and Cheating

1 Melanie Heath, *Forbidden Intimacies: Polygamies at the Limits of Western Tolerance* (Stanford: Stanford University Press, 2023).

2 Anne Lorene Chambers, *Misconceptions: Unmarried Motherhood and the Ontario Children of Unmarried Parents Act, 1921 to 1969* (Toronto: University of Toronto Press, 2007); Joan Sangster, "Incarcerating 'Bad Girls': The Regulation of Sexuality through the Female Refuges Act in Ontario, 1920–1945," *Journal of the History of Sexuality* 7, 2 (1996): 239–75.

3 Robin Jarvis Brownlie, "Intimate Surveillance: Indian Affairs, Colonization, and the Regulation of Aboriginal Women's Sexuality," in *Contact Zones: Aboriginal and Settler Women in Canada's Colonial Past*, ed. Katie Pickles and Myra Rutherdale (Vancouver: UBC Press, 2005), 160–78; Martin Cannon, "The Regulation of First Nations Sexuality," *Canadian Journal of Native Studies* 18, 1 (1998): 1–18.

4 Céline Le Bourdais and Évelyne Lapierre-Adamcyk, "Changes in Conjugal Life in Canada: Is Cohabitation Progressively Replacing Marriage?" *Journal of Marriage and Family* 66, 4 (2004): 929–42.

5 Céline Le Bourdais et al., "Impact of Conjugal Separation on Women's Income in Canada: Does the Type of Union Matter?" *Demographic Research* 35 (2016): 1489–1522.

6 Anne Milan, "Marital Status: Overview, 2011," Ottawa, Statistics Canada, July 2013, https://www150.statcan.gc.ca/n1/pub/91-209-x/2013001/article/11788-eng.pdf.

7 Le Bourdais and Lapierre-Adamcyk, "Changes in Conjugal Life."

8 Rachel Margolis et al., "Capturing Trends in Canadian Divorce in an Era without Vital Statistics," *Demographic Research* 41, 52 (2019): 1453–78.

9 Philip N. Cohen, "The Coming Divorce Decline," *Socius* 5 (2019): 2378023119873497.

10 Karen Benjamin Guzzo, "Trends in Cohabitation Outcomes: Compositional Changes and Engagement among Never-Married Young Adults," *Journal of Marriage and the Family* 76, 4 (2014): 826–42.

11 Le Bourdais et al., "Impact of Conjugal Separation."

12 Daniel Schneider, "Wealth and the Marital Divide," *American Journal of Sociology* 117, 2 (2011): 627–67.

13 Eric Klinenberg, *Going Solo: The Extraordinary Rise and Surprising Appeal of Living Alone* (London: Duckworth, 2012).

14 Rebecca Traister, *All the Single Ladies: Unmarried Women and the Rise of an Independent Nation* (New York: Simon and Schuster, 2016).
15 Jocelyn J. Wentland and Elke Reissing, "Casual Sexual Relationships: Identifying Definitions for One Night Stands, Booty Calls, Fuck Buddies, and Friends with Benefits," *Canadian Journal of Human Sexuality* 23, 3 (2014): 167–77.
16 Jessica Penwell Barnett, "Polyamory and Criminalization of Plural Conjugal Unions in Canada: Competing Narratives in the s.293 Reference," *Sexuality Research and Social Policy* 11, 1 (2014): 63–75; Heath, *Forbidden Intimacies*.
17 Attorney General of Ontario, "About the All Families Are Equal Act, 2016," *Ontario Newsroom* (blog), November 29, 2016, https://news.ontario.ca/en/backgrounder/42854/about-the-all-families-are-equal-act-2016.
18 Miriam Smith, "Homophobia and Homonationalism: LGBTQ Law Reform in Canada," *Social and Legal Studies* 29, 1 (February 1, 2020): 65–84.
19 Statistics Canada, "Same-Sex Couples in Canada in 2016," Census in Brief, Ottawa, Minister of Industry, August 2, 2017.
20 Kathleen Hull, *Same-Sex Marriage: The Cultural Politics of Love and Law* (New York: Cambridge University Press, 2006).
21 Statistics Canada, "By the Numbers: Same-Sex Couples and Sexual Orientation," Ottawa, Minister of Industry, 2015, accessed Sept. 6, 2023, https://www.statcan.gc.ca/eng/dai/smr08/2015/smr08_203_2015.
22 Tina Fetner and Melanie Heath, "Do Same-Sex and Straight Weddings Aspire to the Fairytale? Women's Conformity and Resistance to Traditional Weddings," *Sociological Perspectives* 59, 4 (2016): 721–42.
23 Rachel Allison and Barbara J. Risman, "Marriage Delay, Time to Play? Marital Horizons and Hooking Up in College," *Sociological Inquiry* 87, 3 (2017): 472–500.
24 Lisa Wade, *American Hookup: The New Culture of Sex on Campus* (New York: W.W. Norton, 2018).
25 Jennifer S. Hirsch and Shamus Khan, *Sexual Citizens: A Landmark Study of Sex, Power, and Assault on Campus* (New York: W.W. Norton, 2020).
26 Wade, *American Hookup*.
27 Aziz Ansari and Eric Klinenberg, *Modern Romance* (New York: Penguin, 2015).
28 Danielle M. Currier, "Strategic Ambiguity: Protecting Emphasized Femininity and Hegemonic Masculinity in the Hookup Culture," *Gender & Society* 27, 5 (2013): 704–27.
29 Julie A. Reid, Sinikka Elliott, and Gretchen R. Webber, "Casual Hookups to Formal Dates: Refining the Boundaries of the Sexual Double Standard," *Gender & Society* 25, 5 (2011): 545–68.
30 Nicole Andrejek, "Dating in the Digital Age" (PhD diss., McMaster University, 2020).
31 Courtney Blackwell, Jeremy Birnholtz, and Charles Abbott, "Seeing and Being Seen: Co-Situation and Impression Formation Using Grindr, a Location-Aware Gay Dating App," *New Media and Society* 17, 7 (2014): 1117–36.

32 Janelle Ward, "What Are You Doing on Tinder? Impression Management on a Matchmaking Mobile App," *Information, Communication and Society* 20, 11 (2017): 1644–59.

33 Ansari and Klinenberg, *Modern Romance*.

34 Kath Albury and Paul Byron, "Safe on My Phone? Same-Sex Attracted Young People's Negotiations of Intimacy, Visibility, and Risk on Digital Hook-Up Apps," *Social Media and Society* 2, 4 (2016): 2056305116672887; Rebecca M. Hayes and Molly Dragiewicz, "Unsolicited Dick Pics: Erotica, Exhibitionism or Entitlement?" *Women's Studies International Forum* 71 (2018): 114–20.

35 Monica Anderson, Emily A. Vogels, and Erica Turner, "The Virtues and Downsides of Online Dating," New York, Pew Research Center, February 6, 2020, https://www.pewresearch.org/internet/2020/02/06/americans-personal-experiences-with-online-dating/.

36 Barry D. Adam, *The Rise of a Gay and Lesbian Movement*, rev. ed., Social Movements Past and Present (New York: Twayne, 1995).

37 Steve Valocchi, "Riding the Crest of a Protest Wave? Collective Action Frames in the Gay Liberation Movement, 1969–1973," *Mobilization: An International Quarterly* 4, 1 (1999): 59–73.

38 M.L. Haupert et al., "Prevalence of Experiences with Consensual Nonmonogamous Relationships: Findings from Two National Samples of Single Americans," *Journal of Sex and Marital Therapy* 43, 5 (2017): 424–40.

39 Alicia M. Walker, *The Secret Life of the Cheating Wife: Power, Pragmatism, and Pleasure in Women's Infidelity* (Lanham, MD: Lexington Books, 2018).

40 Judith Treas and Deirdre Giesen, "Sexual Infidelity among Married and Cohabiting Americans," *Journal of Marriage and Family* 62, 1 (2000): 48–60.

41 David C. Atkins, Donald H. Baucom, and Neil S. Jacobson, "Understanding Infidelity: Correlates in a National Random Sample," *Journal of Family Psychology* 15, 4 (2001): 735–49; Camille B. Lalasz and Daniel J. Weigel, "Understanding the Relationship between Gender and Extradyadic Relations: The Mediating Role of Sensation Seeking on Intentions to Engage in Sexual Infidelity," *Personality and Individual Differences* 50, 7 (2011): 1079–83.

Chapter 4: What Are We Doing in the Bedroom?

1 E. Sandra Byers, Joel Henderson, and Kristina M. Hobson, "University Students' Definitions of Sexual Abstinence and Having Sex," *Archives of Sexual Behavior* 38, 5 (2009): 665–74.

2 Laurence Dion and Marie-Aude Boislard, "What 'Counts' as First Sex between Women? Results from a Study of First Sex among Women Who Have Sex with Women," *Canadian Journal of Human Sexuality* 31, 2 (2022): 253–67.

3 Jessica Fields, *Risky Lessons: Sex Education and Social Inequality*, Rutgers Series in Childhood Studies (New Brunswick, NJ: Rutgers University Press, 2008); Jennifer S. Hirsch and Shamus Khan, *Sexual Citizens: A Landmark Study of Sex, Power, and Assault on Campus* (New York: W.W. Norton, 2020).

4 Peggy Orenstein, *Boys and Sex: Young Men on Hookups, Love, Porn, Consent, and Navigating the New Masculinity* (New York: Harper, 2020).

5 Niki Fritz and Bryant Paul, "From Orgasms to Spanking: A Content Analysis of the Agentic and Objectifying Sexual Scripts in Feminist, for Women, and Mainstream Pornography," *Sex Roles* 77, 9 (2017): 639–52.

6 Hannah Frith, "Visualising the 'Real' and the 'Fake': Emotion Work and the Representation of Orgasm in Pornography and Everyday Sexual Interactions," *Journal of Gender Studies* 24, 4 (2015): 386–98.

7 Judith Treas, "How Cohorts, Education, and Ideology Shaped a New Sexual Revolution on American Attitudes toward Nonmarital Sex, 1972–1998," *Sociological Perspectives* 45 (2002): 267–83.

8 Gigi Engle, "How the Normalization of Anal Sex Has Shifted the Conversation about Consent," *Marie Claire*, August 14, 2017, https://www.marieclaire.com/sex-love/a5489/rise-in-anal-sex-statistics/; Alisa Hrustic, "Here's How Many Women Are Actually Having Anal Sex," *Men's Health*, July 28, 2017, https://www.menshealth.com/sex-women/a19527855/how-many-women-are-having-anal-sex/.

9 Mary Bernstein, "Nothing Ventured, Nothing Gained? Conceptualizing Social Movement 'Success' in the Lesbian and Gay Movement," *Sociological Perspectives* 46, 3 (2003): 353–79; Miriam Smith, "Homophobia and Homonationalism: LGBTQ Law Reform in Canada," *Social and Legal Studies* 29, 1 (2020): 65–84.

10 Tom Hooper, "Queering '69: The Recriminalization of Homosexuality in Canada," *Canadian Historical Review* 100, 2 (2019): 257–73.

11 Michael McDonald, "When the Government Apologizes: Understanding the Origins and Implications of the Apology to LGBTQ2+ Communities in Canada" (master's thesis, University of Victoria, 2019).

12 Kelsy Burke, *Christians under Covers: Evangelicals and Sexual Pleasure on the Internet* (Oakland: University of California Press, 2016).

13 Clive M. Davis et al., "Characteristics of Vibrator Use among Women," *Journal of Sex Research* 33, 4 (1996): 313–20; Debra Herbenick et al., "Prevalence and Characteristics of Vibrator Use by Women in the United States: Results from a Nationally Representative Study," *Journal of Sexual Medicine* 6, 7 (2009): 1857–66.

14 Herbenick et al., "Prevalence and Characteristics."

15 Debra Herbenick et al., "Women's Vibrator Use in Sexual Partnerships: Results from a Nationally Representative Survey in the United States," *Journal of Sex and Marital Therapy* 36, 1 (2010): 49–65

16 Mimi Schippers, *Beyond Monogamy: Polyamory and the Future of Polyqueer Sexualities* (New York: NYU Press, 2016); Elisabeth Sheff, *The Polyamorists Next Door: Inside Multiple-Partner Relationships and Families* (Lanham: Rowman and Littlefield, 2015).

Chapter 5: Pleasure, Pain, and Risk

1 Shana Conroy and Adam Cotter, "Self-Reported Sexual Assault in Canada, 2014," *Juristat* 37, 1 (July 11, 2017), https://www150.statcan.gc.ca/n1/en/catalogue/85-002-X201700114842.

2   Sinikka Elliott, *Not My Kid: What Parents Believe about the Sex Lives of Their Teenagers* (New York: NYU Press, 2012).
3   Nicole Andrejek, "Girls' Night Out: The Role of Women-Centered Friendship Groups in University Hookup Culture," *Sociological Forum* 36, 3 (2021): 758–75.
4   Jennifer S. Hirsch and Shamus Khan, *Sexual Citizens: A Landmark Study of Sex, Power, and Assault on Campus* (New York: W.W. Norton, 2020).
5   Hirsch and Khan, *Sexual Citizens*.
6   Statistics Canada, "Uniform Crime Reporting Survey (UCR)," 2019, accessed Sept. 8, 2023, http://www23.statcan.gc.ca/imdb/p2SV.pl?Function=getSurvey&SDDS=3302.
7   Conroy and Cotter, "Self-Reported Sexual Assault."
8   Cristine Rotenberg and Adam Cotter, "Police-Reported Sexual Assaults in Canada before and after #MeToo, 2016 and 2017," Ottawa, Statistics Canada, November 8, 2018, https://www150.statcan.gc.ca/n1/en/catalogue/85-002-X201800154979.
9   Cassia C. Spohn, "The Rape Reform Movement: The Traditional Common Law and Rape Law Reforms," *Jurimetrics* 39, 2 (1999): 119–30.
10   Susan Brownmiller, *Against Our Will: Men, Women, and Rape* (New York: Fawcett Columbine, 1993).
11   Spohn, "The Rape Reform Movement."
12   Diana Holmberg and Karen L. Blair, "Sexual Desire, Communication, Satisfaction, and Preferences of Men and Women in Same-Sex versus Mixed-Sex Relationships," *Journal of Sex Research* 46, 1 (2009): 57–66; Juliet Richters et al., "Sexual Practices at Last Heterosexual Encounter and Occurrence of Orgasm in a National Survey," *Journal of Sex Research* 43, 3 (2006): 217–26.
13   Jessica A. Maxwell et al., "How Implicit Theories of Sexuality Shape Sexual and Relationship Well-Being," *Journal of Personality and Social Psychology* 112, 2 (2017): 238–79.
14   Elizabeth A. Armstrong, Paula England, and Alison C.K. Fogarty, "Accounting for Women's Orgasm and Sexual Enjoyment in College Hookups and Relationships," *American Sociological Review* 77, 3 (2012): 435–62.
15   Emily Nagoski, *Come as You Are: The Surprising New Science That Will Transform Your Sex Life* (New York: Simon and Schuster Paperbacks, 2015).
16   David A. Frederick et al., "Differences in Orgasm Frequency among Gay, Lesbian, Bisexual, and Heterosexual Men and Women in a U.S. National Sample," *Archives of Sexual Behavior* 47, 1 (2018): 273–88.
17   Nicole Andrejek, Tina Fetner, and Melanie Heath, "Climax as Work: Heteronormativity, Gender Labor, and the Gender Gap in Orgasms," *Gender & Society* 36, 2 (2022): 189–213.
18   Alfred C. Kinsey et al., *Sexual Behavior in the Human Female* (Bloomington: Indiana University Press, 1998 [1953]); William H. Masters and Virginia E. Johnson, *Human Sexual Response* (Boston: Little, Brown, 1966).
19   Nagoski, *Come as You Are*; Laurie B. Mintz, *Becoming Cliterate: Why Orgasm Equality Matters – And How to Get It* (New York: HarperOne, 2018).

20 K.R. Mitchell et al., "Painful Sex (Dyspareunia) in Women: Prevalence and Associated Factors in a British Population Probability Survey," *BJOG: An International Journal of Obstetrics and Gynaecology* 124, 11 (2017): 1689–97.

21 David M. Ortmann and Richard A. Sprott, *Sexual Outsiders: Understanding BDSM Sexualities and Communities* (Lanham, MD: Rowman and Littlefield, 2013).

22 Robin Bauer, "Queering Consent: Negotiating Critical Consent in Les-Bi-Trans-Queer BDSM Contexts," *Sexualities* 24, 5–6 (2021): 767–83; Brandy L. Simula, "Pleasure, Power, and Pain: A Review of the Literature on the Experiences of BDSM Participants," *Sociology Compass* 13, 3 (2019): e12668.

23 Christian C. Joyal and Julie Carpentier, "The Prevalence of Paraphilic Interests and Behaviors in the General Population: A Provincial Survey," *Journal of Sex Research* 54, 2 (2017): 161–71.

24 Tony Silva and Tina Fetner, "Men's Feminist Identification and Reported Use of Prescription Erectile Dysfunction Medication," *Journal of Sex Research* 60, 4 (2023): 463–72.

25 William Pratt, "Prostitutes and Prophylaxis: Venereal Disease, Surveillance, and Discipline in the Canadian Army in Europe, 1939–1945," *Journal of the Canadian Historical Association* 26, 2 (2015): 111–38.

26 Public Health Agency of Canada, "Report on Sexually Transmitted Infections in Canada, 2018," Ottawa, Her Majesty the Queen in Right of Canada, June 24, 2021, accessed Sept. 11, 2023, https://www.canada.ca/en/public-health/services/publications/diseases-conditions/report-sexually-transmitted-infections-canada-2018.html.

27 Nisrine Haddad et al., "HIV in Canada – Surveillance Report, 2019," *Canada Communicable Disease Report* 47, 1 (2021): 77–86.

28 World Health Organization, "Global HIV Programme: HIV Data and Statistics," WHO, 2021, https://www.who.int/teams/global-hiv-hepatitis-and-stis-programmes/hiv/strategic-information/hiv-data-and-statistics.

29 Haddad et al., "HIV in Canada."

30 Haddad et al., "HIV in Canada."

31 Hamish McManus et al., "Comparison of Trends in Rates of Sexually Transmitted Infections before vs after Initiation of HIV Preexposure Prophylaxis among Men Who Have Sex with Men," *JAMA Network Open* 3, 12 (2020): e2030806.

32 More information is available on the Government of Canada's website: Public Health Agency of Canada, "HIV and AIDS: Symptoms and Treatments," accessed Sept. 11, 2023, https://www.canada.ca/en/public-health/services/diseases/hiv-aids.html.

33 Conroy and Cotter, "Self-Reported Sexual Assault."

34 Melissa A. Milkie et al., "Time with Children, Children's Well-Being, and Work-Family Balance among Employed Parents," *Journal of Marriage and Family* 72 (2010): 1329–43.

35 Paula England, "The Gender Revolution: Uneven and Stalled," *Gender & Society* 24, 2 (2010): 149–66.

Chapter 6: The Social Organization of Sexuality

1 Patricia Yancey Martin and Robert A. Hummer, "Fraternities and Rape on Campus," *Gender & Society* 3, 4 (1989): 457–73.

2 Laura Hamilton and Elizabeth A. Armstrong, "Gendered Sexuality in Young Adulthood: Double Binds and Flawed Options," *Gender & Society* 23, 5 (2009): 589–616.

3 Lisa Wade, *American Hookup: The New Culture of Sex on Campus* (New York: W.W. Norton, 2018).

4 Elizabeth A. Armstrong, Paula England, and Alison C.K. Fogarty, "Accounting for Women's Orgasm and Sexual Enjoyment in College Hookups and Relationships," *American Sociological Review* 77, 3 (2012): 435–62.

5 Andrew J. Cherlin, "Demographic Trends in the United States: A Review of Research in the 2000s," *Journal of Marriage and Family* 72, 3 (2010): 403–19.

6 Daniel Boothby and Torben Drewes, "Postsecondary Education in Canada: Returns to University, College and Trades Education," *Canadian Public Policy/Analyse de Politiques* 32, 1 (2006): 1–21.

7 Karen Robson et al., "Underrepresented Students and the Transition to Postsecondary Education: Comparing Two Toronto Cohorts," *Canadian Journal of Higher Education* 48, 1 (2018): 39–59.

8 Céline Le Bourdais et al., "Impact of Conjugal Separation on Women's Income in Canada: Does the Type of Union Matter?" *Demographic Research* 35 (2016): 1489–1522.

9 Statistics Canada, "Marital Status and Opposite- and Same-Sex Status by Sex for Persons Aged 15 and Over Living in Private Households for Both Sexes, Total, Presence and Age of Children, 2016 Counts, Canada, Provinces and Territories, 2016 Census – 100% Data," Families, Households and Marital Status Highlight Tables, Ottawa, Statistics Canada, July 8, 2017, https://www12.statcan.gc.ca/census-recensement/2016/dp-pd/hlt-fst/fam/Table.cfm?Lang=E&T=11&Geo=00&SP=1&view=1&sex=1&presence=1.

10 Dawne Moon, *God, Sex, and Politics: Homosexuality and Everyday Theologies* (Chicago: University of Chicago Press, 2004).

11 There is much disagreement about which traditions are evangelical and which are mainline, so we simply asked people to select the category that best fit themselves.

12 Kelsy Burke, *Christians under Covers: Evangelicals and Sexual Pleasure on the Internet* (Oakland: University of California Press, 2016).

13 Tina Fetner et al., "Christian Religious Identity and Sexual Behaviour in Canada Today," *Canadian Journal of Human Sexuality* 32, 2 (2023): 141–50.

14 Carol Hanisch, "The Personal Is Political," February 1969, http://carolhanisch.org/CHwritings/PIP.html.

15 Tina Fetner, "Feminist Identity and Sexual Behavior: The Intimate Is Political," *Archives of Sexual Behavior* 51, 1 (2022): 441–52.

16 Max Stick and Tina Fetner, "Feminist Men and Sexual Behavior: Analyses of Men's Sex with Women," *Men and Masculinities* 24, 5 (2020): 780–801.

17 Daniel L. Carlson and Brian Soller, "Sharing's More Fun for Everyone? Gender Attitudes, Sexual Self-Efficacy, and Sexual Frequency," *Journal of Marriage and Family* 81, 1 (2019): 24–41.

18 Jennifer S. Hirsch and Shamus Khan, *Sexual Citizens: A Landmark Study of Sex, Power, and Assault on Campus* (New York: W.W. Norton, 2020).

19 Jacqueline C. Pflieger et al., "Racial/Ethnic Differences in Patterns of Sexual Risk Behavior and Rates of Sexually Transmitted Infections among Female Young Adults," *American Journal of Public Health* 103, 5 (2013): 903–9; Gregorio A. Millett et al., "Comparisons of Disparities and Risks of HIV Infection in Black and Other Men Who Have Sex with Men in Canada, UK, and USA: A Meta-Analysis," *The Lancet* 380, 9839 (2012): 341–48.

20 Martin Cannon, "The Regulation of First Nations Sexuality," *Canadian Journal of Native Studies* 18, 1 (1998): 1–18.

21 Mariana Valverde, *The Age of Light, Soap, and Water: Moral Reform in English Canada, 1885–1925* (Toronto: University of Toronto Press, 2008).

Conclusion: Sex in Canada

1 CBC Television News, "No Place for the State in the Bedrooms of the Nation," *CBC News*, June 21, 2018, https://www.cbc.ca/archives/no-place-for-the-state-in-the-bedrooms-of-the-nation-1.4681298.

2 Brenda Cossman, "Fifty Years Later: The Legacy of the 1969 Criminal Reforms," *University of Toronto Law Journal* 70, 3 (2020): 223–24.

3 Tom Hooper, "Queering '69: The Recriminalization of Homosexuality in Canada," *Canadian Historical Review* 100, 2 (2019): 257–73.

4 Miriam Smith, "Homophobia and Homonationalism: LGBTQ Law Reform in Canada," *Social and Legal Studies* 29, 1 (2020): 65–84.

5 Katrina Ackerman and Shannon Stettner, "'The Public Is Not Ready for This': 1969 and the Long Road to Abortion Access," *Canadian Historical Review* 100, 2 (2019): 239–56.

6 Thomas Lemieux and David Card, "Education, Earnings, and the 'Canadian G.I. Bill,'" *Canadian Journal of Economics/Revue canadienne d'économique* 34, 2 (2001): 313–44.

7 Amin Ghaziani, *There Goes the Gayborhood?* (Princeton, NJ: Princeton University Press, 2014).

8 Elizabeth A. Armstrong, *Forging Gay Identities: Organizing Sexuality in San Francisco, 1950–1994* (Chicago: University of Chicago Press, 2002).

9 Emily Kazyak, "Disrupting Cultural Selves: Constructing Gay and Lesbian Identities in Rural Locales," *Qualitative Sociology* 34, 4 (2011): 561–81; Miriam Smith, *Lesbian and Gay Rights in Canada: Social Movements and Equality-Seeking, 1971–1995* (Toronto: University of Toronto Press, 1999).

10 Ghaziani, *There Goes the Gayborhood?*; Greggor Mattson, "Style and the Value of Gay Nightlife: Homonormative Placemaking in San Francisco," *Urban Studies* 52, 16 (2015): 3144–59.

11 Adam Isaiah Green, "The Social Organization of Desire: The Sexual Fields Approach," *Sociological Theory* 26, 1 (2008): 25–50.

12 Lisa Duggan, "The New Homonormativity: The Sexual Politics of Neoliberalism," in *Materializing Democracy: Toward a Revitalized Cultural Politics*, ed. Russ Castronovo and Dana D. Nelson (Durham: Duke University Press, 2002), 175–94.

13 Julie Gouweloos, "Intersectional Prefigurative Politics: Queer Cabaret as Radical Resistance," *Mobilization: An International Quarterly* 26, 2 (2021): 239–55; Maurice Kwong-Lai Poon et al., "Queer-Friendly Nation? The Experience of Chinese Gay Immigrants in Canada," *China Journal of Social Work* 10, 1 (2017): 23–38; Sonali Patel, "'Brown Girls Can't Be Gay': Racism Experienced by Queer South Asian Women in the Toronto LGBTQ Community," *Journal of Lesbian Studies* 23, 3 (2019): 410–23; Carmen H. Logie and Marie-Jolie Rwigema, "'The Normative Idea of Queer Is a White Person': Understanding Perceptions of White Privilege among Lesbian, Bisexual, and Queer Women of Color in Toronto, Canada," *Journal of Lesbian Studies* 18, 2 (2014): 174–91.

14 Mimi Schippers, *Beyond Monogamy: Polyamory and the Future of Polyqueer Sexualities* (New York: NYU Press, 2016); Elisabeth Sheff, *The Polyamorists Next Door: Inside Multiple-Partner Relationships and Families* (Lanham: Rowman and Littlefield, 2015).

15 Canton Winer et al., "'I Didn't Know Ace Was a Thing': Bisexuality and Pansexuality as Identity Pathways in Asexual Identity Formation," *Sexualities* (forthcoming): https://doi.org/10.31235/osf.io/agnd8.

16 Tina Fetner, "Feminist Identity and Sexual Behavior: The Intimate Is Political," *Archives of Sexual Behavior* 51, 1 (2022): 441–52; Max Stick and Tina Fetner, "Feminist Men and Sexual Behavior: Analyses of Men's Sex with Women," *Men and Masculinities* 24, 5 (2020): 780–801.

17 Nicole Andrejek, "Dating in the Digital Age" (PhD diss., McMaster University, 2020); Lisa Wade, *American Hookup: The New Culture of Sex on Campus* (New York: W.W. Norton, 2018).

18 Tina Fetner, "The Religious Right in the United States and Canada: Evangelical Communities, Critical Junctures, and Institutional Infrastructures," *Mobilization: An International Quarterly* 24, 1 (2019): 95–113.

19 Céline Le Bourdais and Évelyne Lapierre-Adamcyk, "Changes in Conjugal Life in Canada: Is Cohabitation Progressively Replacing Marriage?" *Journal of Marriage and Family* 66, 4 (2004): 929–42.

20 Andrejek, "Dating in the Digital Age."

21 Statistics Canada, "Same-Sex Couples in Canada in 2016," Census in Brief, Ottawa, Minister of Industry, August 2, 2017.

22 Jean Dumas and Yves Péron, "Marriage and Conjugal Life in Canada," Ottawa, Statistics Canada, 1994, https://publications.gc.ca/site/fra/9.814186/publication.html; Anne Milan, "Marital Status: Overview, 2011," Ottawa, Statistics Canada, July 2013, https://www150.statcan.gc.ca/n1/pub/91-209-x/2013001/article/11788-eng.pdf.

23 Statistics Canada, "Fertility: Fewer Children, Older Moms," Canadian Megatrends, Ottawa, Statistics Canada, 2018, https://www150.statcan.gc.ca/n1/pub/11-630-x/11-630-x2014002-eng.htm; CIA.gov, "The World Factbook-Central Intelligence Agency," Washington, DC, CIA, 2022, https://www.cia.gov/the-world-factbook/field/mothers-mean-age-at-first-birth/.
24 Andrejek, "Dating in the Digital Age."
25 Shana Conroy and Adam Cotter, "Self-Reported Sexual Assault in Canada, 2014," *Juristat* 37, 1 (2017), https://www150.statcan.gc.ca/n1/en/catalogue/85-002-X201700114842.
26 Jennifer S. Hirsch and Shamus Khan, *Sexual Citizens: A Landmark Study of Sex, Power, and Assault on Campus* (New York: W.W. Norton, 2020).

Bibliography

Ackerman, Katrina, and Shannon Stettner. "'The Public Is Not Ready for This': 1969 and the Long Road to Abortion Access." *Canadian Historical Review* 100, 2 (2019): 239–56.

Adam, Barry D. *The Rise of a Gay and Lesbian Movement*. Rev. ed. Social Movements Past and Present. New York: Twayne, 1995.

Aizura, Aren, Marcia Ochoa, Salvador Vidal-Ortiz, Tristan Cotton, and Carsten Balzer/Carla LaGata, eds. "Decolonizing the Transgender Imaginary." *TSQ: Transgender Studies Quarterly* 1, 3 (2014).

Albury, Kath, and Paul Byron. "Safe on My Phone? Same-Sex Attracted Young People's Negotiations of Intimacy, Visibility, and Risk on Digital Hook-Up Apps." *Social Media and Society* 2, 4 (2016): 2056305116672887.

Allison, Rachel, and Barbara J. Risman. "Marriage Delay, Time to Play? Marital Horizons and Hooking Up in College." *Sociological Inquiry* 87, 3 (2017): 472–500.

Andersen, Robert, and Tina Fetner. "Cohort Differences in Tolerance of Homosexuality: Attitudinal Change in Canada and the United States, 1981–2000." *Public Opinion Quarterly* 72, 2 (2008): 311–30.

Anderson, Monica, Emily A. Vogels, and Erica Turner. "The Virtues and Downsides of Online Dating." New York, Pew Research Center, February 6, 2020. https://www.pewresearch.org/internet/2020/02/06/americans-personal-experiences-with-online-dating/.

Andrejek, Nicole. "Dating in the Digital Age." PhD diss., McMaster University, 2020.

–. "Girls' Night Out: The Role of Women-Centered Friendship Groups in University Hookup Culture." *Sociological Forum* 36, 3 (2021): 758–75.

Andrejek, Nicole, Tina Fetner, and Melanie Heath. "Climax as Work: Hetero-normativity, Gender Labor, and the Gender Gap in Orgasms." *Gender & Society* 36, 2 (2022): 189–213.

Ansari, Aziz, and Eric Klinenberg. *Modern Romance.* New York: Penguin, 2015.

Armstrong, Elizabeth A. *Forging Gay Identities: Organizing Sexuality in San Francisco, 1950–1994.* Chicago: University of Chicago Press, 2002.

Armstrong, Elizabeth A., Paula England, and Alison C.K. Fogarty. "Accounting for Women's Orgasm and Sexual Enjoyment in College Hookups and Relationships." *American Sociological Review* 77, 3 (2012): 435–62.

Arnett, Jeffrey J. "Getting Better All the Time: Trends in Risk Behavior among American Adolescents since 1990." *Archives of Scientific Psychology* 6, 1 (2018): 87–95.

Atkins, David C., Donald H. Baucom, and Neil S. Jacobson. "Understanding Infidelity: Correlates in a National Random Sample." *Journal of Family Psychology* 15, 4 (2001): 735–49.

Attorney General of Ontario. "About the All Families Are Equal Act, 2016." *Ontario Newsroom* (blog), November 29, 2016. https://news.ontario.ca/en/backgrounder/42854/about-the-all-families-are-equal-act-2016.

Barnett, Jessica Penwell. "Polyamory and Criminalization of Plural Conjugal Unions in Canada: Competing Narratives in the s.293 Reference." *Sexuality Research and Social Policy* 11, 1 (2014): 63–75.

Bauer, Greta R., and Ayden I. Scheim. "Transgender People in Ontario, Canada: Statistics from the Trans PULSE Project to Inform Human Rights Policy." London, ON, Trans PULSE Project, 2015. https://transpulseproject.ca/wp-content/uploads/2015/06/Trans-PULSE-Statistics-Relevant-for-Human-Rights-Policy-June-2015.pdf.

Bauer, Robin. "Queering Consent: Negotiating Critical Consent in Les-Bi-Trans-Queer BDSM Contexts." *Sexualities* 24, 5–6 (2021): 767–83.

Bearak, Jonathan Marc, Anna Popinchalk, Cynthia Beavin, Bela Ganatra, Ann-Beth Moller, Özge Tunçalp, and Leontine Alkema. "Country-Specific Estimates of Unintended Pregnancy and Abortion Incidence: A Global Comparative Analysis of Levels in 2015–2019." *BMJ Global Health* 7, 3 (2022): e007151.

Beauchamp, Diane L. "Sexual Orientation and Victimization." Ottawa, Statistics Canada, 2004. https://www.tandis.odihr.pl/retrieve/22973.

Berger, Peter L., and Thomas Luckmann. *The Social Construction of Reality: A Treatise in the Sociology of Knowledge.* New York: Anchor Books, 1990.

Berlant, Lauren, and Michael Warner. "Sex in Public." *Critical Inquiry* 24, 2 (1998): 547–66.

Bernstein, Mary. "Nothing Ventured, Nothing Gained? Conceptualizing Social Movement 'Success' in the Lesbian and Gay Movement." *Sociological Perspectives* 46, 3 (2003): 353–79.

Blackwell, Courtney, Jeremy Birnholtz, and Charles Abbott. "Seeing and Being

Seen: Co-Situation and Impression Formation Using Grindr, a Location-Aware Gay Dating App." *New Media and Society* 17, 7 (2014): 1117–36.

Bolton, Melissa, Alexander McKay, and Margaret Schneider. "Relational Influences on Condom Use Discontinuation: A Qualitative Study of Young Adult Women in Dating Relationships." *Canadian Journal of Human Sexuality* 19, 3 (2010): 91–104.

Boothby, Daniel, and Torben Drewes. "Postsecondary Education in Canada: Returns to University, College and Trades Education." *Canadian Public Policy/ Analyse de Politiques* 32, 1 (2006): 1–21.

Bozinoff, Lorne. "US Court Ruling Boosts Approval of Same Sex Marriage in Canada." *Forum Research*, news release, June 29, 2015.

Brown, Larry K., et al. "Condom Use among High-Risk Adolescents: Anticipation of Partner Disapproval and Less Pleasure Associated with Not Using Condoms." *Public Health Reports* 123, 5 (2008): 601–7.

Brownlie, Robin Jarvis. "Intimate Surveillance: Indian Affairs, Colonization, and the Regulation of Aboriginal Women's Sexuality." In *Contact Zones: Aboriginal and Settler Women in Canada's Colonial Past*, ed. Katie Pickles and Myra Rutherdale, 160–78. Vancouver: UBC Press, 2005.

Bruce, Katherine McFarland. *Pride Parades: How a Parade Changed the World*. New York: NYU Press, 2016.

Budnick, Jamie. "The New Gay Science: Sexuality Knowledge, Demography, and the Politics of Population Measurement." PhD diss., University of Michigan, 2020.

Burke, Kelsy. *Christians under Covers: Evangelicals and Sexual Pleasure on the Internet*. Oakland: University of California Press, 2016.

Butler, Judith. *Gender Trouble: Feminism and the Subversion of Identity*. 2nd ed. New York: Routledge, 1990.

–. *Undoing Gender*. New York: Routledge, 2004.

Byers, E. Sandra, Joel Henderson, and Kristina M. Hobson. "University Students' Definitions of Sexual Abstinence and Having Sex." *Archives of Sexual Behavior* 38, 5 (2009): 665–74.

Cannon, Martin. "The Regulation of First Nations Sexuality." *Canadian Journal of Native Studies* 18, 1 (1998): 1–18.

Cano, Jennifer K., and Angel M. Foster. "'They Made Me Go through Like Weeks of Appointments and Everything': Documenting Women's Experiences Seeking Abortion Care in Yukon Territory, Canada." *Contraception* 94, 5 (2016): 489–95.

Carlson, Daniel L., and Brian Soller. "Sharing's More Fun for Everyone? Gender Attitudes, Sexual Self-Efficacy, and Sexual Frequency." *Journal of Marriage and Family* 81, 1 (2019): 24–41.

Carpenter, Laura M. *Virginity Lost: An Intimate Portrait of First Sexual Experiences*. New York: NYU Press, 2005.

CBC Television News. "'No Place for the State in the Bedrooms of the Nation.'" *CBC News*, June 21, 2018. https://www.cbc.ca/archives/no-place-for-the-state-in-the-bedrooms-of-the-nation-1.4681298.

Chambers, Anne Lorene. *Misconceptions: Unmarried Motherhood and the Ontario Children of Unmarried Parents Act, 1921 to 1969*. Toronto: University of Toronto Press, 2007.

Cherlin, Andrew J. "Demographic Trends in the United States: A Review of Research in the 2000s." *Journal of Marriage and Family* 72, 3 (2010): 403–19.

CIA.gov. "The World Factbook-Central Intelligence Agency." Washington, DC, CIA, 2022. https://www.cia.gov/the-world-factbook/field/mothers-mean-age-at-first-birth/.

Clarke, Victoria, and Kevin Turner. "V. Clothes Maketh the Queer? Dress, Appearance and the Construction of Lesbian, Gay and Bisexual Identities." *Feminism and Psychology* 17, 2 (2007): 267–76.

Cohen, Philip N. "The Coming Divorce Decline." *Socius* 5 (2019): 2378023119873497.

Conroy, Shana, and Adam Cotter. "Self-Reported Sexual Assault in Canada, 2014." *Juristat* 37, 1 (July 11, 2017). https://www150.statcan.gc.ca/n1/en/catalogue/85-002-X201700114842.

Copen, Casey E., Anjani Chandra, and Isaedmarie Febo-Vazquez. "Sexual Behavior, Sexual Attraction, and Sexual Orientation among Adults Aged 18–44 in the United States: Data from the 2011–2013 National Survey of Family Growth." *National Health Statistics Reports* 88 (January 7, 2016): 1–14. https://pubmed.ncbi.nlm.nih.gov/26766410/.

Cossman, Brenda. "Fifty Years Later: The Legacy of the 1969 Criminal Reforms." *University of Toronto Law Journal* 70, 3 (2020): 223–24.

Currier, Danielle M. "Strategic Ambiguity: Protecting Emphasized Femininity and Hegemonic Masculinity in the Hookup Culture." *Gender & Society* 27, 5 (2013): 704–27.

D'amico, Emilie, Danielle Julien, Nicole Tremblay, and Elise Chartrand. "Gay, Lesbian, and Bisexual Youths Coming Out to Their Parents: Parental Reactions and Youths' Outcomes." *Journal of GLBT Family Studies* 11, 5 (2015): 411–37.

Davis, Clive M., Joani Blank, Hung-Yu Lin, and Consuelo Bonillas. "Characteristics of Vibrator Use among Women." *Journal of Sex Research* 33, 4 (1996): 313–20.

Davis, Georgiann. *Contesting Intersex: The Dubious Diagnosis*. New York: NYU Press, 2015.

Dekker, Arne, and Gunter Schmidt. "Patterns of Masturbatory Behaviour." *Journal of Psychology and Human Sexuality* 14, 2–3 (2003): 35–48.

DeLuzio Chasin, C.J. "Theoretical Issues in the Study of Asexuality." *Archives of Sexual Behavior* 40, 4 (2011): 713–23.

Diefendorf, Sarah. "After the Wedding Night: Sexual Abstinence and Masculinities over the Life Course." *Gender & Society* 29, 5 (2015): 647–69.

Dion, Laurence, and Marie-Aude Boislard. "What 'Counts' as First Sex between Women? Results from a Study of First Sex among Women Who Have Sex with Women." *Canadian Journal of Human Sexuality* 31, 2 (2022): 253–67.

Dodge, Brian, Debby Herbenick, Tsung-Chieh (Jane) Fu, Vanessa Schick, Michael Reece, Stephanie Sanders, and J. Dennis Fortenberry. "Sexual Behaviors of U.S. Men by Self-Identified Sexual Orientation: Results from the 2012 National Survey of Sexual Health and Behavior." *Journal of Sexual Medicine* 13, 4 (2016): 637–49.

Drescher, Jack. "I'm Your Handyman: A History of Reparative Therapies." *Journal of Homosexuality* 36, 1 (1998): 19–42.

Duggan, Lisa. "The New Homonormativity: The Sexual Politics of Neoliberalism." In *Materializing Democracy: Toward a Revitalized Cultural Politics*, ed. Russ Castronovo and Dana D. Nelson, 175–94. Durham: Duke University Press, 2002.

Dumas, Jean, and Yves Péron. "Marriage and Conjugal Life in Canada." Ottawa, Statistics Canada, 1994. https://publications.gc.ca/site/fra/9.814186/publication. html.

Elizabeth, Autumn. "Challenging the Binary: Sexual Identity That Is Not Duality." *Journal of Bisexuality* 13, 3 (2013): 329–37.

Elliott, Sinikka. *Not My Kid: What Parents Believe about the Sex Lives of Their Teenagers*. New York: NYU Press, 2012.

England, Paula. "The Gender Revolution: Uneven and Stalled." *Gender & Society* 24, 2 (2010): 149–66.

Engle, Gigi. "How the Normalization of Anal Sex Has Shifted the Conversation about Consent." *Marie Claire*, August 14, 2017. https://www.marieclaire.com/sex-love/a5489/rise-in-anal-sex-statistics/.

Fetner, Tina. "Feminist Identity and Sexual Behavior: The Intimate Is Political." *Archives of Sexual Behavior* 51, 1 (2022): 441–52.

–. "The Religious Right in the United States and Canada: Evangelical Communities, Critical Junctures, and Institutional Infrastructures." *Mobilization: An International Quarterly* 24, 1 (2019): 95–113.

Fetner, Tina, Nicole Andrejek, Meghan Bird, and Megan Werger. "Christian Religious Identity and Sexual Behaviour in Canada Today." *Canadian Journal of Human Sexuality* 32, 2 (2023): 141–50.

Fetner, Tina, Michelle Dion, Melanie Heath, Nicole Andrejek, Sarah L. Newell, and Max Stick. "Condom Use in Penile-Vaginal Intercourse among Canadian Adults: Results from the Sex in Canada Survey." *PLOS ONE* 15, 2 (2020): e0228981.

Fetner, Tina, and Melanie Heath. "Do Same-Sex and Straight Weddings Aspire to the Fairytale? Women's Conformity and Resistance to Traditional Weddings." *Sociological Perspectives* 59, 4 (2016): 721–42.

Fields, Jessica. *Risky Lessons: Sex Education and Social Inequality*. Rutgers Series in Childhood Studies. New Brunswick, NJ: Rutgers University Press, 2008.

Flanders, Corey E., Cheryl Dobinson, and Carmen Logie. "'I'm Never Really My

Full Self': Young Bisexual Women's Perceptions of Their Mental Health." *Journal of Bisexuality* 15, 4 (2015): 454–80.

Foucault, Michel. *The History of Sexuality*. Vol. 1. New York: Random House, 1978.

Frederick, David A., H. Kate St. John, Justin R. Garcia, and Elisabeth A. Lloyd. "Differences in Orgasm Frequency among Gay, Lesbian, Bisexual, and Heterosexual Men and Women in a U.S. National Sample." *Archives of Sexual Behavior* 47, 1 (2018): 273–88.

Frith, Hannah. "Visualising the 'Real' and the 'Fake': Emotion Work and the Representation of Orgasm in Pornography and Everyday Sexual Interactions." *Journal of Gender Studies* 24, 4 (2015): 386–98.

Fritz, Niki, and Bryant Paul. "From Orgasms to Spanking: A Content Analysis of the Agentic and Objectifying Sexual Scripts in Feminist, for Women, and Mainstream Pornography." *Sex Roles* 77, 9 (2017): 639–52.

Galupo, M. Paz, Johanna L. Ramirez, and Lex Pulice-Farrow. "'Regardless of Their Gender': Descriptions of Sexual Identity among Bisexual, Pansexual, and Queer Identified Individuals." *Journal of Bisexuality* 17, 1 (2017): 108–24.

Gates, Gary J. "LGBT Demographics: Comparisons among Population-Based Surveys." Los Angeles, Williams Institute, UCLA, 2014. https://escholarship.org/uc/item/0kr784fx.

Ghaziani, Amin. *The Dividends of Dissent: How Conflict and Culture Work in Lesbian and Gay Marches on Washington*. Chicago: University of Chicago Press, 2008.

–. *There Goes the Gayborhood?* Princeton, NJ: Princeton University Press, 2014.

Goldenberg, Shira M., Vivian Liu, Paul Nguyen, Jill Chettiar, and Kate Shannon. "International Migration from Non-endemic Settings as a Protective Factor for HIV/STI Risk among Female Sex Workers in Vancouver, Canada." *Journal of Immigrant and Minority Health* 17, 1 (2015): 21–28.

Gollom, Mark. "Abortion Barriers in Canada Are Back in Spotlight Following Passage of Abortion Bans in U.S." *CBC News*, May 18, 2019.

Gouweloos, Julie. "Intersectional Prefigurative Politics: Queer Cabaret as Radical Resistance." *Mobilization: An International Quarterly* 26, 2 (2021): 239–55.

Government of Canada. "Bill C-16: An Act to Amend the *Canadian Human Rights Act* and the *Criminal Code*." Justice.gc.ca, September 1, 2021. https://justice.gc.ca/eng/csj-sjc/pl/identity-identite/statement-enonce.html.

Green, Adam Isaiah. "Queer Unions: Same-Sex Spouses Marrying Tradition and Innovation." *Canadian Journal of Sociology* 35, 3 (2010): 399–436.

–. "The Social Organization of Desire: The Sexual Fields Approach." *Sociological Theory* 26, 1 (2008): 25–50.

Greenberg, David F. *The Construction of Homosexuality*. Chicago: University of Chicago Press, 1988.

Grzanka, Patrick R. "Intersections and Configurations." *Archives of Sexual Behavior* 45, 3 (2016): 501–3.

Guzzo, Karen Benjamin. "Trends in Cohabitation Outcomes: Compositional Changes and Engagement among Never-Married Young Adults." *Journal of Marriage and the Family* 76, 4 (2014): 826–42.

Haddad, Nisrine, Ashley Weeks, Anita Robert, and Stephanie Totten. "HIV in Canada – Surveillance Report, 2019." *Canada Communicable Disease Report* 47, 1 (2021): 77–86.

Hamilton, Laura, and Elizabeth A. Armstrong. "Gendered Sexuality in Young Adulthood: Double Binds and Flawed Options." *Gender & Society* 23, 5 (2009): 589–616.

Harder, Helena, Rachel M.L. Starkings, Lesley J. Fallowfield, Usha Menon, Ian J. Jacobs, Valerie A. Jenkins, and on behalf of the UKCTOCS Trialists. "Sexual Functioning in 4,418 Postmenopausal Women Participating in UKCTOCS: A Qualitative Free-Text Analysis." *Menopause* 26, 10 (2019): 1100–9.

Haupert, M.L., Amanda N. Gesselman, Amy C. Moors, Helen E. Fisher, and Justin R. Garcia. "Prevalence of Experiences with Consensual Nonmonogamous Relationships: Findings from Two National Samples of Single Americans." *Journal of Sex and Marital Therapy* 43, 5 (2017): 424–40.

Hayes, Rebecca M., and Molly Dragiewicz. "Unsolicited Dick Pics: Erotica, Exhibitionism or Entitlement?" *Women's Studies International Forum* 71 (2018): 114–20.

Heath, Melanie. *Forbidden Intimacies: Polygamies at the Limits of Western Tolerance.* Stanford: Stanford University Press, 2023.

Herbenick, Debra, Michael Reece, Stephanie A. Sanders, Brian Dodge, Annahita Ghassemi, and J. Dennis Fortenberry. "Women's Vibrator Use in Sexual Partnerships: Results from a Nationally Representative Survey in the United States." *Journal of Sex and Marital Therapy* 36, 1 (2010): 49–65.

Herbenick, Debra, Michael Reece, Stephanie Sanders, Brian Dodge, Annahita Ghassemi, and J. Dennis Fortenberry. "Prevalence and Characteristics of Vibrator Use by Women in the United States: Results from a Nationally Representative Study." *Journal of Sexual Medicine* 6, 7 (2009): 1857–66.

Hirsch, Jennifer S., and Shamus Khan. *Sexual Citizens: A Landmark Study of Sex, Power, and Assault on Campus.* New York: W.W. Norton, 2020.

Holmberg, Diana, and Karen L. Blair. "Sexual Desire, Communication, Satisfaction, and Preferences of Men and Women in Same-Sex versus Mixed-Sex Relationships." *Journal of Sex Research* 46, 1 (2009): 57–66.

Hooker, Evelyn. "The Adjustment of the Male Overt Homosexual." *Journal of Projective Techniques* 21, 1 (1957): 18–31.

Hooper, Tom. "Queering '69: The Recriminalization of Homosexuality in Canada." *Canadian Historical Review* 100, 2 (2019): 257–73.

Hrustic, Alisa. "Here's How Many Women Are Actually Having Anal Sex." *Men's Health*, July 28, 2017. https://www.menshealth.com/sex-women/a19527855/how-many-women-are-having-anal-sex/.

Hull, Kathleen. *Same-Sex Marriage: The Cultural Politics of Love and Law*. New York: Cambridge University Press, 2006.

Hunt, Sarah. "An Introduction to the Health of Two-Spirit People: Historical, Contemporary and Emergent Issues." Prince George, BC, National Collaborating Centre for Aboriginal Health, 2016. https://www.ccnsa-nccah.ca/docs/emerging/RPT-HealthTwoSpirit-Hunt-EN.pdf.

Jacobs, Sue-Ellen. "Is the 'North American Berdache' Merely a Phantom in the Imaginations of Western Social Scientists?" In *Two-Spirit People: Native American Gender Identity, Sexuality, and Spirituality*, ed. Sue-Ellen Jacobs, Wesley Thomas, and Sabine Lang, 21–44. Urbana: University of Illinois Press, 1997.

Jacobs, Sue-Ellen, Wesley Thomas, and Sabine Lang, eds. *Two-Spirit People: Native American Gender Identity, Sexuality, and Spirituality*. Urbana: University of Illinois Press, 1997.

Jones, Angela. *Camming: Money, Power, and Pleasure in the Sex Work Industry*. New York: NYU Press, 2019.

Joyal, Christian C., and Julie Carpentier. "The Prevalence of Paraphilic Interests and Behaviors in the General Population: A Provincial Survey." *Journal of Sex Research* 54, 2 (2017): 161–71.

Julian, Kate. "Why Are Young People Having So Little Sex?" *The Atlantic*, November 13, 2018. https://www.theatlantic.com/magazine/archive/2018/12/the-sex-recession/573949/.

Katz, Jonathan Ned. *The Invention of Heterosexuality*. New York: Penguin Group, 1995.

Kavanaugh, Megan L., and Jenna Jerman. "Contraceptive Method Use in the United States: Trends and Characteristics between 2008, 2012 and 2014." *Contraception* 97, 1 (2018): 14–21.

Kazyak, Emily. "Disrupting Cultural Selves: Constructing Gay and Lesbian Identities in Rural Locales." *Qualitative Sociology* 34, 4 (2011): 561–81.

Kinsey, Alfred C., Wardell B. Pomeroy, and Clyde E. Martin. *Sexual Behavior in the Human Male*. Philadelphia: Saunders, 1948.

Kinsey, Alfred C., Wardell B. Pomeroy, Clyde E. Martin, and Paul H. Gebhard. *Sexual Behavior in the Human Female*. Bloomington: Indiana University Press, 1998 [1953].

Kinsman, Gary William. *The Regulation of Desire: Sexuality in Canada*. Montreal: Black Rose Books, 1987.

Klinenberg, Eric. *Going Solo: The Extraordinary Rise and Surprising Appeal of Living Alone*. London: Duckworth, 2012.

Krishnakumar, Priya. "This Record-Breaking Year for Anti-Transgender Legislation Would Affect Minors the Most." CNN.com, April 15, 2021. https://www.cnn.com/2021/04/15/politics/anti-transgender-legislation-2021/index.html.

Lalasz, Camille B., and Daniel J. Weigel. "Understanding the Relationship between Gender and Extradyadic Relations: The Mediating Role of Sensation Seeking on

Intentions to Engage in Sexual Infidelity." *Personality and Individual Differences* 50, 7 (2011): 1079–83.

Laumann, Edward O., John H. Gagnon, Robert T. Michael, and Stuart Michaels. *The Social Organization of Sexuality: Sexual Practices in the United States.* Chicago: University of Chicago Press, 1994.

Le Bourdais, Céline, and Évelyne Lapierre-Adamcyk. "Changes in Conjugal Life in Canada: Is Cohabitation Progressively Replacing Marriage?" *Journal of Marriage and Family* 66, 4 (2004): 929–42.

Le Bourdais, Céline, Sung-Hee Jeon, Shelley Clark, and Évelyne Lapierre-Adamcyk. "Impact of Conjugal Separation on Women's Income in Canada: Does the Type of Union Matter?" *Demographic Research* 35 (2016): 1489–1522.

Lehmiller, Justin J., Justin R. Garcia, Amanda N. Gesselman, and Kristen P. Mark. "Less Sex, but More Sexual Diversity: Changes in Sexual Behavior during the COVID-19 Coronavirus Pandemic." *Leisure Sciences* 43, 1–2 (2021): 295–304.

Lemieux, Thomas, and David Card. "Education, Earnings, and the 'Canadian G.I. Bill.'" *Canadian Journal of Economics/Revue canadienne d'économique* 34, 2 (2001): 313–44.

Lerum, Kari, and Shari L. Dworkin. "The Power of (But Not In?) Sexual Configurations Theory." *Archives of Sexual Behavior* 45, 3 (2016): 495–99.

Lewis, Abram J. "'We Are Certain of Our Own Insanity': Antipsychiatry and the Gay Liberation Movement, 1968–1980." *Journal of the History of Sexuality* 25, 1 (2016): 83–113.

Lindberg, Laura D., Lauren Firestein, and Cynthia Beavin. "Trends in U.S. Adolescent Sexual Behavior and Contraceptive Use, 2006–2019." *Contraception: X* 3 (2021): 100064.

Logie, Carmen H., and Marie-Jolie Rwigema. "'The Normative Idea of Queer Is a White Person': Understanding Perceptions of White Privilege among Lesbian, Bisexual, and Queer Women of Color in Toronto, Canada." *Journal of Lesbian Studies* 18, 2 (2014): 174–91.

Margolis, Rachel, Youjin Choi, Feng Hou, and Michael Haan. "Capturing Trends in Canadian Divorce in an Era without Vital Statistics." *Demographic Research* 41, 52 (2019): 1453–78.

Martin, Patricia Yancey, and Robert A. Hummer. "Fraternities and Rape on Campus." *Gender & Society* 3, 4 (1989): 457–73.

Martinez, Gladys M., and Joyce C. Abma. "Sexual Activity and Contraceptive Use among Teenagers Aged 15–19 in the United States, 2015–2017." NCHS Data Brief. Data Briefs. Washington, DC, National Center for Health Statistics, May 2020. https://www.cdc.gov/nchs/products/databriefs/db366.htm?deliveryName= USCDC_171-DM27640&deliveryName=USCDC_277-DM29489.

Martinez, Michael D., Kenneth D. Wald, and Stephen C. Craig. "Homophobic Innumeracy? Estimating the Size of the Gay and Lesbian Population." *Public Opinion Quarterly* 72, 4 (2008): 753–67.

Masters, William H., and Virginia E. Johnson. *Human Sexual Response*. Boston: Little, Brown, 1966.

Matthews, J. Scott. "The Political Foundations of Support for Same-Sex Marriage in Canada." *Canadian Journal of Political Science* 38, 4 (2005): 841–66.

Mattson, Greggor. "Style and the Value of Gay Nightlife: Homonormative Placemaking in San Francisco." *Urban Studies* 52, 16 (2015): 3144–59.

Maxwell, Jessica A., Amy Muise, Geoff MacDonald, Lisa C. Day, Natalie O. Rosen, and Emily A. Impett. "How Implicit Theories of Sexuality Shape Sexual and Relationship Well-Being." *Journal of Personality and Social Psychology* 112, 2 (2017): 238–79.

McDonald, Michael. "When the Government Apologizes: Understanding the Origins and Implications of the Apology to LGBTQ2+ Communities in Canada." Master's thesis, University of Victoria, 2019.

McKay, Alexander, Christopher Quinn-Nilas, and Robin Milhausen. "Prevalence and Correlates of Condom Use among Single Midlife Canadian Women and Men Aged 40 to 59." *Canadian Journal of Human Sexuality* 26, 1 (2017): 38–47.

McKay, Alexander, Mary-Anne Pietrusiak, and Philippa Holowaty. "Parents' Opinions and Attitudes towards Sexuality Education in the Schools." *Canadian Journal of Human Sexuality* 7, 2 (1998): 139–45.

McManus, Hamish, et al. "Comparison of Trends in Rates of Sexually Transmitted Infections before vs after Initiation of HIV Preexposure Prophylaxis among Men Who Have Sex with Men." *JAMA Network Open* 3, 12 (2020): e2030806.

Milan, Anne. "Marital Status: Overview, 2011." Ottawa, Statistics Canada, July 2013. https://www150.statcan.gc.ca/n1/pub/91-209-x/2013001/article/11788-eng.pdf.

Milkie, Melissa A., Sarah M. Kendig, Kei M. Nomaguchi, and Kathleen E. Denny. "Time with Children, Children's Well-Being, and Work-Family Balance among Employed Parents." *Journal of Marriage and Family* 72 (2010): 1329–43.

Millett, Gregorio A., et al. "Comparisons of Disparities and Risks of HIV Infection in Black and Other Men Who Have Sex with Men in Canada, UK, and USA: A Meta-Analysis." *The Lancet* 380, 9839 (2012): 341–48.

Mintz, Laurie B. *Becoming Cliterate: Why Orgasm Equality Matters – And How to Get It*. New York: HarperOne, 2018.

Mishel, Emma. "Intersections between Sexual Identity, Sexual Attraction, and Sexual Behavior among a Nationally Representative Sample of American Men and Women." *Journal of Official Statistics* 35, 4 (2019): 859–84.

Mitchell, K.R., et al. "Painful Sex (Dyspareunia) in Women: Prevalence and Associated Factors in a British Population Probability Survey." *BJOG: An International Journal of Obstetrics and Gynaecology* 124, 11 (2017): 1689–97.

Monro, Surya. *Bisexuality: Identities, Politics, and Theories*. Genders and Sexualities in the Social Sciences. Houndmills, UK: Palgrave Macmillan, 2015.

Moon, Dawne. *God, Sex, and Politics: Homosexuality and Everyday Theologies*. Chicago: University of Chicago Press, 2004.

Mora, Celeste. "What Is the Singular They, and Why Should I Use It?" *Grammarly Blog* (blog), June 1, 2018. https://www.grammarly.com/blog/use-the-singular-they/.

Nagoski, Emily. *Come as You Are: The Surprising New Science That Will Transform Your Sex Life*. New York: Simon and Schuster Paperbacks, 2015.

Orenstein, Peggy. *Boys and Sex: Young Men on Hookups, Love, Porn, Consent, and Navigating the New Masculinity*. New York: Harper, 2020.

Ortmann, David M., and Richard A. Sprott. *Sexual Outsiders: Understanding BDSM Sexualities and Communities*. Lanham, MD: Rowman and Littlefield, 2013.

Otis, Joanne, et al. "Beyond Condoms: Risk Reduction Strategies among Gay, Bisexual, and Other Men Who Have Sex with Men Receiving Rapid HIV Testing in Montreal, Canada." *AIDS and Behavior* 20, 12 (2016): 2812–26.

Pancham, Anna, and Sheila Dunn. "Emergency Contraception in Canada: An Overview and Recent Developments." *Canadian Journal of Human Sexuality* 16, 3/4 (2007): 129–33.

Pascoe, C.J. *Dude, You're a Fag: Masculinity and Sexuality in High School*. Berkeley: University of California Press, 2012.

Patel, Sonali. "'Brown Girls Can't Be Gay': Racism Experienced by Queer South Asian Women in the Toronto LGBTQ Community." *Journal of Lesbian Studies* 23, 3 (2019): 410–23.

Pflieger, Jacqueline C., Emily C. Cook, Linda M. Niccolai, and Christian M. Connell. "Racial/Ethnic Differences in Patterns of Sexual Risk Behavior and Rates of Sexually Transmitted Infections among Female Young Adults." *American Journal of Public Health* 103, 5 (2013): 903–9.

Poon, Maurice Kwong-Lai, Alan Tai-Wai Li, Josephine Pui-Hing Wong, and Cory Wong. "Queer-Friendly Nation? The Experience of Chinese Gay Immigrants in Canada." *China Journal of Social Work* 10, 1 (2017): 23–38.

Pratt, William. "Prostitutes and Prophylaxis: Venereal Disease, Surveillance, and Discipline in the Canadian Army in Europe, 1939–1945." *Journal of the Canadian Historical Association* 26, 2 (2015): 111–38.

Preves, Sharon E. *Intersex and Identity: The Contested Self*. New Brunswick, NJ: Rutgers University Press, 2003.

–. "Report on Sexually Transmitted Infections in Canada, 2018." Ottawa, Her Majesty the Queen in Right of Canada, June 24, 2021. Accessed Sept. 11, 2023, https://www.canada.ca/en/public-health/services/publications/diseases-conditions/report-sexually-transmitted-infections-canada-2018.html.

Puri, Jyoti. *Sexual States: Governance and the Struggle over the Antisodomy Law in India*. Durham: Duke University Press, 2016.

Reid, Julie A., Sinikka Elliott, and Gretchen R. Webber. "Casual Hookups to Formal Dates: Refining the Boundaries of the Sexual Double Standard." *Gender & Society* 25, 5 (2011): 545–68.

Richters, Juliet, Richard de Visser, Chris Rissel, and Anthony Smith. "Sexual Practices at Last Heterosexual Encounter and Occurrence of Orgasm in a National Survey." *Journal of Sex Research* 43, 3 (2006): 217–26.

Robinson, Brandon Andrew, and Salvador Vidal-Ortiz. "Displacing the Dominant 'Down Low' Discourse: Deviance, Same-Sex Desire, and Craigslist.org." *Deviant Behavior* 34, 3 (2013): 224–41.

Robinson, Margaret. "Two-Spirit Identity in a Time of Gender Fluidity." *Journal of Homosexuality* 67, 12 (2020): 1675–90.

Robson, Karen, Paul Anisef, Robert S. Brown, and Rhonda George. "Under-represented Students and the Transition to Postsecondary Education: Comparing Two Toronto Cohorts." *Canadian Journal of Higher Education* 48, 1 (2018): 39–59.

Rohlinger, Deana A. "Framing the Abortion Debate: Organizational Resources, Media Strategies, and Movement-Countermovement Dynamics." *Sociological Quarterly* 43, 4 (2002): 479–507.

Rotenberg, Cristine. "Prostitution Offences in Canada: Statistical Trends." *Juristat* 36, 1 (November 10, 2016). https://www150.statcan.gc.ca/n1/pub/85-002-x/2016001/article/14670-eng.htm.

Rotenberg, Cristine, and Adam Cotter. "Police-Reported Sexual Assaults in Canada before and after #MeToo, 2016 and 2017." Ottawa, Statistics Canada, November 8, 2018. https://www150.statcan.gc.ca/n1/en/catalogue/85-002-X201800154979.

Rotermann, Michelle, and Alexander McKay. "Condom Use at Last Sexual Intercourse among Unmarried, Not Living Common-Law 20- to 34-Year-Old Canadian Young Adults." *Canadian Journal of Human Sexuality* 18, 3 (2009): 75–87.

Rubin, Gayle. "Thinking Sex: Notes for a Radical Theory of the Politics of Sexuality." In *Pleasure and Danger: Exploring Female Sexuality*, ed. Carole S. Vance, 143–78. Boston: Routledge, 1984.

Rupp, Leila J., and Verta A. Taylor. *Drag Queens at the 801 Cabaret*. Chicago: University of Chicago Press, 2003.

Russo, Vito. *The Celluloid Closet: Homosexuality in the Movies*. Rev. ed. New York: Harper and Row, 1987.

Rust, Paula C. "'Coming Out' in the Age of Social Constructionism: Sexual Identity Formation among Lesbian and Bisexual Women." *Gender & Society* 7, 1 (1993): 50–77.

Rust, Paula C. Rodríguez. "Bisexuality: The State of the Union." *Annual Review of Sex Research* 13, 1 (2002): 180–240.

Sangster, Joan. "Incarcerating 'Bad Girls': The Regulation of Sexuality through the Female Refuges Act in Ontario, 1920–1945." *Journal of the History of Sexuality* 7, 2 (1996): 239–75.

Sauerteig, Lutz D.H. "Loss of Innocence: Albert Moll, Sigmund Freud and the Invention of Childhood Sexuality around 1900." *Medical History* 56, 2 (2012): 156–83.

Savin-Williams, Ritch C. *The New Gay Teenager*. Cambridge, MA: Harvard University Press, 2005.

Scherrer, Kristin S. "Coming to an Asexual Identity: Negotiating Identity, Negotiating Desire." *Sexualities* 11, 5 (2008): 621–41.

Schilt, Kristen. "The Unfinished Business of Sexuality: Comment on Andersen." *Gender & Society* 22, 1 (2008): 109–14.

Schilt, Kristen, and Laurel Westbrook. "Doing Gender, Doing Heteronormativity: 'Gender Normals,' Transgender People, and the Social Maintenance of Heterosexuality." *Gender & Society* 23, 4 (2009): 440–64.

Schippers, Mimi. *Beyond Monogamy: Polyamory and the Future of Polyqueer Sexualities*. New York: NYU Press, 2016.

Schnabel, Landon. "Sexual Orientation and Social Attitudes." *Socius* 4 (2018): 237802311876955.

Schneider, Daniel. "Wealth and the Marital Divide." *American Journal of Sociology* 117, 2 (2011): 627–67.

Scott, Susie, Liz McDonnell, and Matt Dawson. "Stories of Non-Becoming: Non-Issues, Non-Events and Non-Identities in Asexual Lives." *Symbolic Interaction* 39, 2 (2016): 268–86.

Seidman, Steven. "Deconstructing Queer Theory, or the Under-Theorization of the Social and the Ethical." In *Social Postmodernism: Beyond Identity Politics*, ed. Linda Nicholson and Steven Seidman, 116–41. Cambridge Cultural Social Studies. Cambridge: Cambridge University Press, 1995.

Serano, Julia. *Sexed Up: How Society Sexualizes Us, and How We Can Fight Back*. New York: Seal Press, 2022.

Sheff, Elisabeth. *The Polyamorists Next Door: Inside Multiple-Partner Relationships and Families*. Lanham: Rowman and Littlefield, 2015.

Silva, Tony. *Still Straight: Sexual Flexibility among White Men in Rural America*. New York: NYU Press, 2021.

–. "Straight Identity and Same-Sex Desire: Conservatism, Homophobia, and Straight Culture." *Social Forces* 97, 3 (2019): 1067–94.

Silva, Tony, and Tina Fetner. "Men's Feminist Identification and Reported Use of Prescription Erectile Dysfunction Medication." *Journal of Sex Research* 60, 4 (2023): 463–72.

–. "Sexual Identity-Behavior Discordance in Canada." *Canadian Review of Sociology* 59, 2 (2022): 156–80.

Simpson, Sean. "Majority Continue to Support (77%) Abortion in Canada, but behind Sweden (87%), Belgium (87%) and France (86%)." Calgary, IPSOS, May 1, 2017. https://www.ipsos.com/en-ca/news-polls/majority-continue-support-abortion-canada.

Simula, Brandy L. "Pleasure, Power, and Pain: A Review of the Literature on the Experiences of BDSM Participants." *Sociology Compass* 13, 3 (2019): e12668.

Singh, Susheela, Gilda Sedgh, and Rubina Hussain. "Unintended Pregnancy: Worldwide Levels, Trends, and Outcomes." *Studies in Family Planning* 41, 4 (2010): 241–50.

Smith, Miriam. "Homophobia and Homonationalism: LGBTQ Law Reform in Canada." *Social and Legal Studies* 29, 1 (2020): 65–84.

–. *Lesbian and Gay Rights in Canada: Social Movements and Equality-Seeking, 1971–1995.* Toronto: University of Toronto Press, 1999.

–. *Political Institutions and Lesbian and Gay Rights in the United States and Canada.* New York: Routledge, 2008.

Snyder, Howard. "Arrest in the United States, 1990–2010." Washington, DC, Bureau of Justice Statistics, 2012. https://bjs.ojp.gov/content/pub/pdf/aus9010.pdf.

South, Scott J., and Lei Lei. "Why Are Fewer Young Adults Having Casual Sex?" *Socius* 7 (2021): 2378023121996854.

Spohn, Cassia C. "The Rape Reform Movement: The Traditional Common Law and Rape Law Reforms." *Jurimetrics* 39, 2 (1999): 119–30.

Statistics Canada. "By the Numbers: Same-Sex Couples and Sexual Orientation." Ottawa, Minister of Industry, 2015. Accessed Sept. 6, 2023. https://www.statcan.gc.ca/eng/dai/smr08/2015/smr08_203_2015.

–. "Canada Is the First Country to Provide Census Data on Transgender and Non-Binary People." The Daily. Ottawa, Statistics Canada, April 24, 2022. https://www150.statcan.gc.ca/n1/en/daily-quotidien/220427/dq220427b-eng.pdf?st=la_O8FPf.

–. "Fertility: Fewer Children, Older Moms." Canadian Megatrends. Ottawa, Statistics Canada, 2018. https://www150.statcan.gc.ca/n1/pub/11-630-x/11-630-x2014002-eng.htm.

–. "Marital Status and Opposite- and Same-Sex Status by Sex for Persons Aged 15 and Over Living in Private Households for Both Sexes, Total, Presence and Age of Children, 2016 Counts, Canada, Provinces and Territories, 2016 Census – 100% Data." Families, Households and Marital Status Highlight Tables. Ottawa, Statistics Canada, July 8, 2017. https://www12.statcan.gc.ca/census-recensement/2016/dp-pd/hlt-fst/fam/Table.cfm?Lang=E&T=11&Geo=00&SP=1&view=1&sex=1&presence=1.

–. "Portrait of Families and Living Arrangements in Canada." Ottawa, Minister of Industry, 2012. https://www12.statcan.gc.ca/census-recensement/2011/as-sa/98-312-x/2011001/mi-rs-eng.cfm.

–. "Same-Sex Couples in Canada in 2016." Census in Brief. Ottawa, Minister of Industry, August 2, 2017.

–. "A Statistical Portrait of Canada's Diverse LGBTQ2+ Communities." The Daily. Ottawa, Statistics Canada, June 15, 2021. https://www150.statcan.gc.ca/n1/en/daily-quotidien/210615/dq210615a-eng.pdf?st=FTVsCzDb.

–. "Uniform Crime Reporting Survey (UCR)." 2019. Accessed Sept. 9, 2023, http://www23.statcan.gc.ca/imdb/p2SV.pl?Function=getSurvey&SDDS=3302.

Stein, Arlene. "Sisters and Queers: The Decentering of Lesbian Feminism." In *Cultural Politics and Social Movements*, ed. Marcy Darnovsky, Barbara Epstein, and Richard Flacks, 133–53. Philadelphia, PA: Temple University Press, 1995.

Stick, Max, and Tina Fetner. "Feminist Men and Sexual Behavior: Analyses of Men's Sex with Women." *Men and Masculinities* 24, 5 (2020): 780–801.

Stone, Amy L. "The Geography of Research on LGBTQ Life: Why Sociologists Should Study the South, Rural Queers, and Ordinary Cities." *Sociology Compass* 12, 11 (2018): e12638.

Sumerau, J.E., Lain A.B. Mathers, and Dawne Moon. "Foreclosing Fluidity at the Intersection of Gender and Sexual Normativities." *Symbolic Interaction* 43, 2 (2020): 205–34.

Thompson, Sharon. *Going All the Way: Teenage Girls' Tales of Sex, Romance, and Pregnancy*. New York: Hill and Wang, 1996.

Tolman, Deborah L. *Dilemmas of Desire: Teenage Girls Talk about Sexuality*. Cambridge: Harvard University Press, 2009.

Traister, Rebecca. *All the Single Ladies: Unmarried Women and the Rise of an Independent Nation*. New York: Simon and Schuster, 2016.

Treas, Judith. "How Cohorts, Education, and Ideology Shaped a New Sexual Revolution on American Attitudes toward Nonmarital Sex, 1972–1998." *Sociological Perspectives* 45 (2002): 267–83.

Treas, Judith, and Deirdre Giesen. "Sexual Infidelity among Married and Cohabiting Americans." *Journal of Marriage and Family* 62, 1 (2000): 48–60.

Ueda, Peter, Catherine H. Mercer, Cyrus Ghaznavi, and Debby Herbenick. "Trends in Frequency of Sexual Activity and Number of Sexual Partners among Adults Aged 18 to 44 Years in the US, 2000–2018." *JAMA Network Open* 3, 6 (2020): e203833.

Valocchi, Steve. "Riding the Crest of a Protest Wave? Collective Action Frames in the Gay Liberation Movement, 1969–1973." *Mobilization: An International Quarterly* 4, 1 (1999): 59–73.

Valverde, Mariana. *The Age of Light, Soap, and Water: Moral Reform in English Canada, 1885–1925*. Toronto: University of Toronto Press, 2008.

van Anders, Sari M. "Beyond Sexual Orientation: Integrating Gender/Sex and Diverse Sexualities via Sexual Configurations Theory." *Archives of Sexual Behavior* 44, 5 (2015): 1177–1213.

Van Houdenhove, Ellen, Luk Gijs, Guy T'Sjoen, and Paul Enzlin. "Asexuality: A Multidimensional Approach." *Journal of Sex Research* 52, 6 (2015): 669–78.

Vogler, Stefan. *Sorting Sexualities: Expertise and the Politics of Legal Classification*. Chicago: University of Chicago Press, 2021.

Wade, Lisa. *American Hookup: The New Culture of Sex on Campus*. New York: W.W. Norton, 2018.

Waite, Sean, and Nicole Denier. "Gay Pay for Straight Work: Mechanisms Generating Disadvantage." *Gender & Society* 29, 4 (2015): 561–88.

–. "A Research Note on Canada's LGBT Data Landscape: Where We Are and What the Future Holds: Canada's LGBT Data Landscape." *Canadian Review of Sociology* 56, 1 (2019): 93–117.

Walker, Alicia M. *The Secret Life of the Cheating Wife: Power, Pragmatism, and Pleasure in Women's Infidelity.* Lanham, MD: Lexington Books, 2018.

Ward, Janelle. "What Are You Doing on Tinder? Impression Management on a Matchmaking Mobile App." *Information, Communication and Society* 20, 11 (2017): 1644–59.

Warner, Michael. "Introduction: Fear of a Queer Planet." *Social Text* 29 (1991): 3–17.

Watts, Vanessa. "Indigenous Place-Thought and Agency amongst Humans and Non Humans (First Woman and Sky Woman Go on a European World Tour!)." *Decolonization: Indigeneity, Education and Society* 2, 1 (2013): 20–34.

Weeks, Carly. "Ontario, New Brunswick Violating Canada Health Act by Forcing Patients to Pay for Abortions: National Abortion Federation." *Globe and Mail*, July 16, 2019. https://www.theglobeandmail.com/canada/article-ontario-new-brunswick-violating-canada-health-act-by-forcing-patients/.

Weinstein, Emily, and Carrie James. *Behind Their Screens: What Teens Are Facing (and Adults Are Missing).* Cambridge, MA: MIT Press, 2022.

Wentland, Jocelyn J., and Elke Reissing. "Casual Sexual Relationships: Identifying Definitions for One Night Stands, Booty Calls, Fuck Buddies, and Friends with Benefits." *Canadian Journal of Human Sexuality* 23, 3 (2014): 167–77.

Westbrook, Laurel. "Trans Categories and the Sex/Gender/Sexuality System." In *Introducing the New Sexuality Studies*, 4th ed.; ed. Nancy L. Fischer, Laurel Westbrook, and Steven Seidman, 25–34. New York: Routledge, 2022.

Westbrook, Laurel, and Aliya Saperstein. "New Categories Are Not Enough: Rethinking the Measurement of Sex and Gender in Social Surveys." *Gender & Society* 29, 4 (2015): 534–60.

Westbrook, Laurel, Jamie Budnick, and Aliya Saperstein. "Dangerous Data: Seeing Social Surveys through the Sexuality Prism." *Sexualities* 25, 5–6 (2022): 717–49.

Westbrook, Laurel, and Kristen Schilt. "Doing Gender, Determining Gender: Transgender People, Gender Panics, and the Maintenance of the Sex/Gender/Sexuality System." *Gender & Society* 28, 1 (2014): 32–57.

Widmer, Eric D., Judith Treas, and Robert Newcomb. "Attitudes toward Non-marital Sex in 24 Countries." *Journal of Sex Research* 35, 4 (1998): 349–58.

Wilson, Alex. "How We Find Ourselves: Identity Development and Two Spirit People." *Harvard Educational Review* 66, 2 (1996): 303–18.

Winer, Canton, Megan Carroll, Yuchen Yang, Katherine Linder, and Brittney Miles. "'I Didn't Know Ace Was a Thing': Bisexuality and Pansexuality as Identity Pathways in Asexual Identity Formation." *Sexualities* (forthcoming). https://doi.org/10.31235/osf.io/agnd8.

Wong, Day. "Hybridization and the Emergence of 'Gay' Identities in Hong Kong and in China." In *Hybrid Hong Kong*, ed. Kwok-bun Chan, 199–217. New York: Routledge, 2012.

World Health Organization. "Global HIV Programme: HIV Data and Statistics." WHO, 2021. https://www.who.int/teams/global-hiv-hepatitis-and-stis-programmes/hiv/strategic-information/hiv-data-and-statistics.

Young, Pamela Dickey, Heather Shipley, and Tracy J. Trothen. *Religion and Sexuality: Diversity and the Limits of Tolerance*. Vancouver: UBC Press, 2015.

Index

Note: "*f*" after a page number indicates a figure.

having sex, 42–43; divorce rates in, 59; living alone in, 60; masturbation data in, 40; statistics on dating apps in, 67; traditional norms in, 147
university students, 125–28, 126*f*, 149. *See also* young people
unwanted sex, reasons for, 101–2, 101*f*
urban/rural divide, 132–33
US Supreme Court, 8–9

vaginal dryness, 119–20, 120*f*
value systems, 5
vasectomy, 51. *See also* contraception
Veterans' Land Act, 143
Veterans' Rehabilitation Act of 1945, 143
vibrators and toys, 93–95, 94*f*, 95*f*. *See also* sexual behaviour
victimization, 30–31
virginity, 4, 41–42, 43*f*, 116

wage inequality, 30
withdrawal (birth control technique), 51. *See also* contraception
women: age of marriage, 150; enjoying sex, 103; faking orgasms, 115–16; oral sex, 84–85; orgasms of, 78, 83, 109–10; pain during sex of, 117, 117*f*; relationship type and sexual pleasure, 110*f*; sexual desire and, 105; sexual pleasure and, 104*f*, 105; use of vibrators, 93–94, 94*f*. *See also* gender differences; men
Wynne, Kathleen, 30

young people: condom use in, 49, 50; deferring marriage, 60; monogamy and, 70; navigating hookup culture, 64–65, 65*f*, 66–67; rates of sex in, 42–43; using dating apps, 67. *See also* university students

Printed and bound in Canada by Friesens

Set in Sabon and Myriad by Julie Cochrane

Copy editor: Deborah Kerr

Proofreader: Alison Strobel

Indexer: Emily LeGrand

Cover designer: David Drummond